COMPLEXITY and EDUCATION

Inquiries into Learning, Teaching, and Research

COMPLEXITY and EDUCATION

Inquiries into Learning, Teaching, and Research

Brent Davis
University of Alberta

Dennis Sumara
University of Alberta

LEA

LAWRENCE ERLBAUM ASSOCIATES, PUBLISHERS

2006   Mahwah, New Jersey   London

Lawrence Erlbaum Associates, Inc., Publishers
10 Industrial Avenue
Mahwah, New Jersey 07430
www.erlbaum.com

Cover design by Clayton Kropp

Library of Congress Cataloging-in-Publication Data

Davis, Brent.
    Complexity and education : inquiries into learning, teaching,
    and research / Brent Davis, Dennis Sumara.
        p.   cm.
Includes bibliographical references and index.
ISBN 0-8058-5934-9 (cloth : alk. paper)
ISBN 0-8058-5935-7 (pbk. : alk. paper)
1. Education—Research. 2. Learning. 3. Teaching.   I. Sumara,
    Dennis J., 1958–   II. Title.
LB1028.D345   2006
370.7'2—dc22   2006006883
                                                           CIP

Books published by Lawrence Erlbaum Associates are printed on
acid-free paper, and their bindings are chosen for strength and
durability.

Printed in the United States of America   ·
10   9   8   7   6   5   4   3   2   1

CONTENTS

Dedication   *vii*

Preface   *ix*

Part 1 • Complexity Thinking

1. What is "complexity"?   3

2. What is "science"?   17

3. The Shape of Complexity   37

4. The Network of Complexity   57

Part 2 • Complexity Thinking, Education, and Educational Inquiry

5. Descriptive Complexity Research: Qualities of Learning Systems   79

6. Descriptive Complexity Research: Level-Jumping   107

7. Pragmatic Complexity Research: Conditions of Emergence   129

8. Pragmatic Complexity Research: Vital Simultaneities   153

Endnotes   171

References   185

Acknowledgments   193

Name Index   195

Subject Index   199

DEDICATION

We dedicate this book to our mentor and friend,
William E. Doll, Jr.

PREFACE

This book is about the possible relevancies of complexity thinking for educational practice and research.

This sort of project is anything but straightforward. Complexity theory/science/thinking is young and evolving—and as we develop, it refuses tidy descriptions and unambiguous definitions. Indeed, it is not even clear whether it should be called a field, a domain, a system of interpretation, or even a research attitude.

Nonetheless, complexity thinking has captured the attentions of many researchers whose studies reach across traditional disciplinary boundaries. For example, among educational researchers, the following phenomena are currently under investigation:

- How does the brain work? Now that researchers are able to watch brain activity in real time, it has become clear that many long-held beliefs about its structure and dynamics—that is, assumptions about what thought and memory are, how learning happens, and so on—are misinformed if not completely mistaken.
- What is consciousness? Over the past century, many neurologists, psychologists, and sociologists have attempted to present definitions and discipline-specific explanations of self-awareness, but is has become increasingly clear that none of these contributions is up to the task of making sense of human consciousness of self and other-than-self.

- What is intelligence? IQ scores have been climbing steadily for the past century, at a pace that cannot be explained in terms of biological adaptation, improved nutrition, or educational intervention. It appears that the sort of spatio-logical abilities that are measured by IQ tests must be readily influenced and enabled by experience and context. What are the conditions that contribute to increases in IQ? Can they manipulated? How is IQ related to or reflective of a broader, more encompassing conception of intelligence?

- What is the role of emergent technologies in shaping personalities and possibilities? The most creatively adaptive humans—that is, young children— are able to integrate the latest technologies into their existences in ways that older, less plastic adults can only envy. What might this mean for formal education, both in terms of pragmatic activity and with regard to common understandings of the purposes of schooling?

- How do social collectives work? Popular assumption has it that the actions and potentialities of social groupings are sums of individual capacities. Yet it is becoming more and more evident that, on occasion, collectives can vastly exceed the summed capacities of their members. How does this happen? Can these situations be orchestrated? What might this mean for classrooms, school boards, communities, and so on?

- What is knowledge? Even the most static of domains—including formal mathematics, the hard sciences, and fundamentalist religions—can be readily shown to be adapting to the shifting interests and obsessions of societies, being led as much as they lead.

- What is education for? If one seriously considers the range of theories and philosophies invoked in current discussions of education, it is obvious that there is little agreement on what formal education is doing, much less on what it is intended to do.

On first blush, it might appear that the only common theme across such questions is that their answers are less and less self-evident. However, a closer look will reveal some deep similarities among the phenomena addressed.

For example, it might be argued that each of these phenomena is pointing toward some sort of system that learns. Brains, social collectives, bodies of knowledge, and so on can all become broader, more nuanced, capable of more diverse possibilities. Further, each of these phenomena arises in the interactions of many sub-components or agents, whose actions are in turn enabled and constrained by similarly dynamic contexts. In very different terms, it is not always clear where one should focus one's attentions in order to understand these sorts of phenomena. For instance, to research consciousness or intelligence or knowledge, does it make sense to focus on the level of neurological events? Or personal activity? Or social context? Or physical setting?

The emergent realm of complexity thinking answers that, to make sense of the sorts of phenomena mentioned above, one must "level-jump"—that is, simultaneously examine the phenomenon in its own right (for its particular coherence and its specific rules of behavior) and pay attention to the conditions of its emergence (e.g., the agents that come together, the contexts of their co-activity, etc.). This strategy is one of several that has been developed within complexity research, which has arisen over the past few decades as a disciplined and demanding approach to the study of events that defy simplistic analyses and cause–effect explanations. It is becoming more and more evident that complexity thinking now offers a powerful alternative to the linear, reductionist approaches to inquiry that have dominated the sciences for half a millennium—and educational research for more than a century.

Moreover, and as developed throughout this text, complexity thinking not only enables, but compels an attentiveness to the roles of researchers in contributing to the shapes of the phenomena researched. This is a particularly important issue for educators. Consider, for example, the impact of behaviorist psychology on teaching practices through the too-simplified assertion that learning can be understood in terms of chains of stimulus–response reactions ... or, more recently, of constructivism-oriented research that has foregrounded and problematized the mechanical logic of behaviorism, but that does not question the assumption that the locus of learning is the individual human knower. As well-meaning as much of the associated research has been, not all of its consequences can be deemed positive when one is faced with jumping to the level of classrooms. In this text we argue that at least part of the problem has been the absence of a discourse that enables one to attend to different levels of complex dynamics—an absence that does not render recent research irrelevant, but that does limit the utility of much of what has been learned.

To be clear, then, we have a very pragmatic intent in this book. We aim to present complexity thinking as an important and appropriate attitude for educators and educational researchers. To develop this point, we endeavor to cite a diversity of practices and studies that are either explicitly informed by or that might be aligned with complexity research. We also offer focused and practiced advice for structuring projects in ways that are consistent with complexity thinking. To illustrate the discussion, we have attempted to present a broad (but by no means comprehensive) overview of the sorts of studies that have been undertaken within education.

Discussions of such topics comprise the Part II of the book (chaps. 5–8). Part I (chaps. 1–4) is concerned with more global issues around complexity thinking, as read through an educational lens. In these chapters, we interrogate the conceptual backdrop of much of contemporary work in education, all organized around the assertion that complexity thinking is not something that can be pasted into the current mosaic of interpretive possibilities. Rather, complexity represents a profound challenge to much of current theory and practice.

A major aspect of this text is the presentation and development of an emergent vocabulary around the complexities of teaching and educational inquiry. We had at first planned to include a glossary of relevant terms as an appendix, but decided against it when we found ourselves compelled to offer definitions of words whose meanings we were deliberately trying to loosen. Instead of a set of print-based definitions, then, we invite readers to consult (and, if desired, participate in development of) word meanings offered on the "Complexity and Education" website.[2]

And, on this count, we begin by flagging a particular problem with vocabulary that we encountered in our opening paragraph: How does one refer to the complexity research? As a theory? A science? An attitude? For reasons that are developed in chapter 2, where we interrogate conventional understandings of the word *science*, we have opted for the phrase "complexity thinking"[3] to refer to the specific manner in which we position ourselves.

One further point before inviting you to read on: We are witnessing an explosion of interest among educationists in complexity thinking. As such, we expect that many of the ideas represented in these pages will be outdated or superceded by the time the book is in print. The intention, then, is not to offer a complete account of the relevance of complexity thinking for education, but to frame issues that we have personally found to be of significance through our decades of teaching and researching. Our intention is not to prescribe and delimit, but to challenge readers to examine their own assumptions and theoretical commitments, whether anchored by commonsense, classical analytic thought, or any of the posts (e.g., postmodernism, poststructuralism, postcolonialism, postpositivism, postformalism, postepistemology) that mark the edges of current discursive possibility.

PART ONE

COMPLEXITY THINKING

CHAPTER ONE

WHAT IS "COMPLEXITY"?

EVERYTHING SHOULD BE AS SIMPLE AS POSSIBLE,
BUT NOT SIMPLER.

—Albert Einstein[1]

Early in the year 2000, prominent physicist and cosmologist Stephen Hawking commented, "I think the next century will be the century of complexity."[2] His remark was in specific reference to the emergent and transdisciplinary domain of complexity thinking, which, as a coherent realm of discussion, has only come together over the past 30 years or so.

Through much of this period, complexity has frequently been hailed as a "new science." Although originating in physics, chemistry, cybernetics, information science, and systems theory, its interpretations and insights have increasingly been brought to bear in a broad range of social areas, including studies of family research, health, psychology, economics, business management, and politics. To a lesser—but accelerating—extent, complexity has been embraced by educationists whose interests extend across such levels of activity as neurological processes, subjective understanding, interpersonal dynamics, cultural evolution, and the unfolding of the more-than-human world.

This sort of diversity in interest has prompted the use of the adjective *transdisciplinary* rather than the more conventional words *interdisciplinary* or *multidisciplinary* to describe complexity studies. Transdisciplinarity is a term that is intended to flag a research attitude in which it is understood that the members of a research team arrive with different disciplinary backgrounds and often different research agendas, yet are sufficiently informed about one another's perspectives and motivations to be able to work together as a collective. This attitude is certainly represented in the major complexity science think tanks, including most prominently the Santa Fe Institute that regularly welcomes Nobel laureates from many disciplines.[3] By way of more specific and immediate example, as a collective, our (the authors') respective categories of expertise are in mathematics, learning theory, and cognitive science (Davis) and literary engagement, teacher education, and interpretive inquiry (Sumara). This conceptual, methodological, and substantive diversity is not simply summed together in this text. Rather, as we attempt to develop in subsequent discussions of complex dynamics, the text is something more than a compilation of different areas of interest and expertise.

The transdisciplinary character of complexity thinking makes it difficult to provide any sort of hard-and-fast definition of the movement. Indeed, as we develop later on, many complexivists have argued that a definition is impossible. In this writing, we position complexity thinking somewhere between a belief in a fixed and fully knowable universe and a fear that meaning and reality are so dynamic that attempts to explicate are little more than self-delusions. In fact, complexity thinking commits to neither of these extremes, but listens to both. Complexity thinking recognizes that many phenomena are inherently stable, but also acknowledges that such stability is in some ways illusory, arising in the differences of evolutionary pace between human thought and the subjects/objects of human thought. By way of brief example, consider mathematics, which is often described in terms of certainty and permanence. Yet, when considered over the past 2500 years, mathematical knowledge has clearly evolved, and continues to do so. Even more contentious, it is often it is assumed that, while ideas may change, the universe does not. But, the viability of this sort of belief is put to question when ideas are recognized to be part of the cosmos. The universe changes when a thought changes.

The fact that complexity thinking pays attention to diverse sensibilities should not be taken to mean that the movement represents some sort of effort to embrace the "best" elements from, for example, classical science or recent postmodern critiques of scientism. Nor is it the case that complexity looks for a common ground among belief systems. Complexity thinking is not a hybrid. It is a new attitude toward studying particular sorts of phenomena that is able to acknowledge the insights of other traditions without trapping itself in absolutes or universals.

Further to this point, although it is tempting to describe complexity thinking as a unified realm of inquiry or approach to research, this sort of characterization is not entirely correct. In contrast to the analytic science of the Enlightenment, complexity thinking is not actually defined in terms of its modes of inquiry. There is no "complexity scientific method"; there are no "gold standards"[4] for complexity research; indeed, specific studies of complex phenomena might embrace or reject established methods, depending of the particular object of inquiry.

It is this point that most commonly arises in popularized accounts of complexity research: The domain is more appropriately characterized in terms of its objects of study than anything else. In an early narrative of the emergence of the field, Waldrop[5] introduces the diverse interests and the diffuse origins of complexity research through a list that includes such disparate events as the collapse of the Soviet Union, trends in a stock market, the rise of life on Earth, the evolution of the eye, and the emergence of mind. Other writers have argued that the umbrella of complexity reaches over any phenomenon that might be described in terms of a living system—including, in terms of immediate relevance to this discussion of educational research, bodily subsystems (like the brain or the immune system), consciousness, personal understanding, social institutions, subcultures, cultures, and a species.

Of course, the strategy of list-making is inherently problematic, as it does not enable discernments between *complex* and *not-complex*. To that end, and as is developed in much greater detail in the pages that follow (particularly, chaps. 5 and 6), researchers have identified several necessary qualities that must be manifest for a phenomenon to be classed as complex. The list currently includes:

- SELF-ORGANIZED—complex systems/unities spontaneously arise as the actions of autonomous agents come to be interlinked and co-dependent;
- BOTTOM-UP EMERGENT—complex unities manifest properties that exceed the summed traits and capacities of individual agents, but these transcendent qualities and abilities do not depend on central organizers or overarching governing structures;
- SHORT-RANGE RELATIONSHIPS—most of the information within a complex system is exchanged among close neighbors, meaning that the system's coherence depends mostly on agents' immediate interdependencies, not on centralized control or top-down administration;
- NESTED STRUCTURE (or scale-free networks)—complex unities are often composed of and often comprise other unities that might be properly identified as complex—that is, as giving rise to new patterns of activities and new rules of behavior (see fig. 1.1);
- AMBIGUOUSLY BOUNDED—complex forms are *open* in the sense that they continuously exchange matter and energy with their surroundings (and so judgments about their edges may require certain arbitrary impositions and necessary ignorances);
- ORGANIZATIONALLY CLOSED—complex forms are *closed* in the sense that they are inherently stable—that is, their behavioral patterns or internal or-

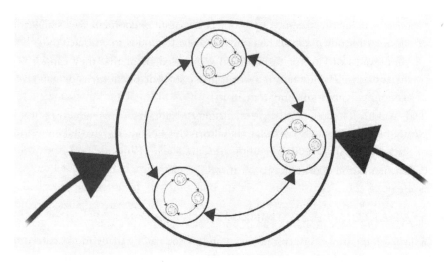

FIGURE 1.1 FIGURATIVE REPRESENTATION OF THE NESTEDNESS OF COMPLEX UNITIES
We use this image to underscore that complex unities are composed not just of smaller components (circles), but also by the relationships among those components (arrows). These interactions can give rise to new structural and behavioral possibilities that are not represented in the subsystems on their own.

ganizations endure, even while they exchange energy and matter with their dynamic contexts (so judgments about their edges are usually based on perceptible and sufficiently stable coherences);

- STRUCTURE DETERMINED—a complex unity can change *its own* structure as it adapts to maintain its viability within dynamic contexts; in other words, complex systems embody their histories—they learn—and are thus better described in terms of Darwinian evolution than Newtonian mechanics;

- FAR-FROM-EQUILIBRIUM—complex systems do not operate in balance; indeed, a stable equilibrium implies death for a complex system.

This particular list is hardly exhaustive. Nor is it sufficient to distinguish all possible cases of complexity. However, it suffices for our current purposes—specifically, to illustrate our core assertion that a great many phenomena that are currently of interest to educational research might be considered in terms of complex dynamics. Specific examples discussed in this text include individual sensemaking, teacher–learner relationships, classroom dynamics, school organizations, community involvement in education, bodies of knowledge, and culture. Once again, this list does not come close to representing the range of phenomena that might be considered.

Clearly, such a sweep may seem so broad as to be almost useless. However, the purpose of naming such a range of phenomena is *not* to collapse the diversity into variations on a theme or to subject disparate phenomena to a standardized method of study. Exactly the contrary, our intention is to embrace the inherent complexities of diverse forms in an acknowledgment that they cannot be reduced to one another. In other words, these sorts of phenomena demand modes of inquiry that are specific to them.

Yet, at the same time, there are distinct advantages—pragmatic, political, and otherwise—to recognizing what these sorts of phenomena have in common, and one of our main purposes in writing this book is to foreground these advantages. But first, some important qualifications.

WHAT COMPLEXITY THINKING ISN'T

One of the most condemning accusations that can be made in the current academic context is that a given theory seems to be striving toward the status of a *metadiscourse*—that is, an explanatory system that somehow stands over or exceeds all others, a theory that claims to subsume prior or lesser perspectives, a discourse that somehow overcomes the blind spots of other discourses. The most frequent target of this sort of criticism is analytic science, but the criticism has been leveled against religions, mathematics, and other attitudes that have presented themselves as superior and totalizing.

Given our introductory comments, it may seem that this complexity science also aspires to a metadiscursive status—and, indeed, it is often presented in these terms by both friend and foe. As such, it behooves us to be clear about how we imagine the nature of the discourse.

To begin, we do not regard complexity thinking as an explanatory system. Complexity thinking does not provide all-encompassing explanations; rather, it is an umbrella notion that draws on and elaborates the irrepressible human tendency to notice similarities among seemingly disparate phenomena. How is an anthill like a human brain? How is a classroom like a stock market? How is a body of knowledge like a species? These are questions that invoke a poetic sensibility and that rely on analogy, metaphor, and other associative (that is, non-representational) functions of language.

In recognizing some deep similarities among the structures and dynamics of the sorts of phenomena just mentioned, complexity thinking has enabled some powerful developments in medicine, economics, computing science, physics, business, sociology … the list goes on. But its range of influence should not be interpreted as evidence of or aspiration toward the status of a metadiscourse. In fact, complexity thinking does not in any way attempt to encompass or supplant analytic science or any other discourse. Rather, in its transdisciplinarity, it explicitly aims to embrace, blend, and elaborate the insights of any and all relevant domains of human thought. Complexity thinking does not *rise over*, but *arises among* other discourses. Like most attitudes toward inquiry, complexity thinking is oriented by the realization that the act of comparing diverse and seemingly unconnected phenomena is both profoundly human and, at times, tremendously fecund.

An important caveat of this discussion is that complexity thinking is not a ready-made discourse that can be imported into and imposed onto education research and practice. That sort of move would represent a profound misunderstanding of the character of complexity studies. Rather, educational researchers interested in the discourse must simultaneously ask the complementary questions, "How might complexity thinking contribute to educational research?" and "How might educational research contribute to complexity thinking?" This reflexive, co-participatory attitude is well represented in the emergence of the movement.

THE ORIGINS OF COMPLEXITY THINKING

As has been thoroughly described in the many popular histories of the movement, complexity thinking arose in the confluence of several areas of Western research, including cybernetics, systems theory, artificial intelligence, chaos theory, fractal geometry, and nonlinear dynamics.[6] Many of these branches of inquiry began to develop in the 1950s and 1960s, emerging mainly out of physics, biology, and mathematics. More recently, certain studies in the social sciences, especially within sociology and anthropology, have come to be included under the rubric of complexity. Given this range of disciplinary influence, it is impossible to do justice to even one aspect of the "field."

It is thus that one of our strategies in this text is to use complexity thinking itself as a case study of the sort of phenomenon that is of interest to a complexivist: It is an emergent realm in which similar but nonetheless diverse elements—in this case, sensibilities and research emphases—have coalesced into a coherent, discernible unity that cannot be reduced to the sum of its constituents. A sense of this diversity might be gleaned from the varied terms for complex systems that arose in different domains, including "complex adaptive systems" (physics), "nonlinear dynamical systems" (mathematics), "dissipative structures" (chemistry), "autopoietic systems" (biology), and "organized complex systems" (information science). These names are attached to fairly specific technical meanings within their respective disciplines, but nonetheless refer to phenomena that share the sorts of qualities identified above.

Use of the word *complexity* to label this class of self-organizing, adaptive phenomena dates back to the middle of the 20th century. In particular, a 1948 paper by physicist and information scientist Warren Weaver[7] is regarded by many as critical to current usage. Weaver was among the first to provide a rubric to distinguish among complex and not-complex forms and events. In brief, he identified three broad categories of phenomena that are of interest to modern science— *simple, complicated,* and *complex*[8]—which he linked to different emphases and tools in the evolution of post-Enlightenment thought.

Weaver's first category, *simple systems,* included those phenomena in which only a few inert objects or variables interact. Examples include trajectories, satellites, and collisions—in effect, the sorts of forms and events that captured the attentions of Galileo, Descartes, Bacon, and Newton in the early stages of the Scientific Revolution. Along with their contemporaries, these thinkers developed a set of *analytic* methods to reduce such mechanical phenomena to basic laws and elementary particles. The guiding assumption was that a more thorough knowledge of such fundamentals would make it possible for researchers to extrapolate their understandings to explain more complicated phenomena.

The meaning of the word *analytic* is critical here. Derived from the Greek *analusis,* "dissolving," analytic methods were literally understood in terms of cutting apart all phenomena and all claims to truth to their root causes and assumptions in order to reassemble them into complete and unshakeable explanatory systems. During the early stages of the emergence of modern science, there seemed to be ample reason to have faith in this approach, given the tremendous predictive power of achievements like Newtonian mechanics. Although now several centuries old, these particular tools remain the principal means to examine and manipulate simple systems. Indeed, they were so effective that, by the early 1800s, confidence in analytic methods had reached an extreme, as is evident in mathematician Pierre Simon de Laplace's bold assertion:

> Given for one instant an intelligence which could comprehend all forces by which nature is animated and the respective situations of the beings which compose it—an intelligence sufficiently vast to submit these data to analyses—it would embrace in the same formula the movements of the greatest bodies and those of the lightest atom; for it, nothing would be uncertain and the future, as the past, would be present to its eyes.[9]

This passage is frequently cited as the quintessential statement of *determinism*—that is, the philosophical attitude that there are no accidents. Everything that is going to happen is absolutely determined (fixed) by what has already happened; everything that has already happened can in principle be determined (calculated) by careful scrutiny of current conditions.

The belief in a deterministic universe and faith in analytic methods persist within the scientific establishment—and rightly so. However, as evidenced by

Laplace's assertion, it had already been acknowledged 200 years ago that the approach was not entirely pragmatic, given that a "vast" intelligence would be needed to understand the universe in such terms. In fact, even earlier, Newton himself recognized that the calculations associated with simple systems that involve three or more interacting components can quickly become intractable. In the 19th century, as scholars met up with more and more such phenomena, a new set of methods were developed. Based on probability and statistics, these tools were more useful for interpretation of the gross or global dynamics of *complicated systems*—situations such as astronomical phenomena, magnetism, molecular interactions, subatomic structures, and weather patterns that might involve millions of variables or parts.

Significantly, the development of statistical and probabilistic methods represented more a resignation than a shift in thinking. These methods did not arise from or prompt a change in the fundamental assumption that phenomena are locked in a fixed trajectory and reducible to the sums of their parts. The universe was still seen as determined. The new tools were understood to provide only a veneer of explanation, not a deep understanding. Lacking a sufficiently vast intelligence and constrained by frustratingly limited perceptual capacities, humans were grudgingly compelled to rely on coarse characterizations. The move to statistical methods was merely an acknowledgment that no flesh-based intellect would ever be sufficient to measure and calculate even a very small part of the intricate universe. The more complicated the phenomenon, the more one was compelled to rely on quantified and averaged descriptions of gross patterns rather than precise analyses of interacting factors.

By the early 1900s, however, belief in the general utility of probabilistic and statistical representations of phenomena had begun to wane. Perhaps, some suggested, neither analytic nor statistical methods could ever be adequate for the interpretation and prediction of some phenomena. For instance, in an early articulation of the important notion of "sensitivity to initial conditions"—or what is now more popularly known as "the butterfly effect"—French mathematician Henri Poincaré explained:

> [E]ven if it were the case the that natural laws no longer held any secret for us, we could still only know the initial situation approximately. If that enables us to predict the succeeding situation with the same approximation, that is all we require, and we should say the phenomenon had been predicted, that is governed by laws. But it is not always so; it may happen that small differences in the initial conditions produce very great ones in the final phenomenon. A small error in the former will produce an enormous error in the latter. Prediction becomes impossible.[10]

In this assertion, Poincaré problematized the prediction-oriented project of modern science. His two-pronged argument—that is, that human measurements are necessarily approximate and that errors in such approximations are not only cumulative but self-amplifying—meant that even the most precisely measured simple phenomena and the most rigorously verified statistical descriptions of complicated phenomena could (and probably would) become wildly inaccurate over time.

However, there is a subtler and more important point to be drawn out of Poincaré's statement—namely the implicit suggestion that the actions of some systems themselves contribute to the transformations of their own possibilities. That is, a linear causal model of reality, one that is based on the assumption that a knowledge of inputs is adequate to predict outputs, does not work for all systems. In some cases, systems are self-transformative.[11]

Put differently, although a complicated system might have many components, the relationship among those parts is fixed and clearly defined. If it were carefully dismantled and reassembled, the system would work in exactly the same, predictable way. However, there exist some forms that cannot be dismantled and reassembled, whose characters are destroyed when the relationships among components are broken. Within these sorts of *complex systems*, interactions of components are not fixed and clearly defined, but are subject to ongoing co-adaptations. The behaviors of simple and complicated systems are mechanical. They can be thoroughly described and reasonably predicted on the basis of precise rules, whereas the rules that govern complex systems can vary dramatically from one system to the next. Moreover, these rules can be volatile, subject to change if the system changes. Such precariousness arises in part from the fact that the "components" of the complex system—at least for all of the systems that are considered in this text—are themselves dynamic and adaptive.

The point is perhaps more apparent through an example. Consider a social unity, in which the "parts" must clearly abide by some reasonably coherent system of rules if that unity is remain viable. As any socially competent human will attest, the rules of interaction are neither stable nor universal. Codes of conduct evolve; roles, responsibilities, and liberties are always differentiated to some extent; acceptable behaviors vary dramatically from one context to the next. Moreover, if such rules could somehow be fixed and uniformly applied, the result would probably not be a utopia. More likely, the system would atrophy and die in short order.

These realizations of the necessary and inevitable internal variability and adaptability of complex unities are of immense importance. In particular, they represent a more-than-subtle challenge to much of the research in the humanities and social sciences that unfolded through the 1800s and 1900s—oriented by either a quasi-mechanical frame or by probability and statistics. Of particular relevance to educational research, for example, the cause–effect logic that underpinned behaviorist psychology is not only rendered problematic by complexity thinking, but almost irrelevant in efforts to understand phenomena as complex as individual understanding and collective knowledge. Specifically, the behaviorist notion that learning is somehow "caused by" or "due to" experience is challenged by the complexivist sensibility that what is learned is more appropriately attributable to the *agent* than to the *agent's context*. For example, the manner in which you are responding to this text is more appropriately understood in terms of your complex structure than in terms of the black markings on these pages, which only act to trigger various aspects of your embodied history. With regard to pedagogy, then, complexivists tend to follow Freud's assertion that teaching, understood in terms of determining learning, is one of the impossible professions. (We explore this point in much greater detail in subsequent chapters, particularly chaps. 6 and 7.)

This sensibility, consistent with Poincaré's insight into the impossibility of certain sorts of predictability, came to be more widely embraced in the physical sciences through the 1900s. It culminated in the formal articulation of the concepts of "self-organization" and "structure determinism," introduced above. Toward the close of the 1900s, complexity scientist Stuart Kauffman flagged the significance of such notions:

> Since Darwin, we have come to think about organisms as tinkered-together contraptions and selection as the sole source of order. Yet Darwin could not have begun to suspect the power of self-organization. We must seek our principles of adaptation in complex systems anew.[12]

In other words, the prevailing belief that adaptations can be understood in terms of environmental causes, while appropriate for simple and complicated (i.e., mechanical) systems, is utterly unsuited to complex systems. Entirely new principles of adaptation—that is, *learning*—are needed.

It is thus that we arrive at one of our central assumptions and assertions: In this discussion of educational and research implications of complexity thinking, we are concerned with are *learning systems*. Moreover, following Kauffman,[13] we seek our principles of *learning* in complex systems anew.

WHAT IS "LEARNING"? WHAT ARE "LEARNERS"?

To reemphasize the point, this text is framed by the assumption that learning is not simply a matter of "modification in behavior," as asserted in much of 20th-century psychology-oriented educational research. This deeply entrenched assertion, along with its orienting notion that "experience causes learning to happen" are argued here to be, quite simply, impractical and unproductive. Experience, rather, is better understood in terms of triggers than causes. Learning, then, is a matter of transformations in the learner that are simultaneously physical and behavioral—which is to say, in biological terms, *structural*. Learning is certainly conditioned by particular experiences, but it is "due to" the learner's own complex biological-and-experiential structure, not an external stimulus.

Such assertions represent a rejection of deep-seated assumptions about linear causality, an aspect of determinism, that were transposed from the analytic sciences onto discussions of teaching through the 19th and 20th centuries. Cause–effect interpretations make little sense when learning is understood in terms of recursive and elaborative processes. To be clear, the issue here is *not* whether the universe is deterministic; it is whether attempts at deterministic explanations are relevant and applicable in a domain like education. The issue of determinism presses into the realms of cosmology and philosophy, and it is a matter of continuing debate, even among complexivists. It is less contentious within education, where the assertion that teaching cannot cause learning is broadly (but certainly not universally) accepted.

The complexivist reconsideration of learning goes even further. Not only are the assumptions about the dynamics of learning challenged, so is the prevailing belief about what a *learner* is. To discuss this issue, we need to be a bit more deliberate about the meaning of the word *structure*, which we have already used several times. It turns out that the concept is vital to broader appreciations of complexity, adaptability, and related notions.

The word *structure* is subject to diverse, even flatly contradictory interpretations. In English, two of the most prominent uses of the word are manifest in discussions of architecture and biology, and it is its biology-based meanings that are invoked here. To elaborate, when used in reference to buildings, structure prompts senses of fixed organization, preplanning, and step-following—which are in turn caught up in a web of associations that includes such notions as foundations, platforms, scaffolds, basics, hierarchies, and so on.

The biological meaning of structure is quite different. Heard in such phrases as "the structure of an organism" and "the structure of an ecosystem," the word is used to point to the complex histories of organic forms. Structure in this sense is both caused and accidental, both familiar and unique, both complete and in process. This usage is closer to the original meaning of the word, as suggested by its etymological links to *strew* and *construe*. Indeed, when the word was first applied to architecture some 400 to 500 years ago, it was at a time when most buildings were subject to continuous evolution as parts were added, destroyed, or otherwise altered. The structure of a building was most often understood in terms of its immediate use, not its original purpose.

A very different way of explaining the distinction between architectural and biological meaning of structure is to point out that, in the biological sense, structure is *incompressible*. The unique structure of a living system arises from and embodies its history. Although many of that structure's traits might be characterized in global or general terms, the finer details—and, perhaps, most of the vital details, in terms of understanding the system's general character—can never be known or replicated precisely. In contrast, the vital aspects of a building or other static form can be specified with considerable precision, and usually in highly compressed forms such as blueprints or maps.

Returning to the issue at hand, then, a *learner* in this text is understood to be a structuring structured structure, to borrow from Dyke.[14] A learner is a complex unity that is capable of adapting itself to the sorts of new and diverse circumstances that an active agent is likely to encounter in a dynamic world.

For us, this conception of a learner alters the landscape of educational discourse. Overwhelmingly, the word *learner* is used to refer to the assumed-to-be isolated and insulated individual. By contrast, in complexity terms, learners can include social and classroom groupings, schools, communities, bodies of knowledge, languages, cultures, species—among other possibilities. One might also move in a micro direction, extending the list to include organs and bodily subsystems, cells, neurons, and so on.[15] In this way, complexity thinking suggests, it is not at all inappropriate to say that a discipline "argues" or a cell "knows" or a culture "thinks." Such phrasings are not so much anthropomorphisms as they are acknowledgments of a deep similarity of dynamical structures of many phenomena.

Importantly, in the sorts of cases just mentioned, the named learner can be considered simultaneously a coherent unity, a complex of interacting unities, or a part of a grander unity. On this point, and of considerable relevance to both education and educational research, complexity thinking foregrounds the role of the observer in the phenomenon observed.

COMPLEXITY OF RESEARCH AND COMPLICITY OF RESEARCHERS

As mentioned, a necessary quality of complex systems is that they are open. They constantly exchange energy, matter, and information with their contexts. In the process, they affect the structures of both themselves and their environments.

The term *environment* must be used carefully. In complexity terms, it is not meant to imply the presence of a clear, unambiguous physical boundary between an agent and its context. For complex systems, agents are necessarily parts of their environments. It is not always possible (or useful) to determine with certainty which components are part of the system (i.e., "inside") and which belong to the setting (i.e., "outside").

In fact, the closer one looks at the boundary of a complex/open system, the more troublesome the issue becomes. For example, at the cellular level, it is usually not clear which molecules belong to the system and which to the setting when one zooms in on a cell membrane. The same is true when attempting to distinguish between *person* and *not-person* at the level of the skin, or when attempting to unravel origins and authorship of a particular insight. One cannot specify simply—or, perhaps more appropriately, simply cannot specify—the locations of such boundaries in objective terms. Thus, for the purposes of studying a complex form, the physical or conceptual boundaries of a complex/open system are always contingent on the criteria used to define or distinguish the system from its backdrop.

The critical point here is not that researchers must define boundaries of the phenomena that they study (although this is a vital point). Rather, the main issue here is that complexity thinking compels researchers to consider how they are implicated in the phenomena that they study—and, more broadly, to acknowledge that their descriptions of the world exist in complex (i.e., nested, co-implicated, ambiguously bounded, dynamic, etc.) relationship with the world.

In this sense, and as is developed in greater detail in chapter 4, complexity thinking rejects scientific *objectivity*, relativist *subjectivity*, and structuralist or poststructuralist *intersubjectivity* as satisfactory foundations for any claim to truth. The notion of objectivity—that is, of god's-eye truths or observerless observations—is deemed an impossible fiction. Conversely, the suggestion that individual experience is sufficient for claims of facticity is rejected because it ignores the linguistic bases and other collective aspects of interpretations. At the same time, the notion of intersubjectivity—that is, the belief that truths that are manufactured and sustained strictly through social accord—is also deemed inadequate. Such accord is necessarily nested in the grander physical world. As the argument goes, by orienting attentions, a knower's knowledge necessarily affects the ways a phenomenon is perceived and how the knower acts in relation to that that phenomenon. And so, rather than striving for an impossible objectivity, embracing a self-referencing subjectivity, or holding to a culture-bounded intersubjectivity, for the complexivist truth is more about *interobjectivity*. It is not just about the object, not just about the subject, and not just about social agreement. It is about holding all of these in dynamic, co-specifying, conversational relationships while locating them in a grander, more-than-human context. It is about emergent possibility as a learner/knower (e.g., individual, social collective, or other complex unity) engages with some aspect of its world in an always-evolving, ever-elaborative structural dance.

Complexivists Ian Stewart and Jack Cohen make the point through a clever play on words. They recombine the roots of the common terms *simplicity* and *complexity* to generate *simplexity* and *complicity*. For them, *simplexity* refers to "the process whereby a system of rules can engender simple features. Simplexity is the emergence of large-scale simplicities as direct consequences of rules."[16] Examples of simplexities include Newtonian mechanics and formal mathematics, whose "properties are the direct and inescapable consequences of the rules."[17]

As we develop in greater detail in chapter 2, a prominent issue among complexivists is that simplexities have often been (mis)taken as descriptions of "the way things truly are." In an effort to interrupt this entrenched habit, Cohen and Stewart propose the notion of *complicities* as a category of phenomena in which "totally different rules converge to produce similar features, and so exhibit the same large-scale structural patterns."[18] In other words, they propose a definition that is fully compatible with the meaning of complexity that we have been using in this chapter.

However, with their development of the word *complicity* (to refer to what we are calling *complexity*), they powerfully foreground the fact that the researcher is always already entangled in the phenomenon researched. Researchers are aspects of even grander systems, shaped by and contributing to the shapes of the phenomena in ways and to extents that they simply cannot know. Such realizations render research a profoundly ethical undertaking, and this is an issue that we explore in greater detail in all of the subsequent chapters.

Complexity thinking helps us actually take on the work of trying to understand things while we are part of the things we are trying to understand. It foregrounds that we can never develop an objective appreciation of something of which we are part. Complexity suggests that rather than standing back from the world, we must get involved (and acknowledge our implication/complicity) in the unfoldings of the cosmos.

Indeed, *implication, complicity*, and *complexity* are all derived from the Indo-European *plek-*, "to weave, plait, fold, entwine." Such, then, is a first lesson of complexity thinking. As researchers interested in issues swirling about human knowledge—what it is, how it is developed and sustained, what it means to know, and so on—we are woven into what we research, just as it is woven into us.

CHAPTER TWO

WHAT IS "SCIENCE"?

THERE IS NO SUCH THING AS PHILOSOPHY-FREE SCIENCE;
THERE IS ONLY SCIENCE WHOSE PHILOSOPHICAL BAGGAGE
IS TAKEN ON BOARD WITHOUT EXAMINATION.
—Daniel Dennett[1]

Currently, the movement that we are referring to as "complexity thinking" is more commonly called *complexity science*, a term that was adopted at the end of the 20th century to replace "complexity theory." The reasons for the shift from "theory" to "science" revolved around the desire to represent complexity research as a scholarly and rigorous approach to research. Somewhat ironically, our decision to speak in terms of "complexity thinking" rather than "complexity science" in this text is motivated by a pervasive suspicion of the physical sciences among educators and educational researchers. This suspicion is not entirely unfounded, as we develop in this chapter.

In the context of contemporary discussions of education, the word *science* is usually taken to refer to *both* a collection of established principles on the nature of the universe *and* the particular methods of investigation and verification by which those principles are established. These methods, at least in the manner that they are most commonly presented, are organized around the standard of proof through replication: Hypotheses become facts and theories become truths as researchers are able to demonstrate that predictable and repeatable results can be obtained.

If this were the only sense of the word *science* at play in the contemporary world, then studies of complexity could never be considered scientific. Complex phenomena present two immediate problems around the criterion of replication:

First, very similar systems under virtually identical circumstances and subjected to virtually identical stimuli can respond in dramatically different ways—as any teacher will attest. One simply cannot predict with any great confidence how one pupil or class will make sense of some learning event based on another pupil's or class's interpretations. The second problem is even more troublesome. The *same* system—or, at least, a system that seems to have preserved its character and identity—can and will respond very differently to sets of conditions that appear identical. For example, one cannot reliably predict how a student or a classroom collective will act based on responses in an earlier lesson, or sometimes a few minutes previous. In other words, strict predictability and reliability of results are unreasonable criteria when dealing with systems that learn.

What, then, is meant by *science* in the term *complexity science* if, as noted in chapter 1, the analytic bases of inquiry are deemed inadequate and, as just mentioned, the criteria for verification are rendered impracticable?

To begin to answer this question, we need to underscore once again that no unified response is possible. In fact, a range of perspectives on the character and status of scientific truth is represented among complexity researchers. Indeed, there is likely as much conflict and contradiction among complexivists as there is within almost any area of academic inquiry. In contrast to some other areas, however, complexity researchers tend to appreciate such tensions as necessary and productive sites of insight—not matters to be flattened out, but potential triggers for richer understandings.

Richardson and Cilliers[2] sum up some of the variations in sensibilities that are represented across complexity research by identifying three broad schools of thought that have been represented, these being:

a) HARD (OR REDUCTIONIST) COMPLEXITY SCIENCE—an approach dominated by physicists that, in effect, maintains the same desire as analytic science to uncover and *understand the nature of reality*, oriented by the assumption that such a reality is determined and hence determinable.

b) SOFT COMPLEXITY SCIENCE—an approach more common in the biological and social sciences that draws on the metaphors and principles developed within hard complexity science to describe living and social systems. In this case, complexity is more *a way of seeing the world*, an interpretive system rather than a route to or representation of reality.

c) COMPLEXITY THINKING—an attitude that lies somewhere between the hard and soft approach. It is concerned with the philosophical and pragmatic implications of assuming a complex universe, and might thus be described as representing *a way of thinking and acting*.

Consistent with a complexivist sensibility, Richardson and Cilliers acknowledge the artificiality and illusory neatness of this classification. The varied attitudes are highly intertwined and sometimes simultaneously manifest. In fact, we suspect that a reader intent on taxonomizing parts of this book could readily classify varying portions as fitting firmly in one or another of the above categories. The purpose of the heuristic, then, is not to insist that one commit to a category, but to provide a useful device for making sense of some of the inevitable inconsistencies in the field—in the process, offering a more nuanced picture of complexity and the powerful-although-conflicted character of this particular attitude toward inquiry.

It is important to underscore that, although there are clear disagreements around matters of research emphasis and approach, there remains a reasonable consensus among complexivists as to what constitutes a complex phenomenon or entity. That is, there is a broad agreement on the meaning of *complexity* and a somewhat shakier accord around the meaning of *science*. To render this issue less opaque, and to make clearer our own positionings, in this chapter we move through brief discussions of the three categories of complexity studies suggested by Richardson and Cilliers.

SOME ORIENTING COMMENTS ON THE EVOLUTION OF COMPLEXITY SCIENCE

Before moving into some of the specifics around the different sensibilities represented among complexivists, it may be useful to highlight some of the phases that complexity science research has passed through over recent decades. Here we draw on Waldrop's and Johnson's popular accounts of the emergence of the field.[3]

Early studies of complex phenomena were undertaken well before the coining of the phrases "complexity theory," "complexity science," and "complexity thinking." In the main, this work consisted of disparate and largely unconnected investigations of specific phenomena. Examples include Jane Jacobs' examinations of the rise and decline of cities,[4] Deborah Gordon's multi-year observations of the life cycles of anthills,[5] Friedrich Engels' studies of the emergence of social structures in the free-market world,[6] Rachel Carson's examinations of the ecological implications of industrialized societies,[7] Humberto Maturana's research into self-producing and self-maintaining biological unities,[8] and many similarly minded inquiries. Such studies were principally *observational and descriptive* in nature. The theme that unites these diverse projects is the desire to generate rich accounts of specific phenomena, oriented by a suspicion that anthills, cities, biological unities, cultures, and so on must be studied at the levels of their emergence, not in terms of their sub-components—and certainly not in terms of fundamental particles and universal laws. Gordon, for instance, demonstrated that the lives of anthills could not be reduced to the characters or life cycles of individual ants. Rather, something qualitatively different arose in the interactions of many ants—coherences that were maintained for periods that lasted many times longer than any single ant.

As more and more such studies were published, a handful of researchers undertook to identify some of the qualities and conditions that seemed to be common across the range of phenomena studied. For instance, there seems to be tremendous redundancy among the agents that come together within most complex systems. (As developed in greater detail in chap. 7, such redundancy is not only one of the important markers used to distinguish complex systems from complicated mechanical systems—which tend to be composed of highly specialized, minimally redundant components—it is also one of the conditions that can be manipulated to affect the character of a complex unity.) Phrased differently, the emphasis in complexity studies moved beyond a focus on detailed descriptions of specific instances toward efforts to articulate more generalized characterizations.

With the advent of more powerful and readily available computer technologies in the 1970s, researchers with an interest in complex phenomena were given a tool with which they could begin to test some of their suspicions and hypotheses around the emergence and ongoing coherence of different systems. Very quickly, computer simulations became a major focus in complexity research—and, in fact, this emphasis served as the site around which complexity theory coalesced in the late 1970s and early 1980s. It was also one of the vehicles by which complexity research was popularized through the 1980s and 1990s as simulations of flocking birds, growing cities, anthills, neural nets, and other complex phenomena were made available through popular software, video games, and interactive websites.[9]

By the 1990s, complexity research was a clearly discernible domain, evidenced by the appearance of institutes and conferences designed to bring together researchers who previously had little occasion to interact, along with the publication of several popular histories of the nascent field.[10] By then, prompted by the accumulation of inter-case comparisons, the focus of complexity research had begun to shift again. Investigators had begun to turn their attentions to the prompting and manipulation of complex systems. Could one occasion the emergence of a complex unity? If so, how? Once emergent, could a complex phenomenon be deliberately manipulated? If so, how and to what extent? Phenomena subjected to this manner of questioning varied from ecosystems to immune systems, from social groupings to interneuronal networks.[11]

Such questions were (and are) investigated through a variety of means. For example, increasingly sophisticated computer simulations have been developed to model the complex relationships among neurons in the brain or species in an ecosystem. More pragmatically, some researchers have applied newly established principles of complexity to revive vanquished ecosystems, to rethink established medical orthodoxies, and to re-organize major companies.[12] This emergence of a *pragmatics of transformation* within complexity research is associated with the change in title of complexity research, from *complexity theory* to *complexity science*. This shift was a deliberate one made by complexivists to flag the fact that research had achieved a certain rigor and respectability, if not the requirements of replication that are better suited to studies of mechanical phenomena.

In our view, the shift toward considerations of pragmatics of transformation has also rendered the discourse much better fitted to the particular concerns of educators and educational researchers, given educationists' societal responsibilities for deliberately affecting learners and communities. That said, the perceived utility of this sort of pragmatics varies considerably across the diverse schools of thought among complexity researchers. Returning to the three sensibilities identified by Richardson and Cilliers, then, we now turn to the conceptual commitments implicit in these sensibilities as well as their possible relevancies and utilities for educators and educational researchers.

HARD COMPLEXITY SCIENCE

As mentioned in chapter 1, the strands of inquiry that have come to be knitted together into complexity science first arose within the physical sciences in the mid-1900s. These domains have a long history of being oriented toward the articulation of complete, unambiguous, and objective accounts of the universe, at least insofar as popular beliefs go about the scientific project.[13]

The desire for these sorts of accounts predates modern science by more than two millennia. It is anchored in an ancient assumption that the universe is governed by fixed, immutable laws. In this view, although dynamic, the universe is essentially unchanging—at least in terms of the sorts of phenomena that can occur and the sorts of forms that can exist.[14]

Of course, this view no longer prevails in either the scientific realm or the popular imagination. On the contrary, contemporary theories and worldviews tend to be infused with an evolutionary sensibility—not only an acceptance, but an expectation that things will change. Yet, it is important to underscore that widespread embrace of this notion is recent. Even in the sciences, broad incorporation of evolutionary principles happened barely 100 years ago. Prior to Darwin's articulation of a scientifically defensible, evidence-based theory of evolution and subsequent adoption/adaptation of that theoretical frame within geology, sociology, psychology, and other domains, the project of science was understood in rather straightforward terms of parsing up, categorizing, and labeling the pieces of the assumed-to-be complete and dismantle-able universe. This sensibility, although thoroughly critiqued, has persisted and underpins the continued assumption that science is aimed at a totalized, fully consistent theory of everything.

There is a bit of a contradiction—even paradox—here. Modern science gave rise to and has embraced a frame (i.e., evolutionary theory) that compels at least a problematization, if not outright rejection, of the very foundations of the scientific project that prompted the emergence of the theory of evolution. As it turns out, hard complexity science seems to be positioned within this contradiction, in its desire to assemble an objective account of the universe even while acknowledging the possibility of emergent forms that simply could not be anticipated on the basis of the current state of affairs.

A preferred means of investigation within the hard approach is computer simulation, in which complex systems are modeled in attempts to uncover the conditions that underlie their emergence and to make sense of the transcendent capacities that arise once emergent. These simulations are, of course, rooted in mathematics, which hard complexivists typically argue to be a means to enhance one's appreciation and understanding of the phenomenon at hand.[15] Osberg,[16] however, argues that mathematics can be as obfuscating as illuminating, and so we present the issues in nonmathematical terms here. To summarize Osberg's argument, while mathematics provides powerful tools that should not be ignored, the project of bottom-up computer simulations is necessarily oriented toward the identification of essential rules or principles that can then be recombined to generate complex happenings (or, at least, convincing simulations of complex happenings). There is no disagreement that mathematics and mathematical tools are useful *for these sorts of endeavors*. However, as helpful as a rule-based approach may be, it is inadequate for understanding all dimensions of complexity and it can in fact be a hindrance to these understandings. A key issue is, of course, that merely complicated tools (i.e., computers) are used to model complex phenomena—or, to invoke the vocabulary developed by Cohen and Stewart, simplexities are being substituted for complicities.[17] Such a strategy can be challenged as necessarily limited and limiting. At best, some argue, simulation operates on the level of analogy, thus perhaps obscuring critical aspects of complex behavior.[18]

Of course, computer simulation is not the only approach used within hard complexity science. Other prominent strategies include close observation and controlled experimentation—and, indeed, most of the pre-computer-era studies that have come to be seen as complexity-oriented fall into one or both of these categories. These studies of beehives, cell assemblies, and other physical systems have been vital for prompting broad appreciations of the existence of complex phenomena. However, as noted above, they have also been frustrated by problems with replicability, a criterion that comes along with the methods developed with analytic traditions.

The importance of these issues is perhaps more evident when one considers the potential usefulness of complexity science within educational research. Clearly, there are important things to be learned by close observations of, for example, brain functioning, individual learning, and classroom collectivity. And, clearly, there are things to be learned by experimenting with, for example, varied teaching emphases, different school conditions, and so on. Further, a well crafted simulation of, say, brain function or interpersonal dynamics can contribute significantly to teacher knowledge. However, even if one were to accept the dubious premise that such phenomena are knowable in excruciating detail, is it reasonable to expect that the resulting knowledge would be of much use to educators? Might the collective biological, experiential, social, and cultural issues that contribute to the shape of every classroom event serve to undermine the utility of such knowledge?

To be clear, we are arguing here that a hard approach to complexity science, while relevant, powerful, and appropriate for certain emergent phenomena, is of limited value to educators and educational researchers. Further, a major premise of the hard approach—namely the assumed stability of the phenomenon studied—is inherently problematic for educationists. The conditions and purposes of schooling are constantly shifting, and an attempt, for example, to characterize classroom dynamics in absence of this realization engenders a sort of head-in-the-sand attitude. In particular, it compels investigators to ignore their own contributions to the ongoing evolutions of the phenomenon studied. In arguing for different conceptions of engagement and outcomes, researchers oriented by hard complexity science cannot help but trigger unpredictable shifts in the very phenomena that they might hope to capture in their webs of interpretation. An attitude that is fitted to the study of insects and neurons, then, might be ill-suited to phenomena that evolve at the paces of human actions and interactions.

SOFT COMPLEXITY SCIENCE

Regardless of which school of complexivist thought is embraced, the movement has drifted a long way from the conceptions of the universe and knowledge that framed the early moments of the Scientific Revolution. At that time, the philosophies of René Descartes and Francis Bacon, and the predictive powers of the principles laid out by Isaac Newton and Johannes Kepler supported the emergent belief that the universe was a grand machine. It followed that the systems designed to make sense of this machine would be understood as (Newtonian) mechanics. And, as we discuss in more detail in chapter 3, the foundational image of the age was the *line*, implicit in discussions of (linear) causality, (linear) relationships, and (linear) dynamics.

By contrast, the core metaphors and images for complexivisits are more toward ecosystems, co-determined choreographies, and scale-independent fractals. For the most part, these figurative devices were first articulated by complexivists within the hard sciences and mathematics, but they have come to be increasingly embraced by researchers in education and other social sciences of the past few decades.

The shift has been prompted in large part by the realization that the metaphors and methods borrowed from analytic science, especially those tools drawn from statistics (such as linear regression), are of limited use in efforts to unravel and characterize constantly shifting phenomena. This is not to say that these interpretive tools are useless in the study of complex phenomena, however. True to the etymological root *stasis*, meaning "stationary, stopped," many statistical methods are appropriate, for example, to provide snapshot images of learning and living systems. The difficulty lies in the overapplication of methods that cannot take into account that living and learning systems can and do change. By the time a statistical analysis of a complex unity is completed, its conclusions may no longer be valid. (This point is powerfully demonstrated in election polls. It is also an issue with intelligence tests and most other norm-based reference tools. For the most part, these devices are intended to measure phenomena that are far too volatile for any sort of summary statistic.)

Soft complexity science, then, refers to an increasingly popular movement within the social sciences toward an embrace of images and metaphors to highlight the intricate intertwinings of complex phenomena. For example, personal memories might be characterized in terms of a fractal structure in which virtually any recollection, when closely inspected, can explode into a vast web of associations.[19] In a similar vein, neurologists and sociologists have drawn on a subdiscourse of complexity science—namely network theory—to redescribe interneuronal structures and interpersonal relationships in terms of "scale-free networks"[20] (see chap. 3).

These efforts at redescription have not yet had as significant an impact within educational research as in neurology, psychology, sociology, and other areas of human science research. Nevertheless, there have been some notable contributions to discussions of the nature of learning,[21] teaching,[22] schooling,[23] and educational research[24]—mostly on the descriptive level, but the emphasis does seem to be shifting toward more pragmatic recommendations for educationists (see chaps. 6 and 7). A prominent feature of these writings is an attentiveness to the figurative bases of these discussions, in contrast to popular educational discourse in which the illustrative value of metaphors have often decayed into literalness. For example, Sawada and Caley have offered the notion of *dissipative structures* (a term coined by Nobel laureate Ilya Prigogine to refer to certain complex unities) to describe learners and classrooms.[25] Doll has interrogated the metaphoric roots of the word *curriculum* and foregrounded its etymological relationship to the notion of *recursion*.[26] (Both are derived from the Latin *currere*, "to run.") He develops this idea to problematize the popular tendency to interpret curriculum in terms of linear, unidirectional programs or movements, arguing that learning is never a simple matter of directed progress.

Much of our own research within education might be characterized as fitted to a soft complexity science sensibility, having characterized learning, classrooms, schools, curricula, and administrative structures in terms of nested, open, self-organized systems that operate far from equilibrium (see chaps. 5 and 7). That said, we do not regard the bulk of our work—or the bulk of the work of other educational researchers with an interest in complex dynamics—in "soft" terms. Rather, to our reading, most of it would more appropriately be described in terms of what Richardson and Cilliers call "complexity thinking."

COMPLEXITY THINKING

To reiterate, complexity thinking might be described as a way of thinking and acting. Linking it to a term introduced in chapter 1, complexity thinking might be understood as an acknowledgment of one's *complicity*—not just complicity with/in one's research interests, but with/in the grander systems that contribute to the shape of and that are shaped by those research interests.

As such, complexity thinking has a much more pragmatic emphasis than hard and soft attitudes toward complexity science. Its principal orienting question is neither the fact seeking "What is?" nor the interpretation-seeking "What might be?", but the practice-oriented "How should we act?"

Significantly, complexity thinking in no way represents an abandonment of *science*. However, it does reject an uncritical—and, at times, as unjustified—faith in the analytic method, its mechanical and statistical tools, and other features of much of educational research through the 20th century. Such uncritical embrace of analytic scientific emphases, often dubbed "scientism," is a primary site of critique and response by those whose work might be described in terms of complexity thinking.

Complexity thinking is fully consistent with a science that is understood in terms of a disciplined, open-minded, evidence-based attitude toward the production of new, more useful interpretive possibilities. On this count, complexity thinking is compatible with pragmatist philosophy,[27] in which truth is understood in terms of *adequacy*, not *optimality*. A claim is deemed truthful if it enables knowers to maintain their fitness—and so, in contrast to the demands for validity, reliability, rigor, and generalizability, complexity thinking is more oriented toward truths that are viable, reasonable, relevant, and contingent. Once again, this attitude foregrounds the role of the knower in the known, in contrast to the efforts of analytic science to erase any trace of the observer from the observation.

As such, complexity thinking acknowledges that "compression" and "reduction" of information are necessary in order to make sense of experiences. Humans *must* differentiate, interpret, draw analogies, filter, discard, and generalize in order to deal with the vast amounts of information that confront them at every moment. Complexity thinking thus recognizes the limitations on human consciousness,[28] but does not equate such constraints with limitations on human possibilities.

On the contrary, complexity thinking within education is oriented toward the means by which humanity seems to have transcended its biological limitations. Some principal sites of inquiry oriented in this way are studies that focus on language, writing, mathematics, and other technologies that enable groups of individuals to couple their perceptions and consciousnesses, in effect, creating grander cognitive unities—collective intelligences—whose possibilities simply cannot be determined in terms of the summed capacities of individuals.

In the preceding paragraphs we have made reference to several different instances of phenomena that "know" something, including science, social collectives, and individuals. Complexity thinking prompts this level-jumping between and among different layers of organization, any of which might be properly identified as complex and all of which influence (both enabling and constraining) one another. Complexity thinking also orients attentions toward other dynamic, co-implicated, and integrated levels, including the neurological, the experiential, the contextual/material, the symbolic, the cultural, and the ecological. Each of these levels/phenomena can be understood as enfolded in and unfolding from all of the others. For instance, science cannot be understood without considering social movements and societal obsessions, nor in ignorance of the subjective interests and personal histories of individual scientists.

These points can be rather difficult to appreciate, in large part because prevailing manners of expression in English tend to cast matters of objective knowledge and individual knowing as separate, non-overlapping regions. Hence the

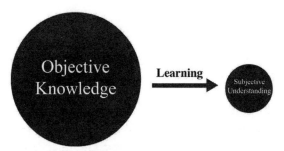

FIGURE 2.1 POPULAR METAPHORS OF KNOWLEDGE AND KNOWING
In common figurative language, objective knowledge and subjective understanding tend to be framed in terms of two isolated domains that must somehow be bridged.

prominence of such phrases as "getting things into your head," "soaking things up," and "taking things in." The implicit imagery here seems to be something toward the image presented in figure 2.1, of two separate spheres linked by the unidirectional arrow of "learning."

Critiques of this figurative grounding, along with associated "banking" or "transmission" approaches with pedagogy, have been extensive and condemning over the past century. In their place, a new orthodoxy has arisen in which subjective understanding is nested within objective knowledge (see fig. 2.2). Their forms are understood to exist in mutual relationship and both are understood to be dynamic and adaptive, albeit operating in much different time frames.

In this emergent figurative framing, learning is understood more in terms of ongoing renegotiations of the perceived boundary between personal knowing and collective knowledge. Understood to unfold from and to be enfolded in one another, both are construed in terms of maintaining fitness. As such, learning is

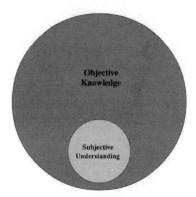

FIGURE 2.2 EMERGENT METAPHORS OF KNOWLEDGE AND KNOWING
In complexity-oriented frames, objective knowledge and subjective understanding are described in terms of nested, co-implicated dynamics.

not understood in terms of a directed movement of information or knowledge (as suggested in fig. 2.1), but in terms of continuous adaptation or coping as these co-implicated phenomena maintain their respective coherences.

As will be further developed in chapter 4, the principal theories of learning that have arisen in education are subject-centered constructivisms (which focus on the individual's efforts to maintain coherence) and social constructionisms (which are more concerned with how individual knowers are shaped by and positioned within collective knowledge systems). And, as further developed in chapter 4, complexity thinking compels a significant elaboration of this manner of nested imagery as it presses attentions in both micro- and macro-directions. We have found nested images of the sort presented in figure 2.3 to be particularly useful in underscoring that, for example, the project of formal education cannot be understood without considering, all-at-once, the many layers of dynamic, nested activity that are constantly at play.

Consistent with the fact that the boundaries of complex systems are difficult to determine, it is impossible to draw tidy lines between these sorts of organiza-

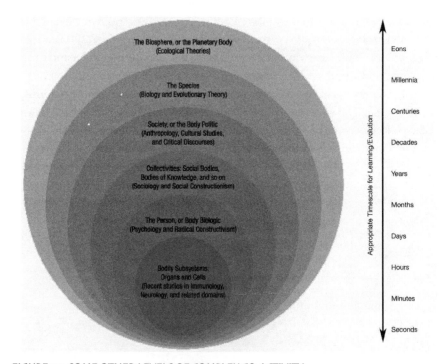

FIGURE 2.3 SOME OTHER LEVELS OF COMPLEX CO-ACTIVITY
Nested systems that are of interest to educational researchers extend well beyond the phenomena of collective knowledge and individual understanding.[29]

tional/organismic layers. However, pragmatically speaking, they can be and often are distinguished according to the paces of their evolutions (as suggested by the time scale, on the right of fig. 2.3) and their relative "sizes." For example, individual cognition tends to be seen as highly volatile (hence readily affected), whereas a body of knowledge or a body politic is usually seen as highly stable (hence as pregiven and fixed, at least insofar as curriculum development is concerned). By way of a more specific example, one might compare the centuries-long period that was needed for Western mathematics to incorporate a "zero concept"[30] to the rapid pace at which a typical child comes to appreciate a number system that includes zero. When considered on the appropriate scales, both can appear as sudden insights that not only open up new vistas of possibility, but that also transform what had previously been accepted as true or factual.[31]

(By way of side note, the time scale in fig. 2.3 is also useful for understanding why some strategies of hard complexity science research cannot be unproblematically imposed on phenomena that are studied by educators. For example, methods developed to study ecosystems, biological phenomena, or medical issues are typically focused on traits at the species level—that is, phenomena that are highly stable, owing to their relatively slow evolutionary pace.)

Of course, in practical terms, an educational researcher could not possibly account simultaneously for several levels of dynamic activity. Our suggestion is not at all that one must accomplish or even attempt such a feat. Rather, we are arguing for an awareness that habits of interpreting particular phenomena as fixed or fluid are dependent on the level of observation and the observer's purposes, *not* on the phenomenon. For example, a neurophysiologist might choose to regard an individual's understanding of "red" as fixed in order to study that person's brain activity when objects recognized as red are encountered. A psychologist, in contrast, is more likely to consider the individual's understanding of red as mutable, and might thus seek to unravel the experiences, emotions, and anticipations that contribute to the person's subjective interpretation of redness. A sociologist might ignore subjective experiences, seeking to understand the social and cultural significance of color. An anthropologist might attempt to link the sociologist's and the neurophysiologist's insights in an effort to understood the intertwined dynamics of biology and culture in a society's habits of distinction. And so on. As such, what red *is* can only be discussed in terms of the immediate worry, not in terms of some absolute, unchanging, observer-free aspect of the universe.

A point to underscore here is that, with specific regard to educational research, complexity thinking does not permit a simplistic separation of *established knowledge* and *how knowledge is established*. Both obey similar, evolutionary dynamics.

As such, in complexity terms, the key distinction is not between *product* and *process*, but between relatively stable aspects of collective knowledge and the somewhat more volatile dynamics that underpin that stability.

Of course, such sensibilities are not entirely new. They might be argued to have been represented by post-structuralist, critical, socio-cultural, social-constructionist, and other discourses. We would not dispute this point. However, complexity thinking takes the discussion to realms that these discourses often ignore or evade. For the past few hundred years at least, the topics that have predominated within educational discourse have overwhelmingly been book-ended by the phenomena of the individual's concerns at one extreme and society's needs at the other. Often, in fact, these two extremes have been cast as oppositional, as evidenced in the ever-popular debates over whose interests schooling should most serve (i.e., the individual's or society's interests).

Complexity thinking presents two challenges here. First, as suggested by figure 2.3, it looks beyond the bookends of the popular debate. Second, it introduces the biological across all phenomena—from the subpersonal to the personal, through the interpersonal, across the social and cultural, past the species level, to the interspecies space of the biosphere. In other words, complexity thinking embraces much of structuralist, post-structuralist (see chap. 4), and critical thinking, but counters that these discourses often do not go far enough. A key issue for instance, is the nature of knowledge. Complexity thinking understands knowledge to refer to systems' stabilized but mutable patterns of acting—and thus supports the commonsense usages of the word *knowledge* to refer to what humans, nonhumans, and human collectives know. By contrast, at least some branches of structuralist, post-structuralist, and critical thought cannot accommodate such notions—with a few oriented by the extreme assertions that either "all knowledge is socially constructed" or "individuals construct their own knowledge." Complexity thinking recognizes the "truth" of such claims, insofar as they are noted in relationship to specific systems. But it also suggests a limited utility to these assertions when thinking in terms of the necessarily transphenomenal enterprise of formal education (see chap. 8).

WHAT IS "SCIENCE"?

We have not yet answered the question that serves as the title of this chapter. To review, we have indicated that there is a significant difference between analytic and complexivist sensibilities, that complexity science nonetheless both derives from and relies on analytic science, that complexity research is hardly unified, that complexity thinking embraces a pragmatist attitude toward truth, that researchers oriented by complexity thinking within the social sciences and humanities must be attentive to their complicities, and that complexity science compels one to be aware of physical-biological contexts and not merely social-cultural situations. Three additional issues remain to be developed: the quest of science, the nature of a scientific theory, and the relationship of science to other modes of Western knowledge production.

The first of these issues, regarding the particular foci of scientific inquiry, can only be addressed by looking at the history and evolution of scientific research. To perhaps overtruncate the discussion, modern analytic science arose at a time that the universe was assumed to be fixed and finished. The project of all inquiry, scientific or otherwise, was thus understood in terms of naming what *is*. Science, true to its etymological roots of "separating one thing from another" (from the Latin *scire*, related to scissors, schism, and so on) or, even more anciently, to a "splitting, rending, cleaving, dividing, separating" (cf. the Greek *skhizein*), was oriented toward the project of classification. It was aimed at parsing up and naming the universe though the identification of essential traits, key distinctions, and all-encompassing taxonomies. Basic laws and fundamental units were actually byproducts of this attitude, arising as finer and finer distinctions were made.

A prominent example of this distinction is the still-employed system of biological classification developed by Linnaeus in the 1700s. He grouped species together into genera according to resemblances, genera into families, and so on until, at the apex of an organizational pyramid, he arrived at six kingdoms that encompassed all living forms. Similar examples can be found in all other classical branches of science, underscoring that the scientific project was originally understood in terms of tracing out the fault lines of the universe. Further, this project was assumed to be an accumulative one, pointed toward a complete and exhaustive knowledge of all things.

The nature of the project changed dramatically through the 1800s as mounting bodies of evidence in geology, biology, astronomy, linguistics, and other domains pointed toward the likelihood that the universe was neither fixed nor finished. Rather, it seemed to be evolving—and not in entirely predictable ways. That made at least parts of the universe moving targets, not subject to totalized taxonomies or universal laws.

In brief, the evolutionary sensibilities that emerged in the sciences through the 19th century were organized around a very different attitude toward understanding the differences and relationships among phenomena. As a result, science changed. Dramatically. It shifted from an emphasis on *dichotomization* to an emphasis on *bifurcations*. Dichotomization is derived from the Greek *dikha+tomie*, "two parts." To dichotomize is to generate two independent and unambiguously defined pieces. By contrast, bifurcation is derived from the Lation *bi+furca*, "two-pronged" or "forked." A bifurcation is a growth into two branches, as opposed to a fragmenting into two pieces.

An immense conceptual difference between dichotomization and bifurcation is that the former assumes proper distinctions are unproblematic, whereas the latter always incorporates a rationale for any distinction that is made. In effect, when a bifurcation is noted—in, for example, an evolutionary tree, a genealogy, a history of the emergence of languages—the result is not merely two new categories, but a common origin for those categories. In other words, a bifurcation flags the complicity of the distinction-maker: *someone* is making a distinction for *some reason*. Bifurcations highlight not just difference, but relationship[32] and the conceptual shift toward them that occurred in the latter half of the 19th century thus marked a key evolution in what science was all about.

The emergence of complexity marks a further evolution. It attends not only to the bifurcations that might have contributed to the rise of a range of forms and phenomena that are currently observed, but also to the manners in which those forms and phenomena can self-organize into other, transcendent forms—entities that do not arise by branching off from other entities, but that spontaneously emerge in the mutually specifying dynamics of already existing forms.

These two transformations in the project of science—first, the shift from dichotomization to bifurcation, and second, the recognition of evolving, emergent, and embedded forms—unfolded alongside transformations in the nature and status of scientific knowledge. This pair of shifts might also be characterized as a movement from *correspondence theories* to *coherence theories* to *complexity theories*.

Correspondence theories of truth are not only associated with the original scientific project of parsing and naming the world, they actually underpinned it. In this frame, words are uncritically understood as tags that one attaches to forms, hence the usage of the term correspondence. Word-objects were (and are—the perspective persists in popular discourse) assumed to correspond to physical objects and events. Language, it follows, was/is a means to represent things as they are.

In the early 1900s, Ferdinand de Saussure famously critiqued the belief that language comprised a collection of word-objects that correspond to real-world artifacts and actions.[33] Embracing the evolutionary dynamics of Darwin rather than the separating logic of Aristotle, Saussure and many of his contemporaries argued that language is not a mapping or labeling system, but a means by which humans *collectively* establish and maintain coherence with one another and the grander world. As Saussure developed, a language is the product of circular (recursive) interactions between two or more agents. Linguistic symbols, then, are not tagging tools, but go-betweens that allow minds to connect.

As will be further developed in chapter 4, Saussure described language as a closed, self-referential system—that is, as a self-contained set of cross-references in which meaning arises in the contrasts and gaps among words, not in their references to external objects or events. As such, language is subject to continuous transformation as prompted by changes in collective obsessions, the introduction of new forms, and so on. The vital criterion for the persistence of linguistic forms was thus a sort of evolutionary fitness. Survival did not depend on correspondence to something outside the language system, but to internal fitness or consistency.

This sort of *coherence theories* might be distinguished from correspondence theories on two principal counts. First, since the theories focus on *internal fit* rather than *external match*, the important qualities of truth are viability and utility. Consistent with pragmatist philosophy, as already mentioned, truth is what works, and it is subject to constant modification with new experiences and changing circumstances. On this count, the influence of a shift in the project of science (as prompted by Darwin) is obvious. Second, the evolution of truth is most often a matter of tinkering, not massive revision. Moreover, these adjustments are made "on the fly" with little or no fanfare. Individual and collective construals of the world, that is, are rooted in the human capacity to *rationalize* rather than to be *rational*.

As might be expected, this shift in understanding of the nature of language is associated with a shift in the status of scientific truths. Rather than *representations*, coherence theories suggest that the "facts" of science are more matters of *presentations*. Phrased differently, claims to truth are understood as means to orient perceptions and frame interpretations, not as hard-and-fast assertions about some aspect of reality. As such, a claim to truth, like a science that is attentive to evolutions and bifurcations, can shift and adjust. Indeed, it must be flexible in order maintain its own internal coherence.

For the most part, coherence theories were developed within the humanities and social sciences, and they were thus imposed on the physical sciences from the outside—in particular, through such notable contributions as those of Kuhn[34] and Popper.[35] Occasionally the sensibilities announced have met with harsh, even damning (and occasionally justified) critiques from those scientists who maintain a more correspondence-based sense of their work.[36] Given this backdrop, it is thus interesting to note that complexity science has prompted the emergence of coherence-like sensibilities among many scientists over the past several decades.[37]

The common ground of coherence theories and complexity theories is that both are concerned with the internal relational dynamics of systems as conditioned by events outside of those systems. This focus has prompted a realization that the elements or agents of a system, as Cilliers comments, "have no representational meaning by themselves, but only in terms of patterns of relationships with many other elements."[38]

However, complexity theories embrace not only Darwinian dynamics, but also the phenomenon of self-organization. That is, complexity theories are also attentive to the possibility of emergent, transcendent forms, and this interest compels an attentiveness to the manner in which efforts at representation are co-implicated in experiences of the phenomenon at hand. As Cilliers puts it, context is "always already part of the representation."[39] This means that, in a complex network, no part of the system has any meaning in isolation from the rest of the system (an assertion shared by coherence theorists), and so one must take into account the structure of the whole system. In other words—and it is here that complexity theories split from coherence theories—complexity is incompressible and ever-expanding. Thus, although complexivists agree with coherence theorists in the assertion that representations cannot be considered atomistic units or accounts of fundamental laws or elements, they part company around the assumption that representations are part of a self-contained system. For complexivists, representations have no meaning or identity in themselves, but are part of a greater distributed network of meaning. Theories of reality and the vocabularies developed to describe the world are not independent from it.

The distinction between coherence theories and complexity theories is subtle, but significant. The point is that complexity theories understand that they are not hermetically sealed from the universe, but part of—responsive to and responsible to—grander webs of relationship. Science in this frame is a participation is the emergence of reality, and hopefully a conscientious one in which its partialities are routinely foregrounded.

The notion of *distributed representation*, taken seriously, compels a realization that there are no universal truths. The representations that are used to make sense of the world are products of the frames that have been chosen in order to generate meaning; they are not a pure characteristic of things in themselves, but neither are they completely dissociated with those things. Rather, they are evolving and ever-expanding conversations between sense-makers, the sense made, and sensorial encounters with the universe. Returning to a notion introduced earlier, then, complexity thinking posits that truth is not strictly a matter of intersubjectivity—coherences among humans—but of interobjectivity—conversations between a dynamic humanity within a dynamic more-than-human world. Rather than search for truth, complexity thinking suggests that the best that a knowing agent can do is to take a pragmatic stance toward the representations made. How useful are they? What do they do? What do they entail? What do they foreground and what do they defer? These questions apply as much to how one teaches, what one teaches, and the intentions of formal education as they do to the projects of science.

Such assertions bring us very close to the postmodern mistrust of overarching theoretical paradigms, a suspicion encapsulated in Lyotard's emphatic statement, "I define *postmodern* as incredulity toward metanarratives."[40] Our invocation of this statement might seem somewhat paradoxical within this discussion of complexity science—a movement that is often accused of assuming the status of a new metanarrative.

Indeed, this accusation is perhaps a fair one when applied to the emphases and attitudes of some involved in hard complexity science. However, it is not a justified criticism when applied to complexity thinking. As elaborated throughout this text, complexity thinking makes no claim to be a "theory of everything." Rather, it is an attitude toward the interpretation of particular sorts of phenomena, one that foregrounds its own implicatedness in those interpretations and, hence, in shapes attitudes and actions toward those phenomena. It is particularly attentive to the figurative devices that are employed in its representations, especially the metaphors, analogies, and images that are implicit in efforts to represent. On this count, complexity thinking abandons the rationalist premise of modern science—that is, the assumption that there are irrefutable, foundational truths out of which other truths might be constructed. Quite the contrary, complexity thinking argues, humans are not logical creatures, but association-making creatures who are capable of logic. One must thus look at the constantly shifting web of associations to make sense of what meaning is.

We undertake this project in chapter 3 through a discussion of the *geometry* of complexity. To frame that discussion, our purpose here is to emphasize the metaphorical structures of complexity thinking in contrast to the assumed-logical foundational of analytic thought.

CHAPTER THREE

THE SHAPE OF COMPLEXITY

CLOUDS ARE NOT SPHERES, MOUNTAINS ARE NOT CONES,
AND LIGHTNING DOES NOT TRAVEL IN A STRAIGHT LINE.
THE COMPLEXITY OF NATURE'S SHAPES DIFFERS IN KIND,
NOT MERELY DEGREE,
FROM THAT OF THE SHAPES OF ORDINARY GEOMETRY.

—Benoit Mandelbrot[1]

A few years ago, in the United States, the George W. Bush administration introduced the *No Child Left Behind Act of 2001*.[2] This proposed legislation brought
with it many implications for educators and educational researchers. For the latter, a key issue was flagged by a renewed emphasis on the distinction between
quantitative and qualitative methods.

A major trigger in the discussions the time was a symposium hosted by the
United States Department of Education on the topic of "scientifically based
research," during which it was asserted:

> Clinical trials ..., the gold standard in medicine ... are the only way to be
> sure about what works in medicine.... [The] rules about what works and
> how to make inferences about what works ... are exactly the same for edu-
> cational practice as they would be for medical practice.[3]

The thinly veiled assertion here is that "to be sure about what works," educational
research must be experimental in design and quantitative in nature.

In chapter 2, we noted one major problem with this manner of assertion
(i.e., a failure to attend to the dramatically different time scales used to measure
the evolutions of the phenomena under study). In this chapter, we offer another
criticism, arguing that the qualitative/quantitative distinction implicit in asser-

tions like the one above emerge from profound misreadings of what it means to conduct research. In particular, they are anchored in outdated conceptions of science and evidence, ones that are oblivious to their own figurative grounds. However, to develop this argument, we do not focus on matters of *quantity*, but on the issue of *shape*. In terms of branches of mathematical inquiry, we argue that debates over what is and is not scientific should be more concerned with matters of implicit geometry than with matters of explicit arithmetic or statistics.

Drawing on the post-structuralist strategy of deconstruction, we begin by interrogating some of the foundational metaphors of current discourses within educational research, seeking to demonstrate their origins and alignments with ancient Greek thought. Arguing that the same sensibilities were carried uncritically into modern science, we then explore the very different metaphors and images that are invoked within complexity thinking. In the process, we seek to explicate not just the simplistic character of quantitative/qualitative distinctions, but the inherent flaws of the assumptions that give shape to projects like the *No Child Left Behind* legislation. In particular, we seek to develop the assertion that "rules about what works and how to make inferences about what works" are in fact *not* "the same for educational practice as they would be for medical practice"—or any other domain for that matter. Complex phenomena cannot be so simple-mindedly collapsed into the same categories.

PLANE GEOMETRY AND ANALYTIC SCIENCE

One of the important conclusions about languages by 20th-century thinkers—shared by structuralists, post-structuralists, psychoanalytic theorists, and pragmatists—is that meanings tend to be caught up in complex webs of association, tangled metaphors, and forgotten referents. The best one can hope to do is to tug at some of the frayed strands in these tight weaves of signification, hoping that the right pull in the right place at the right time might start to unravel the webs. Phrased differently, meaning emerges more from what is absent, tacit, literalized, and forgotten than from what is present, explicit, figurative, and conscious. Attentions are thus prompted toward the usually-not-noticed aspects of language and other interpretation practices that support and constrain meanings and perceptions. A powerful and pervasive instance of this sort of deferral is the manner in which notions extracted from Euclidean geometry have come to be knitted through the English language and, correspondingly, through conceptions of truth, justice, and other core social ideals.

Euclid's geometry of the plane was developed in the third century BCE, and it is the version that is called to mind for most when the word *geometry* is mentioned.

But it is not the only geometry, nor is it the first geometry. Euclid's contribution was to gather together a broad range of established (i.e., generally accepted) mathematical conclusions into a coherent, internally consistent field of mathematical study. A century prior to this effort, Plato identified geometry—then understood more generally in terms of the logico-deductive argument—as the hallmark of scholarly thought. Plato's geometry was not solely concerned with figures drawn on the plane, but more broadly with a mode of reasoning that he felt could be used to uncover the deepest secrets of the universe. As such, he used the word geometry to refer to a manner of inquiry *in any domain* that sought a totalized knowledge through systematic reduction of a phenomenon or argument to fundamental elements or original principles.

Euclid's major contribution was to assign a visual form to this manner of inquiry with the refinement of the case of plane geometry. Using 23 definitions (e.g., "a point is that of which there is no part") and five axioms (e.g., "a straight line can be drawn from any point to any point"), he demonstrated the power of logical argument for deriving and linking a diversity of known forms and isolated truths. In so doing, he contributed to a transformation of the meaning of geometry.

Euclidean geometry, then, privileges not just a particular set of elements and images, but a rational, deductive mode of argumentation. This mode has been central to the past few centuries of scientific development. Few debate its power or significance to matters of knowing and knowledge. The over-application of the logico-deductive argument has been subject to extensive critique, particularly among postmodernist[4] and pragmatist[5] thinkers over the last several decades— and, more recently, by researchers oriented by studies in neurology, psychology, and linguistics[6] who have rejected the deeply engrained assumption that human thought is mainly logical. However, largely tacit geometry associated with modern rationality has escaped such broad criticism.

For example, consider the web of immediate etymological associates of the word *plane*. Along with *plain, plan*, and other terms, *plane* is derived from the Latin *planus*, "flat." "Plain language," "plain truth," "plain and simple," "master plan," and related phrases, that is, are entangled in the same conceptual weave as Euclid's plane—as are the contemporary desires to plan ahead, to keep things on the level, to explain (etymologically, "to lay flat"), and so on. The uniting theme across these ideas might be characterized as a collective hallucination—that being, as Rorty[7] describes, taken-for-granted beliefs that reality has a developmental structure, that there is a master plan that is becoming ever more plain as it surrenders to the prying gazes of scientists and their plane-based logic.

A defining feature of the implicit geometry is an assumption of reducibility. Phenomena, it is presupposed, can be broken down into a finite set of simpler elements, as illustrated by the objects and proofs of Euclidean geometry. A plane, for instance, can be uniquely defined by—that is, conceptually reduced to—any pair of lines that intersect at exactly one point. Correspondingly, a line can be uniquely defined by two distinct points. One might thus expect notions associated with lines and points to be at least as pervasive as the logical argument in the knit of modern thought—and such is indeed the case. In table 3.1 we have listed some of the sorts of words and phrases that are clustered around line-based notions derived from Latin, Greek, and German roots.

The words and phrases presented in table are just the tip of the iceberg. Other words and notions that are tangled in this web of Euclidean linearity include *align, explain, extend, justify, limit, ordinary, project, prominent, strict,* and *truth*— and we did not have to work very hard to generate this short and partial list.

The *point* (note the Euclideanism) here is not that the presence of this particular web of associations represents some sort of collective error or hidden conspiracy. It is, rather, that this family of terms derive from and support particular habits of interpretation. In the process, they contribute to the maintenance and projection of what is "normal" or "natural." For instance, as we hope is evident in the table below, beneath the literal surface of these terms is a mesh of *right*ness and wrongness, of *correct*ness and falsehood, of *regular*ity and oddness, or *direct*ness and evasion. In other words, the priority of lines and linearities in the

Term	Derivation	Some current usages and associations
right	>Latin *rectus*, straight	right angle, righteous, right handed, right of way, right/wrong, human rights, right wing
rect-	>Latin *rectus*, straight	rectangle, correct, direct, rectify, rector, erect
regular	>Latin *regula*, straightedge	regulation, regulate, irregular
rule	>Latin *regula*, straightedge	ruler, rule of law, rule out, rule of thumb, broken rule
line	>Latin *linum*, flax thread	linear, timeline, line of text, line of argument, linear relation, sight line, linear causality, toe the line
ortho-	>Greek *orthos*, straight	orthodox, unorthodox, orthodontics, orthogonal, orthopedic
straight	>German *streccan*, stretch	straight up, go straight, straight answer, straight shooter, straight talk, straight and narrow, straight-laced

TABLE 3.1 SOME STRAIGHT-LINE-BASED NOTIONS

language is nested in the contested spaces of good and evil, truth and deception, morality and deviance, clarity and obfuscation.

The claim that lines and line-based interpretations are not neutral can be underscored through reference to any thesaurus. One such volume[8] includes the following entries under "straight": *accurate, candid, continuous, direct, heterosexual, honest, simple, thorough, trustworthy, undeviating, virtuous*. Simply and directly put, to question the cultural priority or social necessity of such qualities is to risk being seen as deliberately provocative and illogical, if not pathological. After all, consider the current connotations of works like *bent, distorted, kinky, oblique, perverse, skewed, twisted*, and *warped*—all of which originally meant an innocent sounding "not straight" or "not level."

This matter comes into even more dramatic relief through similar examinations of the origins, meanings, and contemporary associations of terms linked to 90° (right) angles, some of which are presented in table 3.2. Again, our point is not that this cluster of notions is somehow indicative of some manner of orchestrated deception. It is, rather, that such associations have become pervasive and transparent. Their metaphoric values and intents have been lost as they have become instances of what they name: the normal, the standard, the correct, the orthodox. Analogical usage has decayed into illogical presupposition—a point that is cogently illustrated with the specific example of *normal*.

As taken up in detail elsewhere,[9] the notion of normal originally referred to a carpenter's square. As the adjective version of the noun *norma*, normal was used to describe angles that were reasonably close to 90° in much the same way the word "circular" is used to refer to shapes that are reasonably close to being round. (This precise meaning of normal persists within mathematics.) Several hundred years ago, the notion came to be used as a metaphor for the accuracy of measurements in general. Something was normal if it was sufficiently close to a prespecified or expected value. During the 1800s with the advent of quantitative analyses of

Term	Derivation	Some current usages and associations
standard	>Latin *stare*, stand (i.e., make a right angle to a flat surface)	standardized tests, standard form, raising standards, standard time, rally around a standard, standard units, standard of living, standards of behavior
normal	>Latin *norma*, carpenter's square	normal curve, normalize, normative, normal child, normal development, normality
perpendicular	>Latin *pendere*, to hang (vertically)	pendulum, depend, pending, independent suspend

TABLE 3.2 SOME 90°-ANGLE-BASED NOTIONS

such phenomena as heights and weight—along with less tangible constructs such as intelligence and conscious awareness—the meaning of normal morphed into its current senses of "the way things are" and "the way things should be." These interpretations are held in place by the pervasive application of *normal distributions* (i.e., bell curves) to a range of phenomena, a topic that is addressed in more detail later in this chapter.

Interrogation of the issue of the privileged status of planed, linear, and normal thinking can be carried much further. Another obvious site of inquiry is the word *point*, a fundament of both Euclidean geometry and academic discourse. Our task here, for example, might be construed in terms of making key *points*, linking them with sound, *linear* reasoning as we aim at a fulsome ex*pla*nation, *paralleli*ng the Euclidean imagery in which *points* can be used to define *lines*, which in turn can be used to define *planes*. It is difficult, if not impossible, to escape such a framing in the contemporary culture of academic writing.

To return to our argument, the assertion that orients this discussion is that human thought is enabled and constrained by the conceptual tools that are available. In terms of the visual referents that are most often used to give shape to understandings of truth and acceptability, one need only glance at living spaces to see that the forms of classical geometry are overwhelming in the constructed material world. The influence of Euclid is obvious in homes and offices, in rectangulated cities, in linearized conceptions of time and development, and so on. In schools, Euclid is present in the grids used to lay out curricula, order the school day, organize students in rooms, frame their learning experiences, mark their progress, and so on. Within educational research, it is revealed in the prominence of normal curves and linear regressions. So dominant is this geometry that the unruly and organic are often surprising and even unwelcome. What tend to be preferred are narratives of control, predictability, efficiency, and correlation—such as is demanded by Plato's logic and embodied in Euclid's images.

FRACTAL GEOMETRY AND COMPLEXITY SCIENCE

There are two principal constructs that we challenge in the remainder of this chapter: first, the assumption of linear relations among dynamic phenomena (which underpins much of conventional educational research) and, second, the application of the normal distribution to virtually all phenomena that display some manner of measurable diversity. To frame our critiques of these constructs, we must first describe an alternative to their implicit Euclidean geometries.

Over the past century, a number of mathematicians have focused their attentions on a set of forms whose properties depart radically from the objects studied by Euclid. Late in the 19th century, curious new "pathological" or "monstrous"[10] forms were developed, in part to challenge certain taken-for-granted assumptions about space and dimension. For example, Guiseppe Peano contrived a way to bend a line so that it passed through every point in a plane—that is, a 1-dimensional form was made to completely cover 2-dimensional space. Later, related forms were created that are neither 1-dimensional nor 2-dimensional, but occupy some fractional dimension.

This fracturing of dimensions prompted mathematician Benoît Mandelbrot[11] to coin the word *fractal*, a term that has since been adopted to refer to a rather vigorous branch of geometric inquiry. Since its emergence, in fact, fractal geometry has come to influence work in many fields, including all of the natural sciences, medicine, and economics.[12] Such applications have to do both with the manner in which fractal forms are generated and the qualities of the forms, two aspects that have contributed to such titles as "the geometry of nature,"[13] "the mathematics of the living world," and "the mathematics of complexity."[14]

On these points, fractals are generated through (potentially) infinite recursive processes—in contrast to Euclidean forms, which are built up through finite linear sequences of operations. At each stage in a recursive process, the starting point is the output of the preceding iteration, and the output is the starting point of the subsequent iteration: As illustrated in figure 3.1, every stage in this process is an elaboration, and such elaborations can quickly give rise to unexpected forms and surprising complexity. These recursive processes are noncompressible—meaning that there are no shortcuts to the eventual products (although, for simple examples, such as the tree image in fig. 3.1, the outcomes are sometimes easily foreseen.)

Emergent fractal forms have several unusual properties—unusual, at least, when set against the backdrop of Euclidean geometry. A fractal, for instance, is *scale independent*, meaning that its bumpiness of detail remains constant no matter how much it is magnified or reduced. (The fractal image on the book's front cover is a good example of a scale independent form.) This is a quality that seems to be reflected in the universe, which appears to be no simpler or more compli-

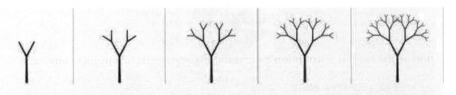

FIGURE 3.1 THE EMERGENCE OF A FRACTAL FORM
Fractal forms, as illustrated in this case of a simple tree image, are generated through recursively elaborative processes.

cated whether examined through microscope or telescope. In contrast, a non-fundamental Euclidean form can always be decomposed into simpler, more basic elements—a quality that analytic science had metaphorically extended and applied to all natural phenomena. The fact that this quality is not even appropriate to all *mathematical* constructs, let alone all complex living forms, should give researchers pause.

Some fractals are also *self-similar*, a curious property by which a well-chosen part can closely or precisely resemble the whole. The "completed" tree image in fig. 3.1 is self-similar, as illustrated in the way that each branch (or each branch of a branch, etc.) looks just like the entire tree. Again, this is a quality that is reflected in many worldly phenomena. By way of familiar examples, a piece broken off a head of broccoli or a sprig of parsley will closely resemble the larger plants. Similarly, a graphical representation of one day's activity on a stock exchange will bear a strong resemblance (at least in terms of erratic detail) to graphs of a week's, a month's, a year's, or a longer period's performance. Perhaps the most familiar example, one that many children notice, is that a well chosen twig often looks very much like the tree it came from.

The quality of self-similarity is well illustrated by the fern leaf in figure 3.2. This example demonstrates that self-similarity is actually a special case of scale independence. For self-similar forms, not only does it become apparent that structural intricacy is not always a function of scale, but that sometimes structure can be level-independent as well. The resulting nestedness might thus serve as a visual metaphor of nested complex forms (cf., fig. 2.1), in which the *dynamics* of

FIGURE 3.2 SELF-SIMILARITY
Some fractal forms are self-similar—that is, a well-chosen and appropriately magnified part precisely matches the whole. Natural forms, such as the fern frond in the image often demonstrate some degree of self-similarity.

systems that emerge from the coupled interactions of other systems are noted to be similar. It is this manner of analogy that contributes to the assertion that, for instance, the evolution of a species and the learning of an individual are dynamically self-similar. They both obey the same complex dynamics, although on different scales and in different temporal frames.

With these sorts of echoes into the realms of natural forms, fractal geometry has found a broad range of applications. The most prominent examples are in medical science (e.g., to describe and study the structures and developments of circulatory systems, nervous systems, brains, and bones), information science and communication technologies (e.g., to compress data and to reduce "noise"), and in economics (e.g., to study market fluctuations). The list of applications is extensive, and growing rapidly, spurred along in large part by the demonstrated utilities of fractal forms and recursively elaborative processes for making sense of the structures and dynamics of complex systems.

Perhaps the most significant contribution of fractal geometry has been conceptual, as a source of new images and metaphors. Complex phenomena, it seems, are much more fractal-like than Euclidean. They are incompressible, recursively elaborated, often surprising. Further, fractal geometry presents a challenge to the pervasive assumption of linearity that has long been inscribed in analytic science.

To be fair, it should be mentioned that the hold of linear forms is not strictly a matter of a cultural preference for lines and planes. Pragmatically speaking, a key reason that linear mathematics held sway in classical times was the fact that it leant itself to calculations that can be done with paper and pencil. Descartes, Newton, and their contemporaries were well aware of nonlinear phenomena. However, owing to the intractability of many nonlinear calculations (the mathematics involved can be extraordinarily labor-intensive and tedious), when such situations arose they were usually replaced by linear approximations.[15] The tendency reached across such phenomena as growth and ecosystemic relations. Mathematician Ian Stewart explains:

> [This] habit became so engrained that many equations were linearized while they were being set up, so that the science textbooks did not even include the full non-linear versions. Consequently most scientists and engineers came to believe that virtually all natural phenomena could be described by linear equations. As the world was a clockwork for the 18th century, it was a linear world for the 19th and most of the 20th century.[16]

Stewart also observes that the situation has recently changed, with the advent of more powerful calculation technologies. Across the physical sciences, the universe has come to be seen as "relentlessly nonlinear."[17]

That said, the deep-seated preference for line-based interpretations of phenomena actually appears to be more than a matter of efficient calculation. Part of the appeal of line graphs and linear correlations might lie in the fact that the straight line is among those shapes that is readily plucked out of the background by human perception. This tendency appears to be rooted in biology, meaning that is has been learned at the species level—although it is clearly amplified by culture. Stewart and Cohen assert that "the standard raw materials of [Euclidean geometry], the notion of a point and a line, match the physiology of our visual systems closely."[18] Others have pointed to the evolutionary advantages that come with the predilection to simplify the world through causal (linear) explanations and efficient (linearized) action schemes.[19] Still others have highlighted that, from the first few hours of birth, humans seek out lines and sensory systems amplify perceived edges of objects.[20] It does not seem unreasonable to suggest that such tendencies would be carried into the articulation of more abstract competencies and constructs. As Cohen and Stewart put it, "Drawing fine lines is a human tendency, an attempt to make our simplified mental labeling system match a differently structured world."[21]

The fractal imagery that is invoked by complexity thinking, then, may represent challenges to both biological predisposition and cultural preference. The crux of this issue is that linear relations and correlations, linear trajectories and forecasts, linear narratives, and linear report formats make for very poor tools to portray complex phenomena. Whether such forms are embedded in quantitative analyses or qualitative descriptions, they are of limited interpretive value and have virtually no predictive value for complex phenomena, as is proven daily in stock markets, classrooms, and personal lives.

To underscore this point, complexity science goes beyond a critique of the use of statistical tools in the study of such self-transforming phenomena as learners, classrooms, communities, and cultures—which is a matter that has long been ensconced in quantitative-versus-qualitative debates among educational researchers. This numerical-versus-descriptive dichotomy is a false one, argue complexivists. Rather, the critical distinction is between *analytic* and *complex*—or, in terms of underlying images, between *Euclidean* and *fractal*. The recursive, nonlinear, dynamic characters of the latter are simply more useful in making sense of phenomena that might be described in similar terms, even if human perceptual systems might be biological-and-culturally predisposed to simpler interpretive tools.

A key to this shift is a recasting of mathematics as a source of models and metaphors, rather than a source of actual descriptions and explanations. Implicit in this redefinition of the role of mathematics is a shift in thinking about the nature of scientific knowledge—one that coincides, but that is not coterminous,

with an epistemological shift in the humanities that was prompted by psychoanalytic, structuralist, post-structuralist, and related discourses through the 20th century (see chap. 2).

Notably, a prominent theme across these discourses over the past 100 years
has been the critique of the use of the normal distribution. As it turns out, this
issue has come to be an important topic within the hard sciences as well.

NETWORKS, POWER LAWS, AND NOT-SO-NORMAL DISTRIBUTIONS

One of the most prominent and important constructs in statistics is the normal
distribution. Its familiar bell-shaped curve (see fig 3.3) is used to illustrate the
manner in which, for many phenomena, data points cluster around a central average in a particular way. The peak at the centre of the curve marks the arithmetic
mean (or average) and the distribution tapers off very rapidly on either side of
that value. That tapering is so rapid that the chances of a data point that deviates
very far from the mean, for all practical purposes, falls to zero quite rapidly. By
way of fictitious, but nonetheless plausible example, the average height of an
adult female in a given region might be 1.7 m. Most adult women would be within
a few cm of that height; a few would be slightly further from the mean, and a very
few would be still further. But no one would be 0.3 m or 21 m tall.

The sensibleness of such examples is one of the reasons that researchers
across domains have tended to assume that all phenomena that can vary do so
according to a normal distribution. It is only recently, with the study of complex
dynamics, that scientists have realized that many commonplace phenomena simply do not follow a normal distribution. For instance, consider the questions,
"How powerful is a normal earthquake?" and "What is the average wealth of a
person on this planet?"

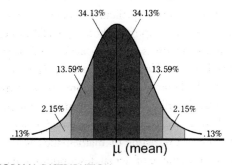

μ (mean)

FIGURE 3.3 THE NORMAL DISTRIBUTION
The percentage values in different regions indicate the portion of data points that are expected to fall inside those parts of the distribution.

These queries actually make little or no sense. Regarding the former, it turns out that minor tremors are pretty much constantly occurring, and these are so frequent and numerous that if they were to be averaged with more major events, a "normal quake" would be calculated to be very minor and scarcely perceptible (to anyone or anything except highly sensitive equipment). The latter is rendered insensible by the fact that wealth is so disproportionately distributed in the world that a simple arithmetic average provides absolutely no useful information.

In current parlance, earthquakes and net worth—along with a host of other *scale-free* phenomena—follow *power law* distributions, not normal distributions. Along with stock market fluctuations, skirmishes and wars, moon craters, fads, extinctions of species, ocean plankton, human heart rhythms, forest fires, avalanches, city sizes, internet hubs, web pages, and epidemics—to name just a handful of instances—earthquakes and wealth obey a distribution similar to the one illustrated in figure 3.4.

In brief, for phenomena that follow a power law distribution, there is no such thing as a "norm"—that is, a "typical" event, instance, member, or fragment. There are no normal-sized cities, there is no representative historical happening, this are no typical catastrophes, there is no characteristic learning event, there are no average insights or discoveries. Relating avalanches and earthquakes to human insight, Buchanan describes the situation in this way:

> Every new idea of science that pops into a theorist's head, or every observation made by an experimenter, is something like a grain falling on a pile of knowledge. It may stick, and merely add to the growing structure, or it may place a portion under such stress that ideas will topple. The toppling may stop quickly or may run for a long while…. [The] avalanches have no inherent or expected size. The smallest revolutions are happening every day, may

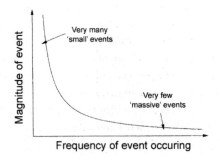

FIGURE 3.4 A POWER LAW DISTRIBUTION
The curve illustrates a very high likelihood of a minor event and a very much smaller probability of a more massive happening.

involve only a few ... and may be virtually invisible ... just like those tiny earthquakes going on all the time beneath our feet. By contrast, the largest revolutions may wipe away much of science as we know it, and are liable to happen at any moment.[22]

Buchanan's analogies between the dynamics of earthquakes and avalanches and the behavior of human systems is more than figurative speculation. These seemingly wildly different phenomena appear to have some deep—and as-yet not well understood—commonalities.

One feature that is well understood, however, is that power law distributions only arise in scale-free phenomena—that is, in phenomena whose organizations might be described in terms of the nested, scale independent qualities of fractal forms. More recent investigations of this category of phenomena have highlighted that they all have a particular sort of strict architecture: They can all be characterized in terms of a specific sort of network structure. For instance, and perhaps somewhat surprising, it appears that social collectivities, the world wide web, food webs in an ecosystem, the network of business links that support a national economy, the network of molecules that interact in a living cell, and the network of a brain's interconnected neurons all seem to be profoundly similar in structure. More bluntly, and perhaps even more surprisingly, the very same organizing principles seem to be at work in both the physical-biological world and the social-cultural world.

A key point here is that, with certain phenomena, "more" is not simply "more," but "different." Watts describes the situation as follows, foregrounding the nested characters of not just varied phenomena, but the realms of inquiry devoted to their study:

> [P]hysics has been reasonably successful in classifying the fundamental particles ... up to the scale of single atoms. But throw a bunch of atoms together, and suddenly the story is entirely different. That's why chemistry is a science of its own, not just a branch of physics. Moving farther up the chain of organization, molecular biology cannot be reduced simply to organic chemistry, and medical science is much more than the direct application of the biology of molecules. At a higher level still—that of interacting organisms—we encounter now a host of disciplines, from ecology and epidemiology, to sociology and economics, each of which comes with its own rules and principles that are not reducible to mere knowledge of psychology and biology.[23]

(We would highlight the last sentence of this citation as the basis of a critique of the sensibilities framing educational research, as embodied in the *No Child Left Behind* initiative of the G.W. Bush administration, discussed at the start of this chapter. The uncritical assertion that a standard of a particular sort of medical research should be the standard for educational research betrays a profound—and, we believe, dangerous—ignorance of the relative complexities of these phenomena.)

It is beyond our purposes here to delve into the "why's" of the profound structural similarities of complex phenomena, but we do provide a few references to some informative and accessible introductions to network theory in our endnotes.[24] As might be expected, given the range of phenomena implicated, the areas of research involved in investigations of networks are diverse, and include physics, mathematics, chemistry, biology, psychology, sociology, medicine, and economics. To date, education has not drawn extensively on the emergent discussions, but we can speculate on some topics that might prove relevant and productive.

To frame these speculations, it is necessary to point to the sorts of organizations or architectures that are studied by network theorists. In figure 3.5, we provide a image of this type of structure in which, briefly, nodes cluster into larger nodes that cluster into larger nodes, and so on. (The image in fig. 3.5 is greatly simplified. A diagram that is appropriate to an actual complex system would look more like a hairball.) Significantly, nodes are not "basic units," but should be understood a subnetworks in themselves as they *link* to one another to form *hubs*. This manner of organization means that most of the interactions of an "agent" (i.e., a node, selected at any level of organization) are with its closest neighbors, consistent with the complexivist insight that most of the information in a complex system is local. However, with the clustered arrangement, every agent is also reasonably well connected to every other agent in the network through a relatively small number of connections.

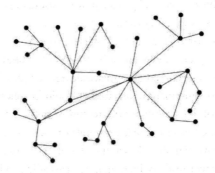

FIGURE 3.5 A SIMPLIFIED REPRESENTATION OF A SCALE-FREE NETWORK
All complex systems are organized in scale-free patterns of nodes noding into grander nodes. The presence of a scale-free organization in a phenomenon is often taken as a critical indicator that it is likely complex.

Perhaps the most familiar articulation of this manner of interconnectivity is the notion of "six degrees of separation," first proposed by sociologist Stanley Milgram and later popularized by the stage play and movie by the same title.[25] The claim here is that, no matter how socially or spatially separate two humans might be, there exists a chain of acquaintances between them that consists of six or fewer persons. This quality is sometimes called the "small world phenomenon," owing to the common expression of the rhetorical question, "Isn't it a small world?!" when new acquaintances discover common associates.

Of course, claims about six degrees of separation and small worlds are often impossible to verify, as conclusive proofs would require a comprehensive knowledge of everyone's social connections. Nevertheless, there is some evidence to support the idea, based on phenomena that are more readily mapped out. The ever-evolving internet is a popular example, and one that is relatively easily studied through electronic means. The resulting maps reveal intricate webs of nodes nodding into nodes, with every computer that is tied into the system separated from every other by no more than 12 degrees.[26] Similarly, studies of neurons in brains reveal they are also organized in a scale-free network. Specifically, as neurologist William Calvin describes,

> [The] factor of 100 keeps recurring: a hundred neurons to a minicolumn, roughly a hundred mincolumns to a macrocolumn, a hundred times a hundred macrocolumns to a cortical area ..., and there are just over a hundred Brodman Areas when you total those in both hemispheres.[27]

This organizational structure means that, in spite of the vast number of neurons in a human brain, the pathway between any two can be surprisingly short—which is a good thing, given the tremendous number of neurons in an adult brain (approx. 10^{12}). More rigidly hierarchical or centralized structures would entail vastly slower response times and much slower paces for adaptation.

Among the advantages of this manner of organization is a tremendous robustness. If a node—or even a relatively major hub—were to fail, there is a strong possibility that a scale-free networked system would remain viable. Alternative routes for the exchange of information and matter could be selected or readily established. It is because of its scale-free architecture that the brain can usually recover from minor strokes. Other familiar examples of such robustness are airlines (if a major hub is delayed or shut down, the rest of the network can usually continue) and electrical power grids (which, massive cascading failures notwithstanding, are able to adapt readily to fluctuations in demands and to deal with sources that go off-line unexpectedly). Importantly, it seems that the robustness of many networks, including social networks and knowledge networks, has as

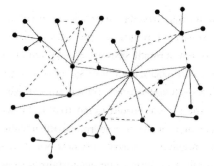

FIGURE 3.6 THE IMPORTANCE OF WEAK LINKS
The addition of a few *weak links* (represented as broken lines) can enhance both the robustness and the flow of information an a network.

much to do with what are called *weak links* (compare fig. 3.5 and 3.6). The addition of a few links among nodes can greatly reduce a network's dependence on its hubs and, hence, decrease its vulnerability. The addition of weak links can also improve the flow of information—which, as developed in subsequent sections and chapters, can have important implications for the intelligence of the system.

In brief then, scale-free networks have two main advantages: First, they are able to move information efficiently because nodes are never too distant from one another. Second, they are usually able to withstand shocks to the system because there are no nodes that are too critical to the global functioning (although failure or destruction of certain nodes can lead to a fragmentation of the network). It is thus that one might contrast a scale-free structure with two other familiar manners of organization, the centralized system and the distributed system (see fig. 3.7).

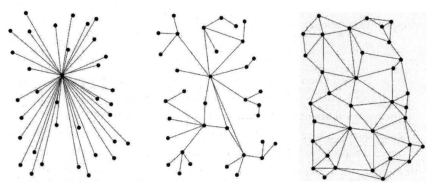

FIGURE 3.7 TYPES OF NETWORK ARCHITECTURES
There are three types of network architectures[28]: (a) centralized, (b) decentralized or scale-free, and (c) distributed.

A centralized system can have highly efficient information flow because nodes can, in principle, be separated by at most one intermediary. The downside of this efficient connectivity is that such systems are vulnerable to massive failures. If the central hub fails to function, the entire systems will go down. In contrast, a distributed, mesh-like system can be extremely robust. Many, many nodes could be removed before the system would begin to fail. However, such robustness comes at the expense of efficient movement of information and resources. The number of "jumps" required to move between nodes at the extremes of such networks can be prohibitively large. The decentralized or scale-free network balances efficient communications with robustness.

Applied to education, this discussion of scale-free networks points to several possible sites of interpretation and study. For example, administrative units—including jurisdictions, schools, and classrooms—tend to be highly centralized. Might a more decentralized structure better serve some educational ends? (We return to this question in chap. 4, in the context of a discussion of the organizations of classrooms.) The physical structures of schools themselves might be reconsidered in terms of complex, networked organizations, as Upitis develops.[29] In a related vein, might network theory prompt reconsiderations of the assumed structures of disciplinary knowledge and the curricula based on varied knowledge domains?

Consider, for example, mathematics. For curriculum purposes, mathematics has been treated not as a nested and evolving network, but as a rigid edifice with fixed associations. The resulting curriculum has been organized around an assumption of an underlying Euclidean geometry, as evidenced in the emphasis on "the basics" (usually seen to be counting, addition, etc.) in the early grades and more abstract concepts at higher grades. The process of moving through topics is most commonly construed as a matter of linear progression through a prespecified sequence of concepts.

For curriculum purposes, what if the architecture of mathematics were reframed in terms of a nested, scale-free network? This shift might prompt attentions away from assumptions of universal basics and linear progress toward notions of highly connected ideas/nodes and neighborhoods of ideas, thus prompting pedagogical attentions toward the need to dwell with concepts/situations. The key question here is not "What is foundational?", but "What are the highly connected ideas?" or "What sorts of notions and competencies are manifest throughout the network?" In turn, the structure of a curriculum would have to be transformed from a directed movement through topics to a study of neighborhoods of concepts—that is, according to the sort of structure illustrated in figures 3.5 and 3.6, rather than the currently ubiquitous line.

This suggestion, while entirely speculative, may not be so far-fetched. Studies of the structure of mathematics have yet to be completed, but it seems reasonable to conjecture that the results will be similar to recent studies of language. As Barabàsi notes,

> Our measurements indicate that language, viewed as a network of synonyms, is hierarchical [i.e., a clustered network] as well, a few highly connected words like "turn," "take," or "go," each with over a hundred synonyms, holding the various lexical modules together.[30]

Similar sensibilities have been applied to other domains. Historians, for example, are beginning to reject the pervasive assumption of (line-based) chains of events that are presumed to precipitate monumental happenings.[31] Rather, invoking notions associated with power laws, the emergent sensibility is focused more on the constant accumulation of small events that trigger cascades of incidents of varying significance. The underlying image is more toward an ever-growing sand pile in which any happening might prompt a landslide—but it would be a gross oversimplification to attribute the slide to the final perturbation. The habit of historians has been to identify such moments as the *keys*, when they may only be *triggers*. They do not *cause*, in the direct linear sense. Rather, the "pile" of accumulated events determines the outcome. In other words, history is being rethought, not in terms of sudden monumental events and "great men," but in terms of slow accumulations and triggers.[32]

Another site in which network thinking is starting to challenge cultural assumption is the manner in which science is (and scientists are) organized. The deeply entrenched belief in the lone genius in solitary pursuit can be shown to be problematic through rather simple examinations of co-authorships and bibliographies. For most of the past century, at least, the bulk of scientific research has involved large teams of investigators. It is now commonplace to encounter scientific papers that have 10 or 20 co-authors. Major discoveries, similarly, are rarely attributed or attributable to single researchers. For example, the 1994 announcement of the "top quark" was credited to 450 different physicists. Surowiecki speculates on the reason for this trend toward collaboration:

> As science has become ever more specialized and as the number of subfields within each discipline has proliferated, it's become difficult for a single person to know everything he [sic] needs to know.[33]

Surowiecki offers several other, more striking examples of shared inquiry, such as the recent discovery of the virus responsible for SARS. This particular effort involved teams around the world that, linked electronically and oriented by the same urgent purpose, detected and verified the role of the virus in mere weeks.

The phenomenon of shared research and joint authorship is perhaps best understood in terms of a shift in the culture of scientific research—in effect, a collective realization that sudden insights are rarely, if ever, matters of solitary genius. The phenomenon is also linked to the simple fact that researchers who collaborate are generally more successful and productive. As de Solla Price and Beaver have shown, "the most prolific man [sic] is by far the most collaborating, and three of the four next most prolific are also among the most frequently collaborating."[34]

Given this situation, it should not be surprising that researchers interested in mapping intellectual influences, theoretical preferences, and research emphases within specific disciplines have started to generate images with the same scale-free architecture as is illustrated in figure 3.4.[35] These maps are decidedly fractal-like, consisting of nodes that connect with other nodes into larger nodes, and so on, to generate patterns reminiscent of frost on window panes, to root systems of poplar groves, the structure of the internet, and the interconnectivity of the human brain. In other words, the notion of an edifice of knowledge—of unambiguous foundations and logical hierarchies of associations—is likely a fiction, and a damaging one when imposed on schools and curricula. Evidence points to the likelihood that collective knowledge, like the individual brain, has an organic, networked structure. The implications for education and for educational research, it would seem, are profound.

CHAPTER FOUR

THE NETWORK OF COMPLEXITY

WHEN WE TRY TO PICK OUT ANYTHING BY ITSELF,
WE FIND IT HITCHED TO EVERYTHING ELSE IN THE UNIVERSE.
—John Muir[1]

Sir Isaac Newton, regarded by many as one of the greatest intellects in the history of Western mathematics and science, once famously attributed his academic successes to having "stood on the shoulders of giants." The quotation has become a familiar one, but it bespeaks an attitude toward knowledge that is decidedly un-complex.

As developed in previous chapters, the prevailing opinion at Newton's time was that a mathematics-informed science was progressing toward a total(ized) understanding of the universe. The growing body of rigorously tested and verified knowledge was thought to be linear—that is, cumulative and forward (or upward).

Complexity thinking troubles the metaphors of accumulations of knowledge and progress toward a foreseeable endpoint that underlie these assumptions. For complexivists, the emergence of new interpretive possibility is framed more in terms of expansiveness and outward movement. The associated image is something more toward the ever-branching possibilities that appear as water flows outward over a surface. In other words, the development of insight seems to be more a matter of expanding the space of the possible by exploring the current space of possibility. As such, the creation of knowledge is "progressive" not because it is moving in a given direction, but because it is constantly elaborating what has already been established. It is expansive, but not directional.

Such progress is decidedly collective, as we began to develop in the final section of chapter 3. Significantly, the purpose of emphasizing collectivity is not to dismiss, diminish, or discount individual identity, subjective knowledge, or personal agency. Rather, the point is that researchers not only depend on the work of their predecessors, they are just as reliant on the insights of their contemporaries—an assertion that is supported by the manner in which increased connectivity among humans has contributed to a rapid expansion of technological possibility.[2] It is not a case of collectivity *versus* individuality, but a situation of collective-possibilities-arising-in-the-mutually-specifying-activities-of-autonomous-agents.

The intention of this chapter is to provide a more detailed, but still unavoidably partial, account of how complexity thinking fits into the contemporary landscape of thought. Our orienting assertion is that complexity thinking is shaped as much by prevailing discourses as by its history. As such, we must be attentive to the sensibilities announced in other domains. Complexity thinking itself compels this attitude, underscoring that new potentials arise in the commingling of existing possibilities. A main purpose of this chapter is thus to flag the emergent character of complexity thinking—that is, to highlight that complexity science is, in fact, an instance of what it purports to study.

The discussion is organized around two important developments: the articulation of a scientifically defensible theory of evolution in the 1800s and the study of self-organizing systems in the 1900s.

THE TRANSITION FROM METAPHYSICAL/SUPERNATURAL TO PHYSICAL/NATURALIST WORLDVIEWS

One of the most significant intellectual shifts in modern times was the development of empirically grounded and rationally defensible theories of evolution. This accomplishment is typically attributed to Charles Darwin and the critical moment is usually identified as his publication of *The Origin of Species* in 1859.

However, although Darwin's contributions were undeniably profound, it is not really appropriate to identify him as the sole author of evolutionary thought. Indeed, his writings can be construed as minor elaborations of extant cultural sensibilities. His grandfather and his father had already published on the topics. As well, 30 years before the appearance of *The Origin of Species*, Charles Lyell published *Principles of Geology* in which he argued that natural landscapes were shaped and continuously reshaped by geological forces, not by the hand of God. In a similar vein, linguists had developed branching tree diagrams to illustrate the bifurcations of European languages from a common protolanguage, and Darwin was certainly aware of their conclusions. With regard to biological evolution, Denis Diderot and Jean-Baptiste Lamarck were among those who had already speculated on the common origins of different forms in the first half of the 1800s. In other words, not only had the stage been set and the audience prepared for Charles Darwin's treatise on the emergence of life itself, he had been exposed to some of the theory's core principles since his early childhood. The publication of *The Origin of Species*, then, was more an instance of elaborated networked thinking than it was a break from established orthodoxies by a rugged individualist.

This is not to say that Darwin offered little new. Quite the contrary, he made a major contribution by knitting together many strands of thinking into a coherent, viable, and evidence-based theory of evolutionary development. The publication of *The Origin of Species* thus triggered (but certainly did not "cause") a considerable acceleration of evolutionary theories in almost all branches of the physical and social sciences, including most obviously botany, astronomy, sociology, and zoology. In an essay to mark the 50th anniversary of the publication of Darwin's major work, John Dewey commented that Darwin had already displaced thousands of years of entrenched assumption within the sciences.[3] In the near century that has passed since Dewey wrote, evolutionary theories have come to serve as the commonsense backdrop of almost all academic and popular discourses.

It is important to be clear about the nature of the conceptual shift wrought by evolutionary thought. Prior to Darwin, the universe was overwhelmingly understood as fixed and finished. As developed in chapter 2, the task of science in this frame was construed in simple and straightforward (i.e., accumulative and directed) terms of naming and classifying parts. More specifically, this project was uncritically organized around a worldview articulated by the ancient Greeks and most commonly attributed to Plato. In brief, the physical universe in which humans dwell was understood as a sort of flawed reflection of a perfect and timeless Ideal realm—a metaphysical (literally, "after or beyond the physical") or supernatural ("above nature") reality. This realm was considered the source and the goal of all *eidos*, or *ideas*, as the word is rendered in current translations of Plato's works.

However, 150 years ago, at the time that Darwin wrote, *eidos* was more commonly translated as *species*, rather than *ideas*. The terms are etymological relatives. Idea and *eidos* derive from the Greek *idein*, "to see," and species from the Latin *specere*, "to look." The Greek *idein* is echoed in contemporary words like *identify* and *ideology*, and the Latin *specere* is heard in words like *spectator*, *spectacles*, and *speculate*. Darwin's proposal of an "origin of species," then, was a deliberately provocative assertion. With that simple phrase, he challenged the prevailing orthodoxy that species-ideas were fixed forms that had no beginnings. In the process, he reduced established classification systems to little more than temporary and flawed conveniences for making sense of differences among organisms.

Much in contrast to the prevailing belief system inherited from the Greeks, Darwin saw change and accident as norms rather than as deviances from perfection. For him, they were the definers of creative possibility, aspects of a grand evolutionary dance, a continuous tinkering with one's own structure and the structure of one's context. Darwin's accomplishment, then, was the description of *physical* or *natural* processes (versus *metaphysical* states or *supernatural* influences) that could not only explain the observed structures of species-ideas, but that could account for their transformations into other species-ideas without the supervision or intervention of an intelligent designer. The physical/natural process itself, Darwin posited, is intelligent, able to produce and select among a range of innovative possibilities in the face of constantly changing circumstances. He suggested that nature could be seen to pull itself up by its own bootstraps through a sort of quasi-random self-assemblage. He further argued that nature is always in the process of becoming something else, constantly (but not deliberately—evolution does not plan ahead, it is merely a process of adapting to immediate contingencies) testing new species-ideas, forever pushing out the borders of possibility and filling the spaces created.

A contrast between the terms *metaphysical* and *physical* is useful to underscore the conceptual shift proposed by Darwin and so many of his contemporaries. As mentioned, the prefix *meta-* means "above or beyond," and in Darwin's time engendered a sort of disdain or disregard for things physical. The word physical, derived from the Greek *physis*, "growth, nature," is a cognate of *phyein*, "to bring forth." (*Phyein* is also the root of the English infinitive *to be*.) In critiquing metaphysics and looking toward the physical, then, Darwin argued that phenomena themselves were sufficient for understanding their forms. Restated, Darwin asserted that scientists should be focusing on the complex interrelationships of forms, not fixing their gazes on an imagined ideal realm in which distinctions are of principal interest. The physical could and should be understood in its own right, not as some imperfect reflection of a metaphysical reality.

EVOLUTIONARY THOUGHT AND EDUCATIONAL THEORIES

One of the major developments in the field of education in the past half-century has been a problematization of an ancient and still commonsensical belief about the relationship between objective knowledge and subjective understanding. To perhaps oversimplify, knowledge tends to be commonsensically cast in terms of some *thing*, "out there," whereas understanding tends to be described in terms of more tentative, ever-shifting, fallible personal interpretations that reside inside one's head. Within this frame, learning is a process of internally representing

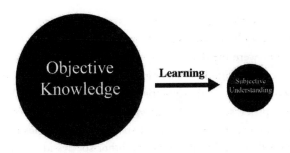

FIGURE 4.1 POPULAR METAPHORS OF KNOWLEDGE AND KNOWING
In common figurative language, objective knowledge and subjective understanding are often framed in terms of two isolated domains that must somehow be bridged.

what is out there—or, less critically, as ingesting knowledge. Phrases such as *acquiring* insight, *grasping* ideas, *exchanging* information, *food* for thought, *solid* foundations, *structured* arguments, *building* knowledge, and *constructing* understandings—to just graze the surface of this web of associations—help to hold these deep-seated assumptions in place.

Graphically, these turns of phrase seem to be organized around the sort of image presented in figure 4.1 (which we first introduced in chap. 2), in which knowledge and understanding are taken to be two discrete regions and, hence, learning becomes a process of taking things in.

Such a frame was famously critiqued by Paulo Freire in his condemnation of "banking education," through which learning and teaching are interpreted in terms of depositing and storing information.[4] Freire's critique was, however, anticipated by at least several centuries in the work of John Locke, who argued that there is clearly nothing that moves from the outside to the inside in moments of learning. What must be happening, he reasoned, is that individual knowers are constructing internal representations of their worlds on the bases of their experiences, constantly revising and updating these models to fit with new circumstances. In other words, Locke argued for a world in which the internal world of understanding was a *reflection* or *mirror* of the external, real world, thus removing the arrow that was thought to connect objective knowledge to subjective understanding (see fig. 4.2). Unfortunately, this model preserved the separation of knower from knowledge, which was still assumed to be "out there," effectively hiding in the bushes waiting to be uncovered.

There were critics of Locke's view—notably a contemporary named Giambattista Vico, as will be developed shortly. But it was not until the 20th century that new conceptions of the relationship between objective knowledge and subjective understandings began to gain broad acceptance. Rejecting two of

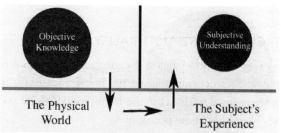

FIGURE 4.2 LOCKE'S IMAGE OF KNOWLEDGE AND KNOWING
John Locke elaborated that commonsense understanding of the relationship between objective knowledge and subjective knowing (as illustrated in fig. 4.1) by suggesting that subjective understanding is rooted in one's physical experiences in the physical world. This sort of image underlies what are depricatingly called "trivial" constructivisms.

Locke's central assumptions—namely that truth is out there and that personal understanding is a matter of internal representation of such truth—these new theories posited a different relationship between understanding. The image was more toward that presented in figure 4.3, in which understanding was suggested to be nested in knowledge. Of course, such a reframing demanded very different conceptions of both knowledge and understanding. As detailed in subsequent sections of this chapter, they came to be understood more in terms of nested dynamics than separated objects, wherein appearances of volatility or stability are matters of temporal scales, not inherent qualities. Correspondingly, learning was recast in terms of the ongoing fitness, whereby both knowledge and understanding were subject to continuous tinkering to maintain viability. We now move into more detailed discussions of these issues.

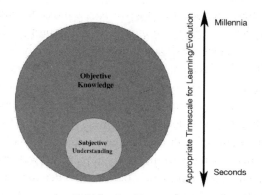

FIGURE 4.3 A COMPLEXIVIST IMAGE OF KNOWLEDGE AND KNOWING
Complexity theories of collective knowledge and individual knowing not only recast these phenomena as enfolded in and unfolding from one another, but posit that they obey similar evolutionary dynamics (albeit on very different time scales).

EVOLVING THINKING:
THE EMERGENCE OF STRUCTURALIST THEORIES

It is not an exaggeration to suggest that, through the 20th century, the gap between the physical sciences and the arts and humanities grew progressively wider. The divergence seemed to climax in the 1970s and 1980s, as social constructionist discourses took hold in the humanities.

Oversimplified, social constructionist discourses are a subset of coherence theories (see chap. 2) that converge around the conviction that all knowledge is socially constructed—that is, that the criterion for facticity is not verification, but intersubjective accord. Things are true because collectives agree that they are true. Of course, such an assertion flies in the face of the project of modern science, which is overwhelmingly framed in terms of *discovering* facts rather than *creating* them. Toward the end of the century, the seeming impasse was the focus of numerous humanities-based critiques modern science and, in response, many (generally vitriolic) science-based critiques of discussions of epistemology within the arts and humanities.[5]

A curious aspect of this situation is that social constructionism and its related discourses actually find their roots in the physical sciences, reliant on the sort of thinking prompted by Darwin. As developed in chapter 2, structuralist discourses rely on a coherence model of truth, as opposed to a correspondence model. The major implication here is that coherence theories are concerned with systems' internal consistencies as the central criterion is for viability, not any sort of match between internal functioning and external conditions.

Those coherence theories that might be called "structuralist" were, in the main, part of a general movement that swept across and through most of the arts and humanities in the early 1900s. The movements' most profound influences were in linguistics, mathematics, psychology, and sociology, largely through the contributions of Ferdinand de Saussure, Nicholas Bourbaki,[6] Jean Piaget, and Lev Vygotsky.

As with all intellectual movements, many of the defining sensibilities of structuralism can be traced back through preceding centuries. For instance, in addition to incorporating the evolutionary dynamics described by Darwin, structuralists also drew on insights of 17th-century thinker Giambattista Vico. Born into the conceptual climate of the Scientific Revolution, which was prompted by thinker such as René Descartes and Francis Bacon, Vico denounced their analytic philosophies. He felt that their emphases on mathematics and the physical sciences undermined the important contributions of other facets of human knowledge, including art, rhetoric, history, and language. Vico saw knowledge-making as entailing a certain level of uncertainty rather than as an inevitable progress toward certainty. As such, he felt that analytic thought served to limit invention and to stifle thinking.

Vico also offered dramatically different views of rationalist mathematics and empiricist science. Departing from the millennia-old belief that mathematics was objectively real (indeed, the epitome of metaphysical truth), he saw mathematics as the product of human minds—that is, as convictions that existed only in human brains. Science he saw in terms of interactions between the brain and the natural world. For him scientific truth was not totally created in the mind, but through experimentation that bridged mental construct and physical constraint.

Vico is often identified as someone who was centuries ahead of his time. Perhaps more than any of his contemporaries, he offered a radically new way to think about knowledge—one that came to be incorporated not only into structuralist sensibilities, but that was to figure prominently in the emergences of existentialism, pragmatism, psychoanalysis, and other academic movements that unfolded more than 150 years after his death. Perhaps his most significant contributions was his argument that knowledge is created, not discovered—a notion that was to gain considerable momentum when it was coupled to the evolutionary dynamics described by Darwin more than a century later.

This point was dramatically demonstrated within Saussurian (structuralist) linguistics, Bourbaki (structuralist) mathematics, and Piagetian and Vygotskian (structuralist) cognitive theories. Each of these projects might be characterized as an effort to describe and assemble a closed and internally consistent system in which terms, propositions, and other constructs are rendered meaningful by virtue of their relationships to other terms and propositions, not because they are associated with some aspect of the "real" world. For example, according to Saussure, a word is meaningful because of its associations and dissociations with other words—with the implication that meanings must be constantly shifting. Invoking the biological sense of structure (see chap. 1), Saussure framed language as a living, organic form composed of ever-evolving and intertwining parts. For him, languages are the products of circular (recursive) interactions between two or more brains. Linguistic symbols are the go-betweens (in the sense of mutual triggers, not in the sense of physical objects) that allow minds to connect.

The biological sense of structure is also useful to interpret the way Piaget used the term to describe learning and the emergence of personal understandings. He borrowed the structuralist qualities of self-reference, self-containment, internal coherence, and no need for external correspondence to articulate his own account of how individuals come to construe a world. In so doing, he offered a *physical* theory of cognition that broke from deeply entrenched metaphysical assumption. Piaget rejected the notion that the "truth is out there" in some higher, not-directly-accessible realm, arguing something more toward the belief that "truth keeps happening" as individuals revise understandings and expectations to maintain their psychological fitness with their experiences. (This point marks the major break with "trivial" constructivist theories, many of which posit a knower-independent, fixed truth.)

Within both psychology and education, Piaget's work has helped to trigger a proliferation of what have come to be called *constructivist* theories. Unfortunately, there are many versions of constructivism that actually have little to do with Piaget's research, owing in large part to resilient metaphysical assumptions on the natures of knowledge, reality, and personal identity.[7] In terms of the relationship of his work to structuralist (and complexivist) sensibilities, the critical point to remember is that Piaget's theory of cognition revolves around the assumption that the sense a person makes of an event is less a function of the qualities of that event and more about the complex history of the agent's linguistically affected, biologically enabled, and culturally infused structure.

In the language of complexity—noting that such vocabulary was not available at the time—Piaget described personal cognition as a self-organizing, adaptive phenomenon. He went even further, to relate the phenomenon of individual cognition to the grander systems of language and culture by speculating that, because each person knits her or his understandings out of unique sets of experiences, those higher order phenomena must obey a similar complex dynamic. Such speculation marks the overlap of Piaget's research into individual cognitive structures and the work of his contemporary, Vygotsky, who was more centrally concerned with the manner in which the world is jointly construed and the manner in which the social world shapes the individual.

Over the past few decades, many, many pages in many, many research journals have been given to comparisons of Piaget's and Vygotsky's theories. For the most part, this literature has been devoted to efforts to reconcile the two bodies of work—a move that is often prompted and frustrated by a failure to appreciate that they were interested in distinct phenomena. Complexity thinking is helpful here, in its suggestion that personal cognition is nested in—that is, enfolded in and unfolding from—collective activity. This frame helps to explicate the relationship between Piaget's interest in how learners incorporate/embody new experiences and Vygotsky's focus on how individuals are incorporated into the body politic. Different processes are at work, and different concerns arise at these two levels of organization.

On this point, it is worth underscoring that almost all structuralist discourses, including those based in the theories of Piaget and Vygotsky, share one more important element. They all tend to employ body-based metaphors to describe their particular interests and foci. Examples include a *body of knowledge*, a *social corpus*, the *body politic*, a *student body*, and the *biological body* (see fig. 2.3). This similarity, of course, also foregrounds some significant divergences among constructivist theories, because the bodies studied vary considerably in structure and form. These differences, in turn, underscore the complexity scientific principle that, while such nested phenomena can be understood to have deep similarities, they cannot be collapsed into or reduced to one another. New laws emerge and new rules apply at each level of complex organization.

EVOLVING THINKING:
THE EMERGENCE OF POST-STRUCTURALIST DISCOURSES

Structuralist theories are principally concerned with the manner in which certain phenomena—including culture, language, and individual cognition—are organized. These theories inquire into the relational webs that afford such phenomena their coherence. While they are, of course, concerned with the dynamics that give rise to and that inhere in their objects of study, in the main those interests are secondary at best.

In the latter half of the 20th century, a complementary set of discourses arose that were more focused on issues of dynamics. These *post*-structuralist theories follow the structuralist argument that terms are rendered meaningful through systems of difference and differentiation, not through unambiguous reference to something real or ideal. However, post-structuralists tend to concern themselves more with the power structures at work—deliberate and accidental, explicit and tacit—within these systems of difference. One might say that the focus is not so much on the weave of the garment of knowledge, but its lining—the usually unnoticed, generally invisible dynamics that give it is shape. One of the terms used to flag this focus is *discourse*.

Discourse refers to the intertwining structures—linguistic, social, and so on—that frame a social or cultural groups' preferred habits of interpretation. A discourse organizes and constrains what can be said, thought, and done. The emphasis here is on language, but post-structuralist theories are also attentive to the activities and traditions that are prompted and supported by specific vocabularies and patterns of language use. Each discourse has its own distinctive sets of (mostly tacit) rules and procedures that govern the production of what is to count as meaningful or senseless, true or false, normal or abnormal.

Discourses always function in relation or opposition to one another. Those that might be labeled *post-structuralist* have the particular quality of being discourses about discourses. For example, they are attentive to the theoretical commitments and personal/social implications of their and other discourse systems. Unlike most other discourses that employ the prefix *post-* in their titles, including postmodernism and postformalism, the post- of post-structuralism is not meant to signal a problematizing or even a rejection of structuralist sensibilities, but an elaboration. Saussure and his contemporaries actually set the stage for the emergence of post-structuralism by arguing that language must be understood as a set of relations rather than in terms of discrete word units. Post-structuralists have extended Saussure's emphases on structural analyses of language, asserting that these structures must not be considered in decontextualized or dehistoricized terms. In other words, for post-structuralists, coherence is a necessary but not a sufficient criterion for the meaningfulness of a system. Rather, they argue that it is immersion in culture that defines the particular mode of human consciousness. Such immersion must be understood not in terms of isolated discourses, but in terms of simultaneous, overlapping, and interlaced discourses.

The most obvious candidates for post-structural critique are religions and metaphysical philosophies, but there are more subtle, seemingly commonsensical discourses (about, for example, science, capitalism, and democracy) that are arguably more important sites for interrogation. One of the major instigators of post-structuralist critique, Michel Foucault, offered several powerful illustrations of this manner of scholarly pursuit as he sought to explicate how systems of meaning are entangled with cultural beliefs around sexuality, sanity, normality, and social order.[8]

Post-structuralist discourses aim to show how absences, slips, misalignments, and other deferrals contribute to the productions and evolutions of meaning. In general, they are also tied to examinations of *power*, a term that is translated from the French words *pouvoir* and *puissance*. The principal meanings of these words have to do with "ability," "wherewithall," "means," and "capacity to act"—that is, *power to*. However, they can also be used to refer to "force" and "strength"—or, *power over*—and the specific connotation varies across post-structuralist discourses.

We have gone into some detail in describing the character and context of post-structuralist theories because, in our assessment, they are readily fitted to complexivist sensibilities, where the complex systems under examination are culture, the body politic, and bodies of knowledge. Close readings of post-structuralist critiques, particularly those from the 1970s and 1980s, demonstrate that they consistently anticipated such complexivist notions as self-organization, self-maintenance, mutual specification of agents, adaptation, nested organization, and so on. In other words, despite the lack of open or direct lines of communication between the sciences and the humanities through the middle part of the 20th century, highly compatible sensibilities emerged around the shared realization that the tools of classical science were inadequate to understand collective activity.

More is said in subsequent chapters on the relevance of post-structuralism for education and educational research. The important point for our immediate purposes is that, although these discourses arose independently of complexity discourses, they rely on very similar understandings of the dynamics and characters of certain sorts of phenomena. In other words, both post-structuralist and complexity theories have a self-awareness of sorts: They both provide insight not only into how other discourses arise, but into how they themselves emerge and operate. Moreover, in post-structuralism's well-developed explications of the natures and roles of discourses, these theories offer important contributions to understandings the complexities of human interaction. Two examples are post-structural theorists' characterizations of the interlaced, co-dependent aspects of discourses and discussions of what it might mean to *represent* knowledge. We address the latter contribution in greater detail at the end of this chapter.

But perhaps the most important contribution of post-structuralist discourses is around their explications of the role of social and cultural norms and conventions. Numerous commentators, many of whom locate their work in education,[9] have offered rich and varied accounts of the hegemonic discourses that support and "naturalize" racisms, colonialisms, sexisms, heterosexisms, classisms, and other manners of oppression, repression, and suppression. Some have also provided accounts of the emergence of these discourses.[10] Consideration of this work is vital in any examination of the relevance of complexity thinking for education.

EVOLVING THINKING:
THE SHIFT IN THE PHYSICAL SCIENCES

By the close of the 20th century, evolutionary assumptions had become so commonsensical and so transparent that they dominated discussions of knowledge and truth within the arts and humanities. At that time, a small group of thinkers that straddled these domains and the physical sciences began to note some deep resonances between emergent sensibilities. Preliminary explications of these resonances were often greeted with skepticism—as evidenced in the varied responses to works such as Lyotard's *The Postmodern Condition*—owing, it seems, to the fact that divergent and non-intersecting evolutionary paths had unfolded through the century. In particular, within the arts and humanities, much of the thinking was explicitly defined in contradistinction from the sciences.

But an important qualification must be made here. The "sciences" that were rejected within much of 20th-century structuralist, post-structuralist, and related theories were the sciences of 1700s and 1800s—the orientations and emphases of which, as developed in chapter 2, were actually dismissed or eclipsed through the 1900s within the sciences. Much of the critique of "scientism" and "positivist science" within the arts and humanities, then, is useful for marking an important bifurcation in thought that occurred over a century ago. However, to assume that those accounts are still appropriately applied to all of contemporary scientific inquiry is to succumb to a crude parody or caricature to the ever-evolving scientific project.

We have ourselves experienced this issue. In different contexts, we have dared to utter the word "science," only to be subjected to the same sorts of critiques that were offered 50 and 100 years ago. Many, it seems, cannot appreciate that not only does science evolve, but that its evolutions are subject to the same sorts of extant cultural sensibilities that render other discourses sensible and insensible. On this matter, a still-irresolvable issue for some seems to be the apparent differences between the humanities and the physical sciences regarding the source of truth: For the former, the current emphasis is on collective accord; for the latter, it is on an attentiveness to the physical world.

It would thus be overly optimistic to suggest that the time has come for these branches of thought to come together. However, it is not unreasonable to suggest a much greater compatibility than was apparent or acknowledged through most of the past century. The enduring difference remains the tension between intersubjectivity and objectivity as the basis of truth. As the popular argument goes, social agreement would not seem to have that much effect on the sum of $1 + 1$, on the speed of the earth's rotation, or on the behaviors of subatomic particles.

Be that as it may, it has become apparent that humanity does indeed have profound effects on some aspects of the physical world—aspects that were previously considered an independent backdrop of scientific inquiry. These effects include the impact of humanity on the genetic pool of the species (e.g., through warfare, migration, medicine, pollution, and genetic engineering), the biodiversity of the planet (e.g., through hunting, disease spread, habitat reduction, and climate change), and weather and climate patterns (e.g., though ozone depletion, farming practices, and deforestation). Such instances are examples of the complex interrelationships between knowledge and the things-known. Knowledge affects perceptions, attitudes, and actions, which in turn can play a significant role in shaping the conditions of that knowledge.

As introduced in chapter 2, the term *interobjectivity* has been introduced by some thinkers, including Humberto Maturana[11] and Bruno Latour,[12] as a sort of conceptual hybrid of *intersubjectivity* and *objectivity*. One of the reasons for this move is to attempt to bring humanities-based and physical sciences-based discussions of truth into greater dialogue. As already developed, the notion of interobjectivity is oriented by the assertion that there is no objective—that is, free-standing, eter-

[handwritten annotation: → "real objectivity" is authentic subjectivity.]

nal, knower-independent—knowledge. Phrased differently, there are no observerless observations or measurerless measurements. Any and every identification entails and implicates an identifier. In reflexive terms, acts of observing and measuring generate observers and measurers at the same time that they generate observations and measurements.

In effect, *interobjectivity* is a restatement of the notion of *complicity*, as developed in previous chapters. The terms point to the emergent realization that the cultural project of knowledge production, whether identified as scientific or otherwise, must be understood in terms of the complicity of the observer in knitting the fabric of relations through which observations are rendered sensible. Efforts at the generation of knowledge are suggested to be not just matters of intersubjective accord, but of the mutually affective relationships between phenomena and knowledge of phenomena—that is, interobjectivity.

An important principle here is that descriptions of the universe are actually *part of* the universe. Hence, the universe changes as descriptions of the universe change—again foregrounding the evolutionary assumption that the universe is not a fixed or finished form. On this count, complexity theories are aligned with ecological discourses and share those discourses' interests in *participatory epistemologies*. Within this category of theories, knowledge is understood to inhere in interactions. That is, knowledge is embodied or enacted in the ever-unfolding choreography of action within the universe. Stated bluntly, the truth isn't out there.

Nor however, is the truth "in here," as some sort of strictly internal, subjective, or even intersubjective, phenomenon. Rather, what is known is acted out in what is done, and what is done contributes to the unfolding of the cosmos. Educationally speaking, this manner of argument mires schooling and research in very complex ethical issues. There is no innocent knowledge, no benign truth, no consequenceless assumption. Deliberate participation in the development and maintenance of knowledge, then, always and already entails a contribution to the unfolding universe. However benevolently conceived, that contribution may exceed its intentions and imagined consequences. Examples are not hard to come by: The move by educational researchers in the mid-1900s to impose behavioral psychological principles on classroom structures is a cogent example. The reduction of teaching to outcome-oriented, reward-administering techniques was undeniably unfortunate. Similarly, the more recent shift toward constructivist discourses may be having similarly problematic outcomes—and, as argued elsewhere, the blame for emergent difficulties might properly rest on the shoulders of educational researchers who seem to pay little attention to the consequences of their studies and reports.[13]

As is no doubt apparent from the preceding few paragraphs, the notion of interobjectivity does not lend itself to simple explanation. One of the reasons for this difficulty is that the word engenders rejections of some of the most deeply engrained cultural assumptions about the nature of the universe. Most obvious is the premise of analytic science that descriptions of phenomena are separate from actual phenomena. To be clear here, interobjectivity does not assert a direct causal connection of descriptions and the things described. The point is *not* that things change because they are noticed and described, but that knowers' actions are altered by virtue of their descriptions. As actions shift, the physical texture of the world is affected, a point that has been dramatically demonstrated over the past century. For example, the illnesses that are currently of greatest concern, the social issues that occupy attentions, and the climates that are now studied are all complexly emergent and, in obvious ways, prompted by entrenched habits of observation, interpretation, and action.

Not to overstate the case, the notion of interobjectivity is far from having captured either the popular imagination or the general attention of the scientific establishment. It is, nonetheless, a corollary of complexity science and, as mentioned, an issue of immense relevance to educators.

All that said, by the time that the notion of interobjectivity had been formally articulated, late in the 1900s, some educational theorists had already embraced the sort of thinking that it announced. Their principal influences, however, were not discussions of the philosophy of science, but the emergent domains of phenomenological and psychoanalytic thought.

BEYOND EVOLVING THINKING: THE CONTRIBUTIONS OF PHENOMENOLOGY AND PSYCHOANALYSIS

One of the critical foundations of Western philosophy has been a deep suspicion of the trustworthiness of human perception. From Plato through Descartes, perception was seen as inaccurate and easily deceived, and this fallibility contributed to insistences for proof, whether via rational argument or empirical demonstration.

Perception, that is, was overwhelmingly cast as the impassible membrane that separated the knower from the known world. However, at the turn of the 20th century, a few new theoretical frames began to emerge in which perception was reinterpreted not as the point of disjuncture, but the site of unification of agent and context. The perceiving body started to be redescribed as the source of meaning and mind, as opposed to some sort of impenetrable biological prison. Two of the most influential movements in the early development of the notion of the embodied mind were psychoanalysis and phenomenology.

From their beginnings, these theories spanned the physical and the social sciences. Indeed, they could be appropriately described in terms of transdisciplinarity. Sigmund Freud drew on and was influenced by studies in neurology, medicine, psychology, sociology, and biological evolution. The authors of phenomenology had a similar list of influences, and it is worth underscoring that these conceptual sources prompted attentions to the complex intertwinings of the experiential/cultural and the genetic/biological in the emergence of knowledge and identity. So oriented, some of the contributions of psychoanalysis and phenomenology have come to be echoed in almost every 20th-century academic movement. For instance, the suggestion that human consciousness is more a passenger than a pilot was revolutionary, introduced as it was at a time when conscious thought was the principal and sometimes exclusive focus of philosophy, psychology, and education. Freud helped foreground the roles of social habitus and nonconscious processes in the shaping of individual and collective characters. An important contribution of psychoanalysis to contemporary thought is its refusal to separate the individual's constitution of the world and the world's constitution of the individual, which could be read as a variant of the notion of interobjectivity. This conceptual move was hinged to a reframing—even a complexification—of individual subjectivity. Freud rejected the radical individualism of modernism, arguing instead that human identities are transitory, fragmented, and interlocked. Experiences of subjectivity are actually manifestations of intersubjective processes.

Similar notions were developed within phenomenology, which was first articulated in the early 1900s by Edmund Husserl. He sought to study phenomena by turning toward "the things themselves"—a phrase he used as a sort of critique of the still-pervasive assumption that the goal of science was to aspire to ideal, metaphysical truths than lay beyond the things themselves. Husserl sought to debunk persistent beliefs in essential qualities and ideal forms, and he developed a means to study how it is that the world becomes evident to awareness. In particular, he sought to foreground the role of intentionality, oriented by the assertion that all perception is oriented to and by objects in context. His phenomenological theory and its associated methods were thus about physical engagement with the world, about the complex intertwinings of concept and percept—about interobjectivity. This work was to be elaborated through the 20th century, and among the most notable contributions were those of Maurice Merleau-Ponty. Although first published in the late 1940s (in French), his *Phenomenology of Perception*[14] remains a standard reference in studies of perception and consciousness.

At the same time that phenomenology was emerging in Europe, pragmatist philosophy was emerging in North America. It too was greatly influenced by

Darwinian thought—perhaps even more so. Some of its principal authors, including Charles Sanders Peirce, William James, and John Dewey, made explicit use of evolutionary notions to describe knowledge and its production. This point is most obvious in their core assertion around the nature of truth. As previously developed, for the pragmatist, truth is what works. This definition that is grounded in Darwin's notion of fitness and it foregrounds the roles of context and timing. During the late 1800s and early 1900s, when pragmatism was cohering as a formal philosophy, there was no shortage of examples to illustrate this suggestion. Most prominently, Darwin's *The Origin of Species* had already toppled libraries of scientific treatises, and Einstein's theories of relativity were poking holes in Newton's seamless fabric of the universe.

The pragmatist movement is notable for its immediate and emphatic assertion that questions of collective knowledge cannot be dissociated from matters of morals, ethics, personal meaning, and cultural standards. No claim to truth was permitted to be construed as inert, simply because all truth was understood to exist in an intricate web of collective meaning. It is thus that truth, the world, and existence, to the pragmatist, are understood as sorts of collective fantasies. They are contrivances in which we all participate and to which we all contribute—and this conclusion of pragmatism is not at all dissimilar from the notion of complicity as developed by complexivists Cohen and Stewart.

In brief, then, it would be an unfortunate and egregious error to suggest that the sensibilities announced by complexity thinking have not been well-represented in the academic literature, generally, or the educational research literature, specifically.[15]

BEYOND EVOLVING THINKING: THE EMERGENCE OF EMERGENT THINKING

One of its most significant contributions to contemporary discussions of education is around the question of how norms and conventions evolve and sustain themselves. On this count, complexity thinking has emerged as an important complement to post-structuralist, psychoanalytic, phenomenological, and pragmatist thought—not just providing support to established critiques of cultural structures, but pointing toward new possibilities for interrupting those structures.

Complexity science, like any domain of academic inquiry, evolves. In one account of the major transitions during its brief history, Steven Johnson[16] describes its early stages in terms of loosely related observational studies of diverse phenomena. The uniting feature was a realization that the structures and dynamics of the forms studied did not lend themselves to established scientific methods, but few if any alternatives had been presented at that point.

The second stage, which unfolded through the late 1970s through the late 1990s, was focused on generalization across examples. Much of this work was organized around increasingly sophisticated computer modeling as researchers sought to identify structural similarities of complex phenomena and to mimic their dynamics, often with surprising success. The third, and current, stage is more concerned with what might be called a "pragmatics of transformation" in which the principal emphasis is on affecting the behaviors and characters of complex phenomena.

These stages, of course, are largely arbitrary heuristic conveniences. There were no sharply defined transitions in the emergence of complexity science. For example, the first stage could be argued to have begun in the early 1800s with the development of an evolutionary sensibility in many branches of academic research. Similarly, a number of studies in the early and mid-1900s could be cited: Friedrich Engels' examinations of the emergence of cities and class structures, John Dewey's (and other pragmatists') critiques of the development of cultural sensibilities, Jean Piaget's research into individual learning and cognition, and Alan Turing's explorations of "morphogenesis,"[17] to mention only a few instances. Such examples, of course, are only identifiable in retrospect, but all were concerned in one way or another with how a unity could assemble itself without direction from a master planner.

An important, consolidating shift occurred in the mid-1900s as researchers across domains began to draw more explicitly on one another's works. Sociologist Jane Jacobs' discussion of the emergence and decay of American cities,[18] for instance, was explicitly informed by information scientist Warren Weaver's categorization of different sorts of systems (as presented in chap. 1). By the 1960s, a host of still-disparate—that is, not-yet identified as conceptually related—studies were being undertaken. Humberto Maturana looked at *autopoietic*[19] biological systems, Evelyn Fox Keller investigated non-equilibrium thermodynamics, Marvin Minsky described the brain in terms of distributed networks, and Deborah Gordon attended to the life cycles of anthills. The list could be easily extended. Across these diverse phenomena, some curious features seemed to be remarkably similar. For example, not only did the unities seem to self-organize, but they seemed to *learn*. Indeed, some of them appeared over time to get more *intelligent*—that is, capable of more flexible, more effective responses to previously unmet circumstances (see chap. 5).

These studies provided the impetus for the emergence of complexity theory, and the phenomenon of self-organization became an object of study in its own right. Equipped with literally hundreds of richly detailed examples of complex forms, and enabled by the recent development of inexpensive and powerful com-

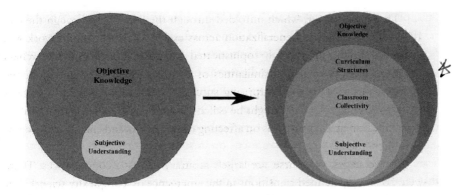

FIGURE 4.4 INTERMEDIARY LEVELS OF COMPLEX COHERENCE
Complexity thinking prompts attention toward possible intermediary levels of complex coherence that occur between subjective understanding and objective knowledge.

puters, researchers set out to investigate the deep similarities of anthills, brains, and social movements.

With regard to discussions in education, this emphasis of complexity research has contributed to an important elaboration of 20th-century discussions of the relationship between collective knowledge and individual understanding, specifically that there are other levels of dynamic and adaptive coherence that must be taken into account in discussions of education. Complexity thinking points to the inadequacy of nesting personal understanding within collective knowledge (see fig. 4.3, above) as it posits the presence of several intermediary layers of nested coherence that are of vital relevance to educators (see fig. 4.4).

All of these phenomena are understood within complexity thinking to be evolving. More provocatively, all are *cognitive*. None is a matter of representing the "real" world at a different scale; rather, each has to do with ongoing adaptation to dynamic circumstances.

A good deal of research, both inside and outside of education, is currently devoted to the study of such nested systems. However, it is the most recent phase of the evolution of the field that we feel is so critical to studies of learning and schooling, with their concerns not just for interpreting the complexities of individuals and collectives, but for deliberately affecting their structures and behaviors. With its current interest in how complexity might be created, maintained, and manipulated, complexity science has come to be well fitted to the specific and explicit concerns of educators and educational researchers.

It is one thing to suggest that complexity discourses have evolved toward the concerns of educators and quite another to explain how emergent insights might be applied to educational research (which is the focus of the Part II). After all, research into molecular biology and slime molds, or even neurophysiology, is a far cry from the sorts of issues and concerns that arise in the work of classroom teachers, school administrators, and curriculum developers.

The contributions of complexity thinking to education and educational research, then, are not necessarily direct ones. Nevertheless, some important principles can be readily adapted to the particular concerns of educationists. For example, one of the topics that we focus on in subsequent chapters is recent research into the processes by which a collection of *I's* becomes a collective of *we*—that is, the transition from a disconnected to a connected structure around a matter of shared concern. These sorts of phase transitions are one of the hallmarks of complex entities, and it turns out that much has been learned about how they can be recognized and described (the foci of chaps. 5 and 6) as well as occasioned (the foci of chaps. 7 and 8).

One of our goals in these discussions is to foreground the complementary characters of post-structuralist and complexity theories. Consistent with complexity thinking, the discussion proceeds with the assumption that a conversation across relevant domains of inquiry is necessary to being able to make sense of the phenomena at hand. As such, while occasional reference is made to, for example, the interactions of atoms, such allusions are in no way intended to suggest that humans interact or behave in ways identical to elemental particles. Rather, the point is that major developments in human understanding usually occur when new and previously unnoticed associations are made between seemingly disparate phenomena.

Put differently, contra Descartes' assumption and assertion that humans are logical, it appears that members of the species are not principally rational creatures. The capacity for logico-rational thought rides on the surface of connection-making systems like the associative structure of the brain or the weave of language. In other words, humans are mainly analogical. We urge readers to bear this realization in mind in the chapters that follow, as our intention in those chapters is to present new associative possibilities, new threads for a more complex weave. For us, the project here is not to represent reality, but to participate mindfully in the unfolding of new possibilities for action and interpretation.

PART TWO

COMPLEXITY THINKING, EDUCATION, AND EDUCATIONAL INQUIRY

CHAPTER FIVE

Descriptive Complexity Research:
QUALITIES OF LEARNING SYSTEMS

EVERYTHING IS WHAT IT IS
BECAUSE IT GOT THAT WAY.

—D'Arcy Wentworth Thomson[1]

As developed in the previous chapter, for most of its brief history, complexity science has focused on observation and description of self-organizing, self-maintaining, adaptive—that is, for our purposes, *learning*—systems. Although new emphases have emerged in the field, this one remains prominent and vibrant. With regard to educational phenomena, given the relatively slow uptake of complexity thinking by educational researchers (relative, at least, to research in sociology, economics, anthropology, psychology, and business), the descriptive aspect of complexity research remains especially relevant.

Indeed, some important preliminary questions remain unresolved. For example, while a handful of theorists have speculated that classroom collectives, schools, and bodies of knowledge might properly be considered as complex emergent phenomena (see chap. 6), the evidence to support such suspicions is sparse and based largely on analogies made to research conducted in other domains. In this chapter, then, we offer more detailed explications of the qualities of complex systems introduced in chapter 1, with a view toward applying those descriptors to a range of educational phenomena in the next chapter.

In the current discussion, we focus on some of the conceptual issues that present themselves in researchers' efforts, first, to recognize and, second, to characterize instances of complexity. To render the discussion manageable, we deal specifically with social collectivity as one instance of complex emergence. Because a broad range of general issues is presented, we use a single illustrative example to link various parts of the discussion. In chapter 6, more concerned with how the descriptive emphasis has been represented in the educational research literature, we use the opposite strategy by citing a broad range of studies and looking across several level of complex organization in an attempt to illustrate some of the issues that can arise in description-oriented complexity research.

In this chapter, our movement through descriptors and our elaborated example is oriented toward the articulation of a preliminary set of assertions around what it might mean for educational researchers to adopt, adapt, and contribute strategies of description and redescription from the complexity sciences. As will become clear through the discussion, these aspects of complex systems cannot be easily pried apart. Each is profoundly dependent on every other. As such, we qualify the discussion by highlighting the artificiality of any attempt to analyze complexity. The suggestion here is *not* that complexity can be reduced to these aspects, but that these aspects are useful for helping observers identify and make sense of complex structures and dynamics.

Discussion Box 5.1 • Understanding Collectives

The illustration that is developed throughout this chapter is based on a collaborative project involving the teaching staff of an inner city school (Valleyview Elementary) and ourselves. It was undertaken in the mid-1990s.[2]

It's difficult to describe exactly how and why the collaboration began, simply because the motivations of participants varied considerably. A major impetus, however, was a recent upheaval in the school. Although the school building itself was a fixture in the community, all but one member of its staff was new in the year that project was undertaken. There had been a series of tensions between the community and the previous staff, and the school board's response was to replace everyone but the vice principal.

That meant that the new principal had opportunity to hand-pick most of the teachers, and the resulting cohort was made up of mainly established and very successful practitioners—who, for the most part, barely knew one another and certainly had few connections to the community. Consequently, among the principal's reasons for welcoming the collaboration were the opportunities she envisioned for establishing collegial relationships within the school and cordial relationships within the community.

As for most of the members of the teaching staff, they seemed to be mainly interested in the advice on pedagogical practices and curriculum structures that we might have had to offer. As dedicated professionals, most had a rich history of participating in in-service activities and they welcomed the fact that the researchers had expertise in two of major strands of elementary school curriculum (i.e., language arts and mathematics).

We had quite different motivations still. We were new to the city, having just moved into our first university positions. Faced with the daunting prospect of establishing a research program in an unfamiliar setting, we embraced the opportunity to work with an entire teaching staff of a school.

SELF-ORGANIZATION

Certainly the most commonly cited quality of a complex system is the manner in which it bootstraps itself into existence. Somehow, these sorts of collectives develop capacities that can exceed the possibilities of the same group of agents if they were made to work independently. Ants self-organize into colonies, birds into flocks, humans into various sorts of social groupings, and so on.

Self-organization is also known as *emergence* and, of the many insights of complexity science, it is simultaneously the most important and the most difficult to appreciate. Somehow, agents that need not have much in common—much less be oriented by a common goal—can join into collectives that seem to have clear purposes.

One of the difficulties in studying instances of emergence is that the specific conditions and mechanisms of its occurrence can vary dramatically across situations. Clearly, for example, the processes at work in the emergence of an anthill are not identical to the processes that give rise to a body of knowledge. Nevertheless, some preliminary generalizations can and have been made about what needs to be in place for self-organization to happen—and our discussions of these points are distributed through the remaining chapters.

Within the education literature, perhaps the most prominent exploration and source of illustrations of self-organization is Peter Senge's *Schools that Learn*[3]— although, notably, neither *self-organization* nor *emergence* (or, for that matter, much of the established vocabulary of complexity science at all) is invoked in the book's near-600 pages. As far as alignment with complexity thinking, the most explicit statement is provided in a chapter on "systems thinking," an academic movement prominent in the 1970s. Systems thinking is focused on the emergence of physical systems (and might be contrasted with cybernetics, which is focused more on ideational or conceptual systems). It was one of the major tributaries of current complexity discourses and the source of the term *self-organization*. As might thus be expected, and as is provocatively suggested by the title, *Schools that Learn* offers numerous discussions of, for example, the joint contributions of parents, teachers, administrators, and students in healthy school systems. For the most part, these discussions are framed in terms of collective possibility rather than individual responsibility, and these emphases are contextualized in supporting anecdotes and explications of the contexts and purposes of schooling.

The book is structured around dozens of case studies that serve to illustrate the central theme that the educational whole can be greater than the sum of its parts. In fact, the book itself is structured to convey this message: The grander theme is intended to arise as the varied anecdotes and interpretations are allowed to "speak" to one another. In these regards, the text offers a potentially vibrant demonstration of self-organization. Conversely, however, it offers relatively little by way of formal explication of complexity thinking. In the context of this discussion of educational research, then, it might be more appropriate to describe the book as a survey of possible self-organizing phenomena that are of interest to educators, as opposed to a reporting of research per se. Further, with its reliance on systems theory, rather than the more general discourse of complexity thinking, the book is mainly concerned with the maintenance of social units and does not address the vital educational issue of the production of complex knowledge.

In fact, although the number of complexity-informed reports appears to be increasing exponentially within the educational research literature, very few of these writings have taken on the actual phenomenon of emergence, opting most often to examine already-emergent understandings, classrooms, schools, and other systems. There have been a few exceptions that will be discussed in more detail in chapters 6 and 7. By way of illustration here, Davis and Simmt[4] report on a few instances of self-organization, the first a teachers' collective that arose around the need to complete some challenging academic tasks, and the second a classroom collective that cohered around the development of a mathematical concept. In each case, they argue, the emergent collective generated insights that surpassed the insights of any individual member. In their discussion of these happenings, Davis and Simmt raise the provocative suggestion that the often-mentioned phenomenon of "the teachable moment" may in fact be a case of emergence on the classroom level—that is, a moment in which a unity of action and purpose arises. They further point out, however, that many of the features of the contemporary classroom, including a fragmented curriculum and radically individualized assessment practices, militate against instances of self-organization.

Once again, however, there are few descriptive studies of self-organized phenomena within the education literature. For the most part, in fact, educational research reports that draw on complexity thinking seem to be written from the realization that instances of self-organized learning systems are so complex and so pervasive within education that focused efforts at description or explication might not be practical or fruitful undertakings. By contrast, researchers in other fields have devoted considerable energies to such descriptions, notably business[5] and sociology.[6] Across these descriptions, a prominent theme is the range of triggers that might prompt the emergence of a social collectivity. To this end, in the case of human systems that it seems, there tends to be a need for a shared identification—an artifact, a belief, a consolidating event, or, most often, the appearance of a common enemy.[7]

Discussion Box 5.2 • Understanding Self-Organizing Collectives

The research group at Valleyview began clumsily and uncomfortably with self-introductions and admissions that the shared trait of group members was that every participant was, in a sense, 'orphaned.' Each had been part of supportive and cohesive work communities the previous year, and although the promise of similar support and cohesion was evident, feelings of connection to one another and to the surrounding community had not yet developed.

Oriented by the conviction that a sense of collectivity was an emergent phenomenon, Sumara and Davis suggested that the group engage in in-service-like sessions around recent developments in the learning and teaching of English language arts and mathematics. Recognizing the professional value of such exercises, if not the community value, members of the group readily agreed.

Based on a suggestion from a colleague who specializes in children's literature, Sumara proposed that the group begin by reading the novel *The Giver*, by Lois Lowry.[8] An interesting shift occurred at this point, as reflected by the transcripts of the research meetings. Whereas most of the articulations prior to the suggestion of a shared reading were "I" statements (i.e., comments about personal interests, backgrounds, responsibilities, expectations, professional anxieties, and so on), the bulk of the subsequent remarks were "we" statements that began to reflect senses of shared projects and shared purposes.

Notably, this shift was not noted in the context of the meetings. In fact, it was only noticed some years afterward when the researchers were rereading parts of the transcripts. Of course, this small happening is not sufficient evidence to claim that a collective had self-organized, but there is little doubt that it coincided with a palpable transition in group dynamics. Senses of collective purpose and activity had arisen, even though the divergent (and somewhat incompatible) reasons of individuals for participating had changed little, if at all.

For example, the researchers' explicit aim in this activity was to open a space to theorize with teachers about what it meant to engage with a piece of literature—that is, they were interested more in *reading* than in *teaching reading*. Nevertheless, the group "decided" that teaching was going to be a major topic of conversation. In particular, Lowry's treatments of such topics as eugenics, euthanasia, and burgeoning sexuality prompted considerable collective discussion and, notably, considerable group cohesion. As these topics were raised, members flagged them as "too controversial," "deals with sex," "too violent." In other words, the group was cohering around an imagined other—specifically the relative unknown of the community served by the school. The families of the community were the *not-us* to the emergent *us* of the reading group.

BOTTOM-UP

A surprising aspect of the phenomenon of self-organization is that it can happen without the assistance of a central organizer. Rather, as epitomized in swarms of bees and traffic jams, coherent unities can arise without the presence of a leader. The same seems to be true of many sorts of human collectivities in events that are sometimes described as "grassroots movements" or, more deprecatingly, "herd" or "mob mentalities."

In popular opinion, such events are often associated with a collapse of rationality and a collective stupidity. However, as Surowiecki[9] argues in his sweeping review of bottom-up social movements, they are most often manifestations of a sort of collective intelligence. Citing instances that range from everyday interactions to the international collaboration that isolated the SARS virus, Surowiecki describes how the *collective* can be smarter than the *collection*. Among the evidence-based assertions presented by Surowiecki, the following have particular relevance to educators and educational researchers:

- Nonpolarized groups can consistently make better decisions and come up with better answers than most of their members and ... often the group outperforms the best member.[10]
- You do not need a consensus in order ... to tap into the wisdom of a crowd, and the search for consensus encourages tepid, lowest-common-denominator solutions which offend no one rather than exciting everyone.[11]
- [The] rigidly hierarchical, multilayered corporation ... discourage[s] the free flow of information.[12]

- [D]ecisions about local problems should be made, as much as possible, by people close to the problem…. [P]eople with local knowledge are often best positioned to come up with a workable and efficient solution.[13]
- [The] evidence in favor of decentralization is overwhelming…. The more responsibility people have with their own environments, the more engaged they well be.[14]
- [I]ndividual irrationality can add up to collective rationality.[15]
- Paradoxically, the best way for a group to be smart is for each person to act as independently as possible.[16]

Some of these conclusions fly in the face of conventional wisdom about "mob mentality"—that is, the pervasive assumption that leaderless crowd will almost certainly override individual wisdom. In fact, the evidence indicates that collectives, most often, have potential for greater and more consistent intelligent action than individuals, whether someone presumes to lead or not. Indeed, mobs with charismatic leaders are the ones that tend to be less intelligent, as responsibilities for individual thought and critical analysis are deferred to the ones in charge.

There are many important caveats to this manner of assertion. For instance, the best collective decisions are most often matters of disagreement and contest, *not* consensus or compromise—a point that immediately renders problematic most current discussion on, for example, classroom collectivity. In particular, the broad and interdisciplinary research that Surowiecki cites could serve as a condemning critique of top-down classroom organizational structures such as "cooperative learning" and other popular collaborative-based and consensus-driven grouping strategies. By his analysis, the groupings that result from such structures are most likely to be decidedly unintelligent—that is, at best, capable of the insights of the brightest individual on her or his own and offering little possibility of surpassing that standard.

A key—and, a paradox—here is that intelligent group action is dependent on the independent actions of diverse individuals. This point is reflective of a core tenet of complexity thinking and a consistent finding across studies of complex unities: Intelligent collective action arises out of the bottom-up, independent (but co-specified) actions of individual agents who act out of self-interest and who may even be motivated by profound selfishness.

To make sense of this assertion, it is important to be clear on what is meant by "intelligence" and "intelligent action." Breaking from technocratic and psychologistic definitions developed through the 20th century, complexity thinkers define intelligence in terms of exploring a range of possible actions and selecting ones that are well-suited to the immediate situation. There are two important criteria here: first, a repertoire of possibilities and, second, a means to discern the relative effectiveness of those possibilities. In other words, in complexity terms, intelligence is not about a rational or comprehensive consideration of immediate circumstances, but a sort of "scouting" of possible responses. So understood, the intelligent unity is the one that generates a diversity of possibilities and that has a mechanism for critically debating the merits of those possibilities.

Given the nested character of complex systems, this conception means that intelligent action must occur simultaneously across several layers of organization. For instance, most dogs will instinctively leap back when encountering a snake or a snake-like object. Such an action is clearly an intelligent one, and has no doubt preserved the existence of many canines. However, it would be inappropriate to attribute the intelligence to the individual animal. Rather, this instance of smart response operates at the species-evolutionary level. The species selected the response, not the individual.

Phrased somewhat differently, and as suggested in previous chapters, what is normally called "evolution" is, in complexity thinking, an instance of cognition on a much grander scale and over a much longer time frame than is typically considered. In terms of educational concerns, this point is of tremendous significance, as it displaces the individual as the sole site of learning/thinking/intelligence/creativity and compels educators and educational researchers to think more broadly about the systems that unfold from and that are enfolded in individual learners.

Discussion Box 5.3 • Understanding Bottom-Up Collectives

One of the traits of the collaborative group was that there was no designated leader, where "leader" is understood in terms of an individual charged with responsibility of making decisions on what would be read or discussed, when it should happen, and so on. But these sorts of decisions were not really matters of consensus, either. What was read and how it was interpreted, rather, might best be described as "just happening."

Through the course of the joint activity, it became clear that what was being collected in this reading of fiction were the teachers' shared worries about their position in the community. They frequently announced their belief that they needed to be very careful with their curriculum selections. Therefore, even though each of them individually indicated a high regard for *The Giver*, reading it with their students was considered impossible. The identity of the community, based on limited interactions and narratives that had circulated for many years, was constructed to be radically conservative—and that imagined identity was used as a basis for judgments about materials selection and teaching strategies.

Informed by complexivist sensibilities, one of the researchers' intentions was to create inquiry structures that would blur boundaries between and among places of learning, especially those places of learning that are considered "school" and "not school." Sumara thus suggested that interested parents might be invited to read *The Giver* and to join the continuing discussion of the book. Spurred by curiosity, and in part by the desire to be proven correct, the group agreed. Copies of the novel were distributed to parents on the school's advisory board, who passed along other copies to some of their friends. As well, the staff invited other parents to take part through the school newsletter. A few weeks later, a discussion group convened consisting of most of the teachers, the researchers, and about a dozen parents. All had read *The Giver*.

This new situation, of course, was the source of tremendous worry and anxiety for all who attended. The primary concern, as was later revealed, turned out to be one of identity: Different factions represented in the assembly wondered about the others' intentions, interpretations, and motivations.

Suspecting that such might be the case, the researchers began by naming some of the worries that they brought to the meeting. In response, several of the parents tentatively pointed to some of their anxieties, most of which revolved around their beliefs about what it means to "do school." As one parent explained, "I don't have many positive memories of studying literature in high school—I mean, I was always afraid that my answers were wrong. I must admit that I'm not sure what's expected of me here or what our purposes are."

In response, the researchers explained their interest in joint reading, which seemed to be sufficient to allow most of the parents to relax. As the focus of discussion shifted to the actual reading of the book, a lively discussion began to unfold. Soon the boundaries separating such identity categories as "university researcher," "classroom teacher," and "parent" began to dissolve, allowing a community dedicated to collective sense-making to emerge. Significantly, what is well known about acts of reading became apparent to everyone in the group: No two readings or interpretations of a given text are alike. And, when the text is a literary one that asks readers to develop identificatory relations with characters and situations, the interpreted responses can say more about the reader than the reader can say about the text. Even though the meeting had begun as a collection of suspicious and worried strangers, the shared interpretive discussions quickly created an event that became deeply interesting to all present. Curiously, without revealing many personal details, members became known to one another in ways that are not typical of teacher/parent interactions. Fictive identities dissolved within the interpretive moment, replaced by identities that were surprising to many. As one parent commented, "I didn't really expect to enjoy this discussion. That hasn't been my experience in school before this."

Teachers in the group were also surprised—mostly at the parents' insistence by the end of the meeting that the *Giver* ought to be taught in some of the Grades 5 and 6 classes. This insistence was tellingly phrased in the language of collectivity: "*Our* kids should read this. *We* should teach it."

The group had thus come to a shared conclusion, one that had not really been suggested by anyone in particular, but seemed to fall out of the shared project of educating children. That is, there was no leader here, merely a form of decentralized control that arose in joint identifications—an emergent us-ness—that surprised everyone present.

SCALE-FREE NETWORKS

Part of what we are presenting here has been argued by anthropologists and sociologists for well over a century—namely that humans are collective creatures. Identities, preferences, abilities, and so on are utterly dependent on contexts that include one another. Complexity studies add more, however, as they offer insights into the dynamics at play that might enable or disable collective possibility. To this end, the branch of complexity research known as network theory, as introduced in chapters 3 and 4, offers some useful principles for recognizing complex structures and describing complex dynamics.

As noted in chapter 3, there are many ways of structuring networks—that is, a set of agents or nodes can be interlinked in a wide variety of ways. Three of the most common, as illustrated in figure 3.7, are centralized, decentralized, and distributed structures. The decentralized network, which consists of nodes noding into grander nodes, usually on several levels of organization, is the "fingerprint"[17] of a complex unity. A decentralized structure has the advantage of being more robust (e.g., in contrast to a more volatile centralized system, if a node of a decentralized systems were to fail, it is unlikely that the whole system will collapse), yet still have a relatively efficient means to distribute information among nodes (e.g., in general, far fewer links are needed to move between any pair of nodes than is the case in a distributed network). This combination of robustness and efficiency means that a decentralized network is a more viable structure for any system that relies on the efficient exchange of information—a category that includes all living and learning systems.

As Barabàsi develops, a decentralized network will decay into a more vulnerable (but informationally efficient) centralized network if stressed. Working from this suggestion, Fuite[18] has hypothesized that the tendency of educators to perceive of *time* as a scarce resource may be one of the main reasons that the most common organizational strategy in the contemporary classroom is the centralized network, with the teacher at the hub and the individual students at the ends of the spokes. Formal, decontextualized examinations may act in a similar manner. As he develops, pressures to cover a broad curriculum in a limited time, imposed evaluations, and other reductions on classroom autonomy prompt many teachers and administrators to believe that their only choice is direct, centralized instruction in which all information is made to pass through the central hub. Of course, this sort of organizational structure militates against an intelligent collective, as it prevents agents from pursuing their own self-interests and obsessions, which in turn prevents the representation and juxtaposition of diverse interpretations and actions.

Whereas the centralized network might be taken as descriptive of the traditional teacher-centered classroom, the distributed network might be applied to some currently popular student-centered approaches. Following Barabàsi, Fuite further suggests that a less efficient (but more structurally robust) distributed network will arise when resources are abundant and stresses relieved. The problem with this architecture when applied to such a group of agents is that it makes it difficult for them to act jointly and cohesively, owing to the diminished need to rely on one another. Individuals might affect or be affected by their nearest neighbors, but for the most part are isolated from the grander collective. By contrast, in the decentralized network, agents have opportunities to specialize and for mutual affect. In brief, and to repeat, the decentralized network is the architecture necessary for an intelligent system.

The implications of this particular aspect of descriptive complexity extend well beyond the organization of the classroom. A few relevant issues are discussed in chapter 6, including educational administrative structures, interpretation of knowledge domains, and applications of cognitive science to schooling.

Discussion Box 5.4 • Understanding Scale-Free Collectives

What was the structure of the reading group? What sort of images would be useful to map out the relationships among members?

At first it is tempting to say that the answer depends on the immediate focus. If, for example, one were to look at established interpersonal relationships, the mapping would likely be different from a representation of, say, a mapping in which the nodes were group members and the links were children in the school (whereby, for example, a parent would be closely lined to a given teacher if her or his child were in that teacher's classroom). On closer examination, however, while it is true that different foci still give different mappings, it is not entirely clear that the structures of those mappings will differ greatly.

Indeed, it appears that most such representations would follow a scale-free, decentralized structure. For instance, consider established personal relationships. The obvious immediate clusters, as revealed in our manner of describing the systems, are the parents, the teachers, and the researchers. But these clusters were hardly uniform (i.e., distributed), nor were they centralized. Rather, they too could be subdivided into clusters. At the same time, there were a number of between-cluster links among participants.

Evidence for the claim that the reading collective was decentralized could be found in the highly efficient lines of communication of the group. This quality was demonstrated when the researchers were compelled to change the meeting time once. They contacted a teacher, who communicated with a single colleague and a single parent, and so on. Within a very small number of steps, everyone had been informed, even though no formal structures had been established for such communications.

Unfortunately, the project has long since ended, so it would be difficult if not impossible to provide formal mappings of this or another set of relationships. (As researchers, we came upon the idea of decentralized networks too late to make use of it in this context.) Nevertheless, the qualities of a robust grouping and an efficient trans-system communication structure are evidence of the distributed structure of the collective.

NESTED ORGANIZATION

An immediate implication of a decentralized architecture, as described above, is that distinct levels of organization can emerge. In other words, and for example, the nodes-clustering-into-nodes structure of figure 3.5 can be interpreted as a representation of a single system, or as many systems that collect into hubs that comprise a grander system.

Complex unities can be (and usually are) simultaneously autonomous unities, collectives of autonomous unities, and subsystems within grander unities. They are nested. A diagram that we have found useful to foreground this feature, with regard to the immediate concerns of educators, is presented in figure 5.1. Developed by Davis and Simmt,[19] each region in this image is intended to flag a coherent, complex phenomenon—in this case, as specifically related to school mathematics. It could be readily adapted for any disciplinary area, however.

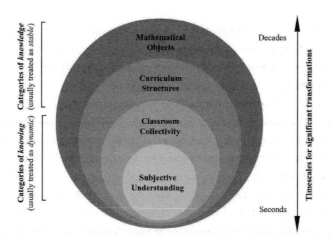

FIGURE 5.1 SOME OF THE NESTED LEVELS OF SCHOOL MATHEMATICS
In addition to collective knowledge and individual understanding, educators might also consider classroom collectivity and curriculum structures in terms of complex phenomena.

As developed at the end of chapter 4, the purpose of this particular diagram is to support the argument that there are levels of complex organization *between* the complex unity of collective knowledge (i.e., in this case, mathematical objects) and individual sense-making (i.e., subjective understandings)—two phenomena that are already generally understood in terms of ever-evolving dynamics, albeit on radically different time scales. Davis and Simmt assert that there are at least two layers of complex organization situated between objective knowledge and subjective understandings, which they identify as an ever-evolving curriculum and the classroom unity.

Davis and Simmt suggest that the phenomena in the outer layers of the diagram—that is established disciplinary knowledge and curricula based on that knowledge—tend to serve as the uninterrogated backdrop of educational research. For the most part, these are seen as relatively fixed and pre-given. By contrast, the phenomena in the inner regions—that is, personal and group understandings—are typically regarded as volatile and relatively easily affected. Hence, teaching comes to be framed in terms of coaxing mutable personal understandings to fit with that standards of established facts, thereby effectively ignoring the nested levels of complex activity that might lie between subjective knowing and objective knowledge.

Complexity thinking occasions a different manner of interpretation. It prompts attentions to, for example, the role of classroom knowledge. What sorts of local conventions, interests, and so on contribute to the shapes (and are shaped by) individual understandings? How are these framed by those aspects of the grander cultural opus of mathematics that is incorporated and organized into curriculum? Conversely, how is the discipline of mathematics shaped by the efforts of individuals to understand, the efforts of teachers to convey, and the efforts of governing bodies to specify the subject matter? Significantly, the point is *not* that all levels must be taken into consideration for each and every event of teaching or educational research. Rather, the issue is that any attempt to understand an educational phenomenon must be understood as *partial*—in the dual sense of incomplete and biased.

More is said on this issue in chapter 6, in specific relation to theories and discourses that have arisen to make sense of different levels of educational organization. In the meantime, we will underscore that the sensibility at work here represents a dramatic departure from analytic studies and their implicit Euclidean geometries. Rather, this is one site where the thinking is explicitly informed by fractal geometry's notion of *self-similarity*, as discussed in chapter 3.

To recap, the fractal geometric concept of self-similarity is an extension of the Euclidean concept of *similarity*. Two figures are similar if, by enlargement or reduction, one can be made to fit exactly on top of the other. For example, all circles are similar to one another, as are all equilateral triangles. The twist added by fractal geometry is that some figures are actually similar to themselves. That is, for a special collection of forms, parts resemble the wholes. Enlarging a well-chosen piece will generate an image that closely matches the original figure—and this is a quality that is manifest in many natural forms, including fern fronds, cauliflower, parsley, clouds, riverbeds, trees, water ripples, and coastlines.

As noted in chapter 3, the property of self-similarity has been used to illustrate that complexity is not necessarily a function of scale. Whether one moves in on or pulls back from such forms, the same level of detail seems to present itself. It also serves as a useful device to flag the nested quality of complex forms. In brief, applying the notion of self-similarity to the dynamics of complex unities, the sorts of nested phenomena identified in figure 5.1 are suggested to operate and unfold in similar ways. Phenomena such as personal cognition, collective action, educational structures, and cultural knowledge are dynamically similar. *All* are learning systems, where learning is understood as a process through which a unity becomes capable of more flexible, more creative activity that enables the unity to maintain its fit to its ever evolving context.

Discussion Box 5.5 • Understanding Nested Collectives

Prompted by the parents' insistence that their children have an opportunity to read *The Giver* in school, it was agreed that Sumara would co-teach a unit with Dolores van der Wey in her Grade 5/6 split class.[20]

Sufficient research funds had been secured to purchase a personal copy of the novel for each student, and they were urged to keep track of their questions and responses to the text as they read. Some opted to write directly on the book's pages, others used Post-it notes, and a few made use of separate response journals. This in-text marking was prompted by theoretical work about literary engagement, in which it has been argued that in order for meaning to be created, the reader must fill in the "gaps" that always exist in a text.[21] It is within this dialogic relation with the text that the reader makes meaning and, at the same time, that the identity of the reader is created through the act of reading. Asking readers to mark their texts while reading provides evidence to the reader of this ever-evolving dialogic relationship.

Because Sumara and van der Wey felt that the novel was somewhat complex and difficult for some readers in the class—and because they wanted to actively participate with readers as they moved through unfamiliar in-text marking practices—they took turns reading the novel aloud in class over the period of one week. Following each chapter, the students were invited to talk about what they had noticed. For example, after reading chapter 1, the children were asked to identify phrases or sentences that had caught their attention. This query sponsored an interesting discussion of the associations and interpretations that readers were making with the text and, as well, provided evidence of how readers never really read the same text. What one reader found significant, others often did not even notice.

However, in the exercise of "pointing" to what had been noticed, a collective site of interpersonal/intertextual recognition and identification was emerging. The usually private act of reading was becoming more publicly constituted. As well, working from the premise that identity emerges from relational identifications, these acts of pointing and discussing broadened the horizons of identification practices for all readers.

Indeed, the conditions for creating knowledge from the reader/text relations were enlarged and complexified as idiosyncratic readings became part of the collective reading. For example, in the middle of the first oral reading, one student theorized aloud that the community in the story must be enclosed in a large plastic dome that prevented travel, limited interactions with other communities, and maintained a constant climate. While this idea is not in any way presented in the novel, its inclusion in the collective space of shared reading rendered it part of the collective understanding of the text. Throughout the subsequent weeks devoted to reading and interpretation activities around *The Giver*, many references were made to the domes. It became part of their commonsense—so much a part that students collectively rejected the suggestion that domes were not part of the story.

Near the completion of the unit of study, Sumara asked the students if they felt that books could change: Was *The Giver* different for having been read? The consensus of class members was that, yes, novels are not static objects. Rather, what a novel *is* only makes sense in the context of bringing it to life through reading and discussion—that is, by weaving it into an ever-evolving fabric of relationships. In other words, prompted by in-text marking practices and discussions of the shifting meanings of the stories they read, these readers came to regard literature not as a fixed backdrop of their in-school activities, but as part of a shifting cultural landscape of which schooling was part.

Correspondingly, for these students, the curriculum around *The Giver* was not a set of mandated facts or skills to be mastered, but an occasion for engagement. It, too, was a shifting, negotiated form. Similar dynamics were clearly at work on the classroom level, with the establishment of collective truths (the example of the domes is one of many that arose) that were valid insofar as they were viable and useful. And, of course, the dynamics of this emergent commonsense was also similar to the dynamics of individual sense, records of which were included in every student's copy of the novel.

AMBIGUOUSLY BOUNDED, BUT ORGANIZATIONALLY CLOSED SYSTEMS

One of the problems with specifying a complex system—for both educational and educational research purposes—is that its boundaries tend to shift. There are many reasons for this fluidity, three of which are of particular relevance here: First, complex systems are "open"; that is, there are constantly exchanging matter and/or information with their contexts. Second, and as noted in the previous section, complex systems usually arise from and are part of other complex systems, even while being coherent and discernible unities. Hence it is not always clear which level(s) should be the focus of one's immediate attentions. Third, and perhaps most confounding, distinguishable but intimately intertwined networks can and do exist in the same "spaces." We discuss these three issues in sequence.

The first point—that complex systems are constantly influencing and being influenced by their context, either through the exchange of matter, the exchange of information, or both—presents different sorts of problems in the study of different sorts of systems. By way of familiar and obvious example, in a situation where a collective is working on a project, it is rarely a simple matter to discern who has contributed what, especially if the final product is at all sophisticated. (It is for this reason that it is not uncommon to encounter scientific publications with literally dozens of co-authors.) Key contributions might be attributable to particular persons, but it may be that those contributions only happened because they were triggered by others' suggestions or by parroting information developed by others elsewhere.

Consider this book, for instance. Two writers are identified, an editor is named, some associates are acknowledged, and a reference list is appended. Do these lists appropriately reflect the text's origins and the authorship of the ideas included herein?

Not at all. It would take a tome far longer than the current volume to even begin to trace out the readily discernible influences, let alone the more subtle conceptual contributions of so many people across so many generations. In the end it would seem that the principal reason that the list of authors is so brief is because we humans seem unable to cope with the grander web of associations and influence that underlie even the most mundane accomplishments.

Indeed, for the most part when a complex system is studied, the researcher is compelled to ignore the origins and eventual destinations of the matter and energy that flow through it, delegating such vital issues to the "context" or the "situation." As is developed in more detail in the next chapter, this tendency has contributed to some significant tensions in the educational research literature, particularly around issues of learning (and especially around the theories of learning that are deemed appropriate for the study of formal education). To reemphasize, the crux of the issue here has to do with the ambiguous boundaries of the system under investigation.

Once again, the relevance and implications of a system-and-context's exchange of matter and/or energy varies according to the system studied. The relative stability of physical unities, such as a biological body or an ecosystem, prompts attentions toward the manner in which they constantly regenerate themselves—that is, how they maintain their patterns in the stream of matter. In a knowledge system, such as mathematics or any other discipline, attentions might be focused on the individuals who "pass through" the system—that is, on the manner in which a discipline or discourse maintains its pattern through the stream of personalities. Analogous statements could be made for any manner of complex system, from cell through biosphere. (Again, this issue resurfaces under the guise of "theories of learning" in the next chapter.)

Whereas the first issue related to efforts to discern the boundaries of complex unities has to do with inter-system exchanges, the second issue has to do with a haziness of definition as one endeavors to distinguish among different levels of organization within a given system. Where, for instance, does an agent stop and a collective begin? This question is sometimes easily answered. After all, the distinction between an ant and an anthill seems relatively straightforward. However, the situation becomes much more difficult as one attempts to investigate more complex systems. Consider, for example, a study of an individual's personality. Clearly, it is inappropriate to impose a boundary on that person's skin. Personal tastes, habits, and tools for interpretation are utterly dependent on the context(s) in which the person has been immersed, and so a strong argument can be made that the system that must be studied in this instance is not the individual, but the culture or society. (Of course, this point has been at the center of research in sociology and anthropology for centuries.)

This issue has emerged as an important one in the educational literature, especially over the past half-century. For millennia, it had been assumed that the individual's preferences and potentialities were *natural* or *innate*—two words that mean, etymologically, inborn. Education was merely a process through which those predetermined possibilities were realized (or frustrated). The actual situation appears to be considerably more complex. As individuals come to be enfolded into various collectives (e.g., families, peer groups, communities, subcultures), those collectives come to be manifest in, and thus to unfold from, individuals. At the same time, one cannot ignore one's biological constitution, since who one is clearly has much to do with one's physical being, especially as that physicality is manifest and interpreted in social settings. Attempts to make sense of these dynamic, co-specifying influences in terms of linear chains and direct causes rarely make sense. Even attempts to use statistical methods to "factor analyze" the relative effects of different influences is highly problematic, not in the least because of the incredible range of influences and the impossibility of effecting sensible measurements of even a small portion of them.

In some ways, this point has been recognized in education through prominent debates on the relative importance of *nature* and *nurture* on individuals' characters, actions, and abilities. "Nature" points to the subpersonal systems that cohere into the biological being; "nurture" nods toward the suprapersonal systems in which one's character comes to form. Unfortunately, as the popular debate tends to be articulated, it is generally assumed that biological structure is separable from cultural influence (usually through some manner of statistical manipulation[22]). The former tends to be cast as fixed and limiting, the latter as dynamic and freeing. Brains, for example, are popularly understood as some sort of pre-given, biologically-determined architecture, whereas the "contents" of brains (e.g., memories and preferences) are seen in terms of contextual influence.

In point of current fact, brains are highly plastic forms. The brain you have at this point in the chapter is different from the brain you had when you began to read it. And it makes no sense at all to attribute those changes to either nature or nurture, or even to attribute percentage influences to these two "factors." The situation is simply, and vastly, more complex—more a case of nested influences than parallel influences.

This issue points to a third difficulty associated with the ambiguous boundaries of complex unities. Not only can it be difficult to distinguish one system from another, or one level from another, systems can unfold within one another.

This point is not an easy one to make, and it is perhaps best introduced through a series of examples that are relevant to educators and educational researchers. Consider the relationship between one's neural system and one's system of understandings, both of which can be understood in terms of decentralized networks, but neither of which can be collapsed into the other. Analogously, consider a domain of knowledge, such as literary criticism, along with the people associated with that domain, the literary critics. Clearly, one cannot be reduced or equated to the other. *A knowledge-producing system and the system of knowledge produced are not the same thing.*

Returning to the image of nested systems presented in figure 5.1, then, it might be more accurately characterized as levels of "knowledge networks" that should not be conflated with the systems and communities that are associated with them. The reason for this point is straightforward: Although a curriculum is clearly situated in a parent discipline, it is clear that the system that produces a curriculum (e.g., a school board or a ministry of education) is not nested in the community of scholars that is most responsible for the maintenance and generation of that knowledge domain. In fact, these systems are often radically disconnected.

One of the reasons that this issue is of particular relevance to education arises from the conventional habit of defining, say, physics in terms of "what physicists study"—and, by correspondence, structuring physics classes after around the sorts of things that physicists are imagined to do in their laboratories. The circularity of the driving definitions are not only uninformative, in complexity terms they are profoundly misleading. In particular, they do a disservice to those interested in questions of education because they deflect attentions away from the particular structural complexities of a given domain—complexities that might inform if not enable efforts to teach if they were better understood. We briefly address this issue in chapter 7.

Discussion Box 5.6 •
Understanding Ambiguously Bounded Collectives

The parent/teacher/researcher group's experience of shared reading and thinking reveals the inadequacy of many of the commonsense beliefs about identity and cognition that continue to underpin much of school practice. Although, for example, researchers working from psycho- and sociolinguistic perspectives have convincingly demonstrated that all language-learning and language-using experiences are inescapably communal,[23] a wide-spread belief in the autonomy of the learner and the corresponding privilege assigned to the 'individual' serves to undermine the potential for these understandings within the context of the public school. And so, although greater numbers of elementary school teachers are subscribing to models of learning that encourage students to develop their thinking within highly social and collaborative environments, the competing desire for children to demonstrate individual mastery persists. Although much of this dissonance might be attributed to the external demands upon school, it seems that a good deal is internal, hinged to entrenched beliefs about identity and cognition.

In spite of dramatic developments in understandings of such matters, these phenomena continue to be conceived in rigidly dichotomous rather than ambiguously bounded terms: Learning, for instance, tends to be seen as an *internalizing* of an *external* world. The emergence of personal identity is popularly thought of as a process of unfolding that occurs apart from the emergence of collective identity. Althrough theorists and researchers from virtually every domain of inquiry[24] have demonstrated one's identity is a dynamic and complex mix of the biological and the experiential, an assumption of individualized and essentialized selves continues to infuse schooling practices. The personal response journal, for example, often functions as a place to record the idiosyncratic experiences and interpretations of particular readers rather than as a location to examine the complex ways in which reading is *always* an act of collective cognition emerging from readers' past, current, and anticipated social relations.

This insight was made evident in the collective readings and rereadings of *The Giver* within the teacher and the teacher/parent reading groups. There it became clear that individual responses to passages were entangled in readers' conversations with one another, with their previous experiences in different settings, and with their students or children. Collected within the responses, then, were not only the markers of reading, but the traces of co-evolving identities and representations of complex, co-emergent patterns of thinking and responding.

Recognizing these emergent patterns meant that the shared reading of *The Giver* became an opportunity for adults and children to become curious about the making of identity and the complex ways in which language and cultural practices contributed to the ongoing, nested, and self-similar evolutions of individual and collective identities. Most importantly, reading the novel helped readers to understand the relationship among the phenomena of learning to perceive, learning to think, and learning to inhabit a particular social identity. Through the shared reading, participants came to wonder whether society was, in fact, more like than unlike the tightly regulated one described in the novel. At the same time, teachers, by interacting with parents in this shared reading location, began to dissolve the well-developed fictionalized identities of "these parents" and "this community." Correspondingly, parents began to express similar re-perceptions and reinterpretations of what they understood as teacher identity and the experience of schooling.

STRUCTURE DETERMINISM

It is one thing to try to make sense of where a complex unity begins and ends. But even if that issue could somehow be unambiguously settled, another at-least-as-difficult issue is the fact that it is the system—and not the system's context—that determines how it will respond to emergent conditions.

Such structure-determined behavior is one of the key characteristics used to distinguish a complex unity from a complicated (mechanical) system. The manner in which a complicated system will respond to a perturbation is generally fairly easy to figure out, simply because its responses are determined by the perturbation. If a block of wood is nudged, for instance, a knowledge of the conditions of the nudge—its force, the shape and mass of the object, friction between surfaces, and so on—is sufficient to both predict and explain the result. The same is true for more complicated systems, such as motors and computers. The perturbation determines the response. But such is not the case for complex systems. If, for example, you nudge a dog, the result will have virtually nothing to do with Newtonian mechanics. Rather, the response will be determined by the dog—or, more descriptively, by the dog's biologically-and-experientially constituted structure. Even more confounding, if a human, who has an even broader repertoire of possible responses, is nudged, the results are even less possible to predict.

What is more, not even experience with nudging will provide an adequate knowledge of what will happen if it is repeated—for two reasons. First, a complex system learns, that is it is constantly altering its own structure in response to emergent experiences. Hence, its response to a virtually identical stimulus may change dramatically in a very brief span of time. Second, systems that are virtually identical will respond differently to the same perturbation. Hence, one cannot generalize the results from one system to another. (This inclination to learn is one of the major, albeit generally unacknowledged, problems with quasi-experimental, statistics-based research in education.)

In brief, the notion of structure determinism stands as a critique of virtually all educational research that is based on a linear cause–effect mentality. In particular, it problematizes the contemporary desire for "best practices" in education—a notion that is anchored in the assumption that what works well in one context should work well in most contexts. That only makes sense when talking about mechanical systems.

Clearly, such assertions render the project of schooling a difficult if not impossible one, at least insofar as formal education is understood in terms of compelling learners to learn what they have been mandated to learn. Complexivists seek to interrupt the implicit causal sensibilities of such attitudes by foregrounding notions of "structural dance," "co-dependent arising," "co-emergence," "establishing a consensual domain," and "mutual specification," all of which are intended to prompt attentions toward the manners in which structurally determined complex unities affect one another.

With regard to pedagogy, for example, a prominent conclusion is that the act of teaching must be understood in terms of a sort of emergent choreography in which the teacher's and students' actions are able to specify one another. Of course, this point is not news to educators. A popular joke among teachers is the inherent foolishness of the claim, "I taught it, they just didn't learn it," often used as a self-mocking reference to less-than-effective classroom events. The point being made is that the teacher's and learners' actions and interpretations were somehow disconnected in that moment and that a different strategy is needed.

In other words, it has been our experience that most experienced teachers have a deep appreciation for the structure-determined nature of their students and their classes. What they have lacked are schooling contexts and curricula that enable them to act responsibly to these embodied understandings.

Discussion Box 5.7 •
Understanding Structurally Determined Collectives

We (Sumara and Davis) have presented reports on our research around the reading of *The Giver* in a number of venues over the past decade. For the most part, fellow researchers and educators who listen to or read about this work seem to have ready appreciations of the event-specific, unrepeatable character of the project. On occasion, however, we will receive a request for more detailed methodological details from researchers who wish to replicate the study.

The desire for (and the belief in the possibility of) replication is deeply inscribed in modern research sensibilities. Unfortunately, however, a truly emergent study—one that comes to reach across different layers of a school community, that is allowed to unfold over months in response to the particular interests and concerns of participants, and that is constantly attentive to the evolving context of its actions—clearly cannot be duplicated.

Inevitably, the responses that are given to replication-oriented requests for further information, then, are frustrating for both questioner and respondent. What can be replicated, at least in a sense, is the research attitude of mindful participation with a community around matters of shared concern, being careful to allow sufficient interpretive space for all members of the research group to act on their particular interests and obsessions. After that point, this sort of action research[25] comes to be very much like deeply engaged pedagogy: It is an ongoing negotiation of possibilities, selecting among the options that present themselves as one moves through the experience.

Such an attitude does not entail an abandonment of one's research interests. The project around *The Giver*, as announced earlier, was explicitly about literary engagement, and for the researchers, that interest was central throughout the event. However, for others, the shared work was undertaken for entirely different purposes. The principal, for example, came to see it mainly as a means to establish better community relations; many of the parents saw it as an opportunity to become more integrally involved in their children's educations, and most of the teachers came to regard it as a study in pedagogy. The project that arose around the study was a complex product of this mix of motivations. In other words, the research event was determined by the structure of the community in which it was undertaken. Replication is thus an impossibility, and the misguided desire to verify through repetition is anchored in a sensibility that is more aligned with Newtonian mechanics that Darwinian dynamics.

FAR-FROM-EQUILIBRIUM

One of the most deeply entrenched assumptions of analytic science is that dynamic systems tend toward equilibrium, toward a steady state. More specifically, the assumption has been that systems in motion must be governed by *negative* feedback mechanisms, by which extreme variations in activity are somehow pushed toward and held in acceptable ranges. The popular illustration of negative feedback is a thermostat. It the temperature of a room falls, the thermostat triggers a furnace that runs until the thermostat triggers it to stop. Negative feedback, then, is a means of maintaining an internal equilibrium, even when external conditions might be volatile and uncontrollable.

The opposite of negative feedback—predictably known as positive feedback—can be profoundly troublesome to a system that seeks equilibrium. Positive feedback serves to amplify (or to extinguish) some dynamic aspect of a system. The manner in which fads and epidemics arise and move through social systems are familiar examples of positive feedback mechanisms at work. Other examples in the human realm include the rush of investment toward (and subsequent bursting) of the dot.com bubble in the late-1990s, sudden riots, outbreaks of war, or (on the more hopeful side of things) peaceful social movements toward more democratic governments as unfolded, for example, in the Ukraine in late-2004 and in Lebanon in early-2005. Positive feedback within social systems is sometimes referred to as the "tell two friends phenomenon," whereby the number of people aware of a situation will increase at an exponential rate.

The popular but uninterrogated assumption that dynamic systems tend toward equilibrium could be concisely restated as: Negative feedback is good, positive feedback is bad. As it turns out, however, mechanisms to amplify small perturbations are essential to the viability of living and learning systems. A system governed by only negative feedback—that is, by mechanisms that drive it toward a steady state equilibrium—is by definition not complex and certainly not alive. This is not to say that negative feedback mechanisms are not important to complex unities. On the contrary, if one looks at human social systems, one could readily identify a number of mechanisms that are in place to prevent personal obsessions and desires to spin out of control. However, at the same time, complex unities must incorporate positive feedback mechanisms that will permit certain perturbations to be amplified so that seemingly small events can come to matter greatly. For instance, the brain is "equipped" with a variety of means— some instinctual, some learned, some hybrids—that can trigger and magnify responses that are much out of proportion to the initial perturbation. Compare the responses of most people to the very similar sensations of a drop of water rolling down an arm to a spider crawling down an arm. The first is likely to be the source of mild interest, if noticed at all; the second can trigger a panicked reaction.

Such extreme responses appear to be vital not only for a system's immediate survival, but for its self-modification—that is, its learning. For example, in the case of individual humans, psychologist Merlin Donald[26] suggests that positive feedback mechanisms in the brain trigger moments of conscious awareness, which he argues are essential to formal learning. To this end, some educators[27] have explored means by which teachers might prompt learners' attentions to specific aspects of a classroom experience—that is, in effect, they have examined how one might go about triggering positive feedback mechanisms in learners' brains.

Considered on the level of social collectivity, positive feedback is commonly associated with "mob mentalities," fads, and other out-of-control responses, whereas negative feedback mechanisms include social mores, legal systems, and other means to regulate behavior. The experienced teacher, of course, is intimately familiar with striking the balance between classroom and lesson structures that are too rigid to allow for innovative responses and structures that are too loose to enable coherent activity. Unfortunately, in the contemporary rhetoric, such structures are most often described in terms of "behavior management," reflecting deeply seated behaviorist (i.e., mechanistic and individualistic) assumptions about human cognition. The balance between positive and negative feedback structures in a living system is necessarily too dynamic to be described in terms of rigid regimes prescribed by behaviorist-oriented programs—which, tellingly, are oriented more toward *classroom control* than to, say, working to sustain the vibrancy of a collective body.

While on the topic of behaviorism, the realization of the presence of positive feedback mechanisms in educational systems should, we believe, prompt a certain mindfulness among educational researchers. The past century is rife with examples of researchers who have introduced notions from other disciplines to inform educational research, but who seem to have paid little attention to the consequences of their efforts to import such ideas. The borrowing of behaviorism from psychology in the 1950s—a move that continues to have troublesome echoes in lesson preparation, regimes of testing, obsessions with classroom control, and so on—was simply unchecked by its champions. Similarly, the more recent embrace of constructivism may be having comparable, although very different, effects.[28] Both of these instances might be characterized as moments in which positive feedback mechanisms (e.g., desires for professional prominence) prompted the system to run unchecked, in the absence of effective negative feedback mechanisms (e.g., evidence of the practical limitations of the theories.)

Discussion Box 5.8 • Understanding Disequilibrated Collectives

During the month in which Sumara and van der Wey co-taught her Grades 5/6 class, the commonplace sponsored by the parent/teacher/school staff readings of *The Giver* continued to grow. Parents who had read the novel passed it on to other parents. Teachers and school staff members (including secretaries, custodians, teacher assistants, and student teachers) read the novel. During the time spent in the staff room, it was not unusual for the researchers to become engaged with a teacher, a parent-volunteer at the school, a student teacher, or a staff member about some aspect of the novel.

Language and concepts specific to *The Giver* began to be used—even when there was no explicit discussion of the book. The researchers encountered, for example, mentions of "the stirrings" (used by Lowry to refer to burgeoning sexuality) in reference to sexual desire, and of "samenesses" (used in the book to point to socially sanctioned traits) in discussing ongoing problems with racial discrimination in the school. As more and more persons came to identify with characters and events presented in the novel, points of identification among readers within the school/community setting became more frequent. Further, because a significant (and constantly growing) proportion of parents had read and were discussing a novel that continued to be the centerpiece of an elaborated, integrated language arts unit, contacts and identifications among adults and children occurred outside the formalized curriculum.

In fact, as was learned later, the effects of the novel spilled beyond the community. Teachers from other schools who were familiar with some of this school's staff began to teach *The Giver*, parent/teacher discussion groups began to spring up across the school district, and community members reported that friends and relatives in other locations had begun to read and discuss the book, prompted by their enthusiastic reportings.

SHORT-RANGE RELATIONSHIPS

The importance of positive feedback mechanisms in learning/research systems is commonly overlooked in current discussions of educational research, where the emphasis is often on careful, top-down organization rather than nurturing healthy local interactions. In complexity terms, the latter is vastly more important, as most of the information within a complex system is exchanged among near neighbors rather than being distributed from a central hub.

It is around this issue that many people find it difficult to appreciate how complex co-activity can arise. How can global behaviors emerge from local interactions? Part of the response has to do with an underlying "win-win logic" of complex unities. In contrast to a zero-sum logic, in which it is assumed that one agent's gain entails another agent's loss, a win-win logic suggests that one agent's situation will likely improve if the situations of his/her/its nearest neighbors improve. A "we" is usually better than an "I" for all involved.

This truth is, of course, abundantly evident in the irrepressible negotiations of status and social relationships within the classroom, a phenomenon that is undeniably complex. However, it is less obvious—and perhaps even rare—around the generation of knowledge and understandings of the subject matters at hand. In brief, for the complex classroom, the teacher must find ways to foster the local exchange of information, which of course entails foregoing a centralized control of that information.

This point moves our discussion toward the pragmatics of pedagogy, and so we will defer its elaboration to chapter 7 where we focus more specifically on the conditions that must be in place for complex emergence. It is mentioned here simply because of its utility for efforts to determine if a phenomenon or form is or is not complex. If agents are able to affect and be affected by their nearest neighbors—as is the case for neurons, ants, species in ecosystems, and so on— then the grander unity has complex, transcendent possibilities. If, however, information is controlled through a central hub—that is, if the architecture of the system is Euclidean—then emergent possibility is unlikely. Such a system is likely a mechanical one (or based on an assumption of mechanics) that is oriented to a replication of existing possibility, rather than an expansion of the space of the possible.

Discussion Box 5.9 •
Understanding Short-Range Relations in Collectives

In one of the closing focus group interviews with the children who were in the class that read *The Giver*, the researchers learned that, in Rebecca's family, both her mother and her older brother had read the novel and that they had "built up conversations" around the book so that they could, according to Rebecca, "learn more about each other." Parents who had been involved in the initial reading of the novel reported in later meetings how much they had valued being able to have conversations with their children about the book and about difficult issues emerging from it. One parent, Helen, suggested that these conversations were unusual in that they dealt with "ideas" rather than the usual daily routines. And as Margaret, another parent, added, these conversations reminded her that her children were complexly intelligent, had views other than hers that they were able to articulate and justify, and were capable of original and interesting thinking. For both parents and children, then, the discussions that sprang up around their shared readings provided evidence of strong thought that helped to scaffold relationships developed around intellectual work.

SEGUE

In this chapter, our emphasis was on the elaboration of some of the principles that have been developed by complexivists who have focused on the identification and description of complex unities. In chapter 6, we turn more specifically to the educational research literature, endeavoring to highlight how many of the same sensibilities have been articulated within education.

CHAPTER SIX

Descriptive Complexity Research:
LEVEL-JUMPING

WE ARE OBSERVING THE BIRTH OF A SCIENCE ...
THAT VIEWS US AND OUR CREATIVITY AS PART OF A FUNDAMENTAL
TREND PRESENT AT ALL LEVELS OF NATURE.

—Ilya Prigogine[1]

We might have subtitled this chapter something like "The Contributions of Educational Research to Complexity Science." Our main purpose here is to review both general trends and a handful of illustrative examples to demonstrate that much of recent educational research is not only compatible with complexity thinking, but elaborates some prominent themes—even if there have been relatively few explicit connections drawn between the two literatures. As such, it can be argued that educational research has made legitimate and significant contributions to complexity thinking.

We also comment on the fact that different aspects of this research are often presented as being "in tension" with one another. We argue that contemporary this-or-that debates have tended to arise from too-narrow an embrace of specific discourses, and further suggest that complexity thinking often provides a means to find the deep complementarities of varied theoretical frames without reducing seemingly oppositional stances to one another or minimizing their particular contributions to educational thought. We use the term *level-jumping* to refer to the device that we use to illustrate this point. In brief, level-jumping refers to the possibility—and, we argue, the necessity—of moving across levels of complex organization to address prominent questions in education.

As such, and consistent with our orienting definition of complex systems—that is, as learning phenomena—this chapter is organized around discussions of different dynamic and adaptive systems within the education literature. Similar to the previous chapter, general themes are addressed in the main text, while illustrative examples are provided in the discussion boxes. By way of disclaimer, we make no attempt to be comprehensive or representative in this review of published studies. The intention here is to provide an introductory impression of the sorts of issues around which complexity thinking might be invoked, not to take on the impossible task of mapping out a rapidly evolving territory.

Finally, the topics of discussion are organized according to the nested image presented in chapter 2 (fig. 2.3), beginning with subpersonal systems and moving though to supracultural systems.

DISCUSSIONS OF NEUROLOGY, BIOLOGY, AND GENETICS WITHIN EDUCATIONAL RESEARCH

With advances in technology that, for example, have enabled researchers to watch the brain's activity in real time and to create electronic simulations of neural nets, it is reasonable to suggest that the cognitive neurosciences have reached the place where they can contribute important and practical insights to discussions of education. However, consistent with complexity thinking, emergent conclusions cannot be understood in simple cause–effect terms. Rather, one's internal, biology-based dynamics must be understood to affect and to be affected by one's physical experiences, which in turn unfold in social and cultural circumstances, which in turn shape and are shaped by intercultural and biospheric circumstances. In other words, although it is necessary to bracket out most phenomena in order to point to some recent developments in understandings of subpersonal phenomena, the intention is in no way to suggest that conclusions out of genetics research, developmental psychology, or cognitive neuroscience provide an adequate basis on which to organize educational practice. They simply do not. And cannot.

The desire to extrapolate beliefs about the worlds of the brain and other bodily organs to the macro-realm of educational action is not a new one. In fact, it is deeply inscribed in commonsense vocabularies that are currently used to talk about learning and teaching. For example, an entrenched cultural habit has been to describe brain structures in terms of the most recent technologies. Thus, over the past few centuries alone, Western cultures have moved through such metaphors as brain-as-writing-tablet, brain as steam-engine, brain-as-telephone-switchboard, brain-as-computer, and, most recently, brain-as-internet. Even more confounding, it has not been the case that one metaphor eclipses another. Rather, old notions have tended to linger as new ones have been added—and so it is not unusual to encounter almost-simultaneous references to recording memories (learning as writing), internal pressures (mind as steam engine), making internal connections (brain as switchboard), inputting, processing, and outputting information (brain as computer), and thought viruses (brain as internet).

The problem with these notions is not their metaphoric character, per se—after all, most of human thought is analogical. Rather, the issue is the tendency to mistake these figurative devices as literal truths. Consider the pervasive assumption that the brain is a computer. This notion is actually profoundly misleading, but it has inspired an entire school of thought in psychology known as *cognitivism*—which has proven both popularly compelling and pedagogically lacking.[2]

Part of the problem to date has been that researchers have lacked the resources and the means to study the "black boxes" of genetic structures and the brain. As mentioned, however, that situation has changed dramatically, particularly in the past 10 years. And, overwhelmingly, the conclusions are consistent with, if not explicitly informed by, complexity science.

A major conclusion of this research is that learning is not about taking things in or soaking things up. Rejecting commonsensical acquisition-, container-, and machine-based metaphors, most current research is oriented by the principle that learning entails physical transformations of the brain. Learning is thus a biological phenomenon, and one that might be explored to enrich the discussions of teaching, schooling policy, and educational philosophy. That said, if one were to rely too heavily on the conceptual contributions of the cognitive neurosciences, one would likely focus one's attentions too narrowly on issues of *how* learning happens (and, hence, be tempted to extrapolate immediately to prescriptions for teaching), potentially eclipsing vital considerations of *what* and *why* one is teaching. We proceed here with this caution in mind.

Perhaps the most educationally significant developments from the cognitive neurosciences are the emergent understandings of the brain as nested and distributed (see chap. 3), and personal understanding as radically contextualized and analogically/associatively structured. In other words, such phenomena as thought, memory, and consciousness cannot be said to occur in a specific site or at a particular level of neurological or social organization. Rather, activity at all levels of organization can be properly described as *cognitive*, as agents (i.e., neurons, minicolumns, macrocolumns, and so on, depending on the level of analysis) affect and are affected by their neighbors' activities.

Significantly, such effects contribute to ongoing physical transformations of the brain, again across all levels of organization, meaning that personal experiences are embodied across all levels of the brain's organization. Phrased differently, the entire cortex is a memory system. This emergent understanding of the human brain, although gaining popular acceptance, still stands in stark contrast to the pervasive belief that the brain is a relatively static form that contains knowledge and that houses identity.[3]

An upshot of the realization that the brain is more than an amalgamation of a 100 billion neurons and trillions of connections[4] is that the popular habit of speculating on the purposes of specific brain areas is somewhat troublesome. As it turns out, when an individual is presented with a novel problem, activity registers throughout the entire brain. As that problem becomes better understood, specific brain regions do indeed "take responsibility" for parts of the task, but these regions are not the same across all learners, and not even necessarily constant within an individual. In other words, discussions of brain modules (and related educational theories, such as those associated with learning modalities and multiple intelligences) do indeed contain a grain of truth, but for the most part are premised on a much-too-rigid and prescriptive conception of a very plastic brain and its constantly changing structure.

The third vital contribution of recent neuroscience to education is the suggestion that the brain is radically contextualized—that is, in terms of the etymology of *radical*, the brain is *rooted* in the context of a biological-and-experiential body. In direct terms, there are at least two different categories of human biology-based memory: those that were learned by the species in evolutionary time (and that are *remembered* in the human genome) and those that are learned by the individual over a lifetime.

There is a further significance to the suggestion that the brain is radically contextualized, one that arrives more from the field of artificial intelligence (AI) than the cognitive neurosciences (although the distinction between these two domains grows ever more blurred). In the 1950s, during the early and wildly overoptimistic days of AI studies, researchers confidently predicted that electronic brains would soon surpass their flesh-based analogs. Such forecasts were based on the tremendous successes of early computers in performing computations that their designers and programmers found conceptually demanding—including mind-numbing calculations and other repetitive processes. Encouraged by such rapid technological achievements, researchers confidently anticipated computers that would blend into human society, able to do anything a human could do, only more efficiently, without tiring, and without complaint.

That AI continues to fall spectacularly short of such lofty goals is instructive, as the problem seems to be rooted in some deep-seated assumptions about the human brain. Further to the two previous points, for example, early AI researchers were unaware of the nested organization of the brain and the manner in which cognition is distributed across levels and areas. They further assumed that intelligence was a straightforward manner of a large data base combined with a powerful processor. Yet even with virtually limitless storage capacities and massively accelerated processing speeds of current computers, none even comes close to a toddler's capacity to discern faces, maintain social relationships, communicate novel thoughts, and extract coherence from moment-to-moment experience. The principal reason for this gap, it seems, has to do with the radically contextualized character of the brain—which is an interactive form that, through the extended structure of the physical body, does not so much "take in information" as it constantly revises its internal structure to maintain its fit within a similarly complex, self-renewing context.

In this sense, an agent's internal dynamics must be coherent with external circumstances, but this does not mean that internal cognition is a reflection or representation of an external reality. It merely means that, whatever is going on inside an agent, it is adequate for it to maintain its viability within its context. And this is where early AI went wrong. It assumed that intelligent action was based on an accurate internal map of an external reality. This theory of thought and memory is decided non-complex.

A secondary, and related, problem with early AI research was the assumption that human cognition was anchored in logical processes (hence the popularity of the brain-as-computer metaphor). In fact, the brain unfolds by establishing physical connections among neurons and coordinated activation patterns of other levels of organization. Once again, it turns out that humans are not logical creatures, but analogical creatures that are capable of logic. The fact that humans find analogy so easy and so natural, but logic so demanding—precisely the opposite of electronic computers—is clear evidence that electronic calculators and flesh-based brains have very little in common.

In terms of educational research and practice, the implications are numerous and profound. Topics that call for further investigation include the pedagogical and curricular implications of the associative/analogical character of human cognition (given that much of modern curricula are organized around the assumption that humans are linear/logical), the structural dynamics that underlie the stability of perception (i.e., How is it that a constantly changing brain supports relatively stable understandings?), the relationship between motor experience and abstract competencies in a radically contextualized cortex, and the relationship between sociocultural context and brain structure. We could go on.

> ### Discussion Box 6.1 • "Increasing Human Potential"
> ### An Example of Complex Educational Research at the Subpersonal Level
>
> The Santa Fe Institute Consortium (SFIC) is a transdisciplinary research collective centered at the Santa Fe Institute, the most prominent complexity science think tank on the planet. The team includes eminent researchers in the fields of neuroscience, imaging, biology, and developmental psychology, among other disciplinary realms.
>
> The SFIC has undertaken the first comprehensive longitudinal study done in human babies and adolescents in which close observations and measurements of structural and physiological changes occurring in the brain will be correlated with cognitive and social development. The Consortium anticipates that the data generated from a series of interconnected studies will provide information that will be useful to convince policy makers and educators that there are fundamental physiological changes that occur early in life and during adolescence that are critical for learning throughout life.
>
> The team is using cutting-edge technologies along with age-specific cognitive tasks (focused on, for example, language development, auditory understanding, and imitative behavior). It departs from similar studies in its longitudinal focus, following a cohort of individuals from birth through their teenage years. Most research studies that are concerned with changes across ages make use of "cross sectional" approaches—that is, different groups of subjects are studied at different ages. A coordinated set of studies that focuses on the same children as they mature is much more difficult, time-consuming, and expensive. However, this approach allows the neural contribution to a cognitive process to be explored by observing how the process changes with development of a given brain structure in the same individual.[5]

DISCUSSIONS OF SUBJECTIVE UNDERSTANDING WITHIN EDUCATIONAL RESEARCH

One of the potential problems of starting this chapter with an explication of the neurological bases of subjective understanding is that the discussion might be taken as foundational—that is, as though we are suggesting that personal knowledge can be reduced to physico-biological processes. Indeed, many have fallen into this trap, as evidenced by Jean Piaget's[6] warning against conflating neurological processes and personal sense-making. These phenomena are inextricably intertwined, but they cannot be equated.

It is significant that Piaget would be so specific on this issue, given his background as a biologist and his extensive use of biology-based analogies and metaphors in his accounts of learning. To state his concern in the vocabulary of complexity thinking, Piaget sought to maintain a clear distinction between the systems that generate knowledge (which, in terms of the foci of his research, were the neurological and nervous systems, as nested within an acting-and-perceiving body) and the systems of knowledge produced and maintained by these systems. The latter served as the specific focus of his theoretical work, in which he drew analogies from the contingent and dynamic qualities of biological development to the contingent and dynamic qualities of subjective conceptual development.

Piaget's scholarship is most often cited as the major influence on current subject-centered constructivist discourses in psychology and education. These discourses, in turn, are among the most prominent and influential theoretical frames in contemporary discussions of curriculum, pedagogy, and research in a number of branches of education. Over the past 30 years, learner-focused constructivist theories have been embraced by researchers in virtually all curriculum areas, especially by those interested in science and mathematics learning. Indeed, "radical constructivism," as it is often called, is commonly cited as the most influential theoretical perspective within a number of branches of educational research. The growing significance of constructivism within education can be readily demonstrated by a search of ERIC, one of the major data bases in the field. Considered across the last three decades, the numbers of items that come up on a search for "constructivist" or "constructivism" follow a smooth pattern of exponential growth. In the 1970s, the numbers of records were in the single digits. By the 1980s, the numbers had increased to two digits, and then to three digits in the 1990s. In 2000, it passed 1,000, and it continues to increase.

Given this rapid growth in popularity, it is perhaps not surprising that, as has been developed by many commentators,[7] interpretations of Piaget's scholarship vary dramatically. Some accounts reflect his implicit complexivist sensibilities; many are decidedly mechanistic. We thus proceed here with a brief explication of the philosophical commitments woven through his work.

Piaget identified himself and his investigations with the French structuralist school of thought, the origins of which are usually associated with the work of Ferdinand de Saussure (as developed in chap. 4). To recap, Saussure focused on language and argued that meaning lies in the manner in which semiotic objects are positioned in relation to one another. In other words, meaning is a matter of the internal coherence of a linguistic system, not of external correspondence of words to objects or events. Piaget believed the same thing of personal understandings: that knowledge was knowledge insofar as it could be rendered coherent with other knowing and insofar as it enabled the knower to remain viable. If incoherences were revealed or viability was threatened, knowings had to be adjusted.

Indeed, Piaget argued that such adjustments were being made continuously in the face of novel experience, albeit that they were usually minor and thus did not often bubble to the surface of conscious awareness. He referred to such ongoing revisions of one's system of knowledge as *assimilations*—shifts that were easily incorporated into an existing system of interpretation. More dramatic changes that triggered broader reorganizations of one's system of knowing he labeled *accommodations*. These two terms could be applied to almost any complex unity and, along with a set of stages of cognitive development, are easily the most prominent aspects of Piaget's legacy within the educational research literature.[8]

The critical point being made here is that, although Piaget's (and constructivists', more generally) accounts of personal sense making are anchored in the same vocabulary, allude to the same sorts of dynamics, and are concerned with similar phenomena as current research in neurology and neurophysiology, they are nonetheless distinct. One of the preeminent authorities on the topic, Ernst von Glasersfeld, notes that, for Piaget, "knowledge is a higher form of adaptation." He goes on to explain that cognition is "an instrument of adaptation the purpose of which is the construction of viable conceptual structures."[9] The theory is sometimes described as *non-representationist* because it explicitly rejects the notion that cognition has to do with constructing an inner model/representation of an outer reality.

In this regard, Piaget can be said to have anticipated the pivotal assertion of complexity science that nested phenomena must be studied at the levels of their emergence. He saw personal understanding as utterly reliant on biological architecture, but he also clearly identified such understanding as transcending that architecture. At the same time, and somewhat ironically, Piaget all but ignored other levels of nesting (the social and culture realms, for example) that are relevant to personal understanding, as discussed in subsequent sections. This is not to say he was unaware of them or discounted their relevance, however. He simply chose to devote his research attentions to the dynamics of personal sense-making and, as such, bracketed social, cultural, and other influences as aspects of the context.

In any case, following both neurological and structuralist insights, Piaget developed his theories around such principles as self-reference, self-containment, and internal coherence. In this regard, his work followed Immanual Kant's suggestion that humans actively engage the world in consciousness, along with Kant's two-world metaphor that split consciousness from an unknown and unknowable reality (hence his decision to bracket off levels of organization beyond the personal in his theories). The individual knower for Piaget was thus engaged in the unrelenting project of assembling a coherent, self-contained interpretive system, constantly updating and revising explanations and expectations to account for new experiences. It is this theoretical commitment that has prompted advocates of individual-centered constructivisms to argue that the theory is *descriptive only*. That is, Piagetian-inspired constructivist discourses are theories of learning, and they should not be construed as theories of teaching, schooling, or any other deliberate, goal-oriented projects. These theories are intended to describe how individuals construe their worlds, not how one might intervene to compel particular pre-selected construals.

We emphasize this issue because a significant number of educationists have mistaken constructivism as a prescriptive rather than a descriptive discourse. By way of analogy, the error is akin to attempting to organize diets around descriptions of digestive systems. The information is of use. In particular, it provides valuable details on what should *not* be consumed. However, it is inadequate for ensuring the well-being of the grander system. By ignoring the original purpose of the discourse, its core assertions and principal contributions can be distorted.

None of this is to say the individual-focused, subject-centered constructivisms have nothing to offer the cultural projects of teaching, schooling, and formal education. On the contrary, they do—but only when considered within a broader matrix of discourses. And, of course, our organizing assertion in this text is that complexity thinking provides just such a matrix.

The problem of forcing descriptive discourses into prescriptive practices is hardly limited to discussions of education that are informed by neurological and constructivist research. When human knowing and knowledge are understood as complexly contingent phenomena in which physical constraints, biological predispositions, idiosyncratic experiences, social situations, and cultural contexts all matter, there are obvious points of disjuncture with the deliberate, outcome-driven project of modern schooling. In this sense, complexity discourses represent a significant departure from earlier waves of theories out of psychology and sociology that were embraced by educationists in the mid-1900s. By way of prominent example, the importation of behaviorist psychology into education, while limited and limiting, was at least conceptually consistent with the project of schooling. Behaviorism is aligned with the desires of analytic science to develop reliable, predictive theories; hence, if one accepts its mechanistic premises, it makes sense to talk about "behaviorist teaching." The discourse is all about relating effect to cause, output to input, consequence to action. Constructivism, by contrast, recasts cognitive systems in terms of internal dynamics rather than external conditions, arguing that a focus on such conditions is virtually useless for making sense of the incredibly complex realm of thought. As such, a phrase like "constructivist teaching" is almost an oxymoron. The first term foregrounds accident and contingency; the latter is typically understood to in terms of deliberate and generalizable action.

Research oriented by radical constructivism has tended to focus on individuals' developments of specific concepts, usually in the context of carefully designed "teaching experiments"[10] in which learners' responses to specific prompts (e.g., elaborations, problems, etc.) are carefully monitored in an effort to track how the individuals incorporate new experiences into established systems of understanding. In this frame, teaching and research are understood in terms of making sense of the sense learners are making through a process of mutual perturbation whereby the learner's actions occasion and are occasioned by the teacher/researcher's actions.[11]

From this brief description, it should be clear why radical constructivism cannot serve as a general theory of teaching. The intention of the theory is to offer a general description of the inevitable complexity of personal understanding, based on viable accounts of how specific learners make sense of specific experiences. If anything, such information points to the impossibility of effective pedagogy, at least in situations where one person is charged with the responsibility of educating many people simultaneously.

Discussion Box 6.2 • "Philosophy in the Flesh"
An Example of Complex Educational Research
at the Level of Subjective Understanding

"The mind is inherently embodied.

"Thought is mostly unconscious.

"Abstract concepts are largely metaphorical."[12]

George Lakoff and Mark Johnson introduce their study and explication of the character of personal meaning-making with these three assertions. They identify these points as major findings in cognitive science and, working from them, assert that they should compel major rethinkings of *both* analytic and postmodern philosophy.

Their wide-ranging discussion is oriented by the major conclusion that much of the subject matter of philosophy (e.g., the natures of time, morality, causation, and mind) is anchored in metaphors derived from bodily experiences. By consequence, they demonstrate that thought not only requires a brain, but a body to experience the world and to provide a basis for metaphors of movement, containment, and so on. These embodied metaphors, in turn, come to serve as the conceptual bases for more abstract notions.

"Cognitive science," as invoked by Lakoff and Johnson, is a transdisciplinary realm that brings together expertise from philosophy, linguistics, neurology, sociology, and anthropology, among other disciplines. In other words, although their explicit focus is subjective understanding, they make it clear that explications of personal knowing must be understood as an emergent phenomenon that is simultaneously embodied and abstract, individual and collective, and biological and cultural.

In other words, personal understanding is a complex phenomenon. Provocatively, Lakoff and Johnson do not explicitly refer to complexity thinking to describe their interpretive frame or their research attitude—a move that might be taken to illustrate that complexivist sensibilities are gaining a broad acceptance in some domains of academic discourse. That is, around some issues, it is no longer necessary to spend the opening chapters explaining what complexity research is all about. The phenomenon under discussion is simply understood to be self-organizing, self-maintaining, self-referencing, recursively elaborated—in a word, complex.

DISCUSSIONS OF COLLECTIVE KNOWLEDGE WITHIN EDUCATIONAL RESEARCH

Exactly the same concerns extend into the use of "social constructionist"[13] discourses within education. This set of theories focus on precisely the sorts of phenomena that subject-centered constructivist discourses set aside as "context," "circumstance," or "perturbation." These phenomena include language itself, various subject matters, social habitus, school cultures, classroom collectives, and so on. Such concerns represent a departure from the long-held beliefs, maintained in Piagetian theories, that the individual is the locus of all cognition and the site of all learning. For the social constructionist, human cognition is something more diffuse, distributed, and collective. Put differently, social constructionists tend to frame subjectivity and objectivity not as two separate worlds, but as existing only in relation to one another. It is thus that the core concern of some branches of the discourse shift from the manner in which the individual constructs the world to the manner in which the world constructs the individual.

Over the past few decades, many, many pages in many, many research journals have been given to comparisons of subject-centered constructivisms and social constructionisms. For the most part, this literature has been devoted to some sort of effort to reconcile the two bodies of work—a move that is prompted and frustrated by the fact that the theories are concerned with different categories of complex phenomena.

Most often, these sorts of discussion are framed in terms of the tensions between the works of Piaget and those of Vygotsky, who typically serve as metonymic reductions of constructivist and constructionist theories. Piaget studied the continuous processes by which learners incorporate new experiences into their expectations of the world. Vygotsky focused on the incorporation of the individual into the body politic. Different processes are at work and different concerns arise at these two distinct levels of complex activity. In point of fact, both theories were developed around such core structuralist principles as internal coherence, self-reference, and ongoing adaptive evolution. As such, both are instances of complexity thinking, and attempts to reconcile them outside the frame of complexity tend to reveal an unfortunate reductionist mindset with a concomitant desire for a totalized account of knowing and knowledge.

Another common element of constructivist and constructionist theories is the use of body-based metaphors to describe different phenomena, evident in discussions of bodies of knowledge, the social corpus, the body politic, or a student body. This element, like the use of evolutionary dynamics, tends to operate more on an implicit than an explicit level. Beyond these sites of intersection, especially as they have been taken up by educational researchers, constructionist theories part company with one another around matters of specific educational concern, core metaphor, and cultural relevance. They also diverge around beliefs about the purposes of education, owing to the fact that social constructionist discourses have been adapted to fit the projects of theorists and researchers situated at all points along the contemporary ideological spectrum. To illustrate such divergences, we mention four strands that have risen to considerable prominence in the literature before looking specifically at their intersections with complexity thinking: activity theory, situated learning, more general sociocultural theories, and actor-network theory.

Activity theory is rooted in the works of Vygotsky and his students (especially Luria and Leont'ev). Activity theorists criticize the individualistic foci of many theories of knowing, including subject-centered constructivisms, and foreground the role of artifacts in cognition. The theory asserts that "mind" can only be understood in terms of goal-oriented, artifact-mediated, and culture-framed interactions between humans and their physical settings. Activity theorists thus call for the simultaneous study of agents, systems of artifacts (e.g., tools, language, signs, gestures), and other individuals—since these forms are tied together in ongoing processes of mutual specification.

Situated learning theory is closely related to activity theory. It was developed mainly in anthropology and sociology, and the theory is directly informed by Vygotsky's work. Situated learning is focused on the processes by which individuals enter into established "communities of practice." Framed principally by the metaphor of apprenticeship, learning is understood in collective terms of coparticipation within and reproduction of the collective. The theory's original authors, Jean Lave and Etienne Wenger, are clear on the point that the theory is strictly descriptive and, in terms of schooling, suited only to the question of how children learn the social role of students. As they comment, the theory "is not itself an educational form, much less a pedagogical strategy or teaching technique. It is an analytical viewpoint on learning, a way of understanding learning."[14] This delimitation, however, has been ignored by many educational researchers—including, for example, some who frame school science or language arts in terms of children apprenticing to be research scientists or published writers. (As noted in previous chapters, profound incongruencies arise when such varied communities of practice are laid atop one another.)

Sociocultural theories, as they are taken up in education, tend to be concerned with matters of the emergence of particular bodies of knowledge and particular social collectives. Commonly, these discourses invoke Vygotsky's main metaphor, influenced by Karl Marx, of shared labor. Central foci include the manners in which language and other cultural tools work to delimit interpretive possibilities, enable interpretive reach, and contribute to the emergence of a social corpus that is united in its common sense. Applied to classrooms, this strand of interpretation has contributed to instructional emphases on group processes and on the means of legitimated or delegitimating claims to truth within specific disciplines (versus the more traditional emphases on the mastery of already-legitimated truths).

Actor-network theory embodies elements and interests from each of the above-mentioned discourses. It is focused on science—or, more descriptively, on the social studies of science—and is specifically concerned with the processes and means through which disputes are settled, ideas are embraced, and methods are accepted. Consistent with activity theory, attention is paid to the roles of symbols, activities, and artifacts—including, for example, journals, conferences, funding agencies, and particle accelerators—that are subject to constant revisions. The discourse is organized around a recognition of the inherent reflexivity of scientific inquiry: Scientists are constantly (re)constructing the social-and-cultural contexts that enable and constrain their work. An "actor-network," then, is a reference to the inextricable intertwinings of a given act and the webs of objects and relationships that affect and that are affected by that act.

Once again, the most frequently cited thinker across these discourses is Vygotsky—and although it is not always clear in the manner in which his seminal works are incorporated into contemporary theories, Vygotsky's thinking can be justly aligned with complexity thinking. In particular, Vygotsky explicitly invoked the metaphor of evolution to describe the learning and development of the individual as a person in a given context. More significantly, Vygotsky was among the first to note the scale independent and self-similar characters of the nested systems of the individual, the cultural context, and the species.

To be clear, Vygotsky departed from the prevailing psychologistic theories of the time, in particular behaviorism. He did not see the *individual* as the locus of learning and development, but the *individual-and-environment* as the dynamic unity. The environment included other persons, artifacts, and so on, hence the pronounced emphasis on interaction and contexts in his work and in theories rooted in his work.

In our assessment, although well over a half-century old, Vygotsky's writings reflect a much more complexivist sensibility than the bulk of recent social constructionist discourses based on his work—at least, interpretations based in educational research. Our principal reason for this assertion is the fact that Vygotsky attended to *both* the system of individual cognition *and* the systems out of which such cognition emerges and within which it is nested. The latter element tends to be ignored or footnoted in contemporary theories that claim a Vygotskian influence, and this ignorance has contributed significantly to the above-noted tensions between subject-centered constructivisms and social constructionisms. There is no indication at all that either Piaget or Vygotsky perceived any sorts of incongruities between one another's theories, as might be expected given the inherently complex characters of their accounts of learning and cognition.

To reiterate, then, a significant contribution of *description*-oriented complexity research within education is the provision of a means to read across these sorts of discourses. Complexity thinking, we believe, should prompt researchers to devote less time to highlighting the differences among theoretical frames and to pay at least as much attention to the complementarities and deep similarities of constructivist, constructionist, and related discourses. It would seem that the vital question here is neither, "How are these discourses different?" nor "How are they alike?", but "At what level of complex organization is this theory a description?"

Discussion Box 6.3 – "Understanding Learning Systems"
An Example of Complex Educational Research
at the Level of Collective Knowledge

What might happen if the classroom collective, rather than the individual student, were understood as the locus of learning—that is, the *learner*—that should occupy most of the teacher's attentions?

Davis and Simmt[15] explore the thesis that mathematics classes might be construed as self-organizing and adaptive systems, based on experiences with a few groups of learners that appeared to operate as coherent knowledge-producing systems—that is, as collective *we*'s rather than collections of *I*'s—around topics of shared interest. Locating their interpretations in contemporary constructivist- and constructionist-oriented studies in mathematics education research, they contend that much of this work is framed by an uninterrogated assumption that the individual is the sole site of cognition and, hence, all pedagogy is oriented toward the development of personal competencies.

Davis and Simmt suggest that such an assumption sets the stage for a seemingly irresolvable tension between teacher-centered and learner-centered teaching approaches. They regard neither of these as viable or particularly effective, suggesting that a more knowledge-centered pedagogy in which the collective is understood as an intelligent entity may be a more sensible approach to organizing a classroom. Such an approach entails certain departures from traditional emphases—including, for example, allowing individual students to specialize. It is in the possibility of diverse interpretations, they suggest, that new possibilities for sense-making and foundations for more robust understandings are established.

They situate this discussion against the backdrop of research in formal mathematics, in which specialized expertise, juxtaposition of diverse concepts, attention to the figurative grounds of abstract concepts, and distributed authority are among the important qualities of the knowledge-producing community.

A number of other studies have attended to the collective character of particular educational systems. For example, Jennifer O'Day[16] draws on complexity to examine how information travels through complex systems. She argues that a key to improving schools is to take the *school* as the unit of accountability, rather than any individual in the school.

Taking quite a different tack, but still focusing on collectivity, an increasingly number of researchers have been exploring the "connected classroom" over the past five years. The phrase *connected classroom* refers to the use of current electronic technologies to mediate contributions from students. Research focuses in large part on how these technologies enable collective senses of topics and issues to arise. The work of James Kaput and Uri Wilensky, who locate their work in mathematics classrooms, is perhaps the most thoroughly developed in this realm.[17]

DISCUSSIONS OF CULTURAL DYNAMICS WITHIN EDUCATIONAL RESEARCH

Constructivist and constructionist discourses, for the most part, are rooted in 20th-century structuralist theories. Cultural studies and critical theory are more commonly aligned with post-structuralism. Elaborating structuralist sensibilities, post-structuralists tend to concern themselves more with the power structures at work—deliberate and accidental, explicit and tacit—within these systems of difference. The point is flagged by their use of the word *discourse*, which as noted earlier refers to the intertwining structures (e.g., linguistic, semiotic, social, etc.) that frame a cultural group's preferred habits of interpretation. A discourse organizes and constrains what can sensibly be said, thought, and done.

As developed in chapter 4, a major emphasis here is on language, but post-structuralists are also attentive to the activities and traditions that are prompted and supported by specific vocabularies and patterns of language use. Each discourse has its own distinctive set of rules and procedures—mostly tacit and unavailable for interrogation—that govern the production of what is to count as meaningful or senseless, true or false, normal or abnormal, sacred or profane. Post-structuralists argue that it is immersion in a dynamic, evolving culture that defines one's mode of consciousness.

Methodologically, much of post-structuralist-oriented research is concerned with *deconstruction*, an interpretive practice used to interrogate the effects of the usually-not-noticed aspects of language, images, and practices. Deconstruction is intended to support new understandings of how meaning is always enabled and constrained by one's ability to perceive (or not perceive) such aspects. As such, deconstruction is always an elaborative process, and it should not be confused with the reductionist emphases of analytic science and analytic philosophy.

Such efforts to show how absences, slips, misalignments, and other deferrals contribute to the productions and evolutions of meaning are common within post-structuralist discourses. As noted in chapter 4, the metaphor of *power* typically invoked around discussions of such topics, and its meaning tends to vary from a more benign sense of "capacity to act" (i.e., power *to*) to a more coercive sense of "dominating force" (i.e., power *over*). This variation in definition is certainly at work within the educational research literature, where a rough—but not at all reliable—distinction might be drawn between cultural studies and critical theory. *Cultural studies* is a title applied to various cross-disciplinary efforts to interpret texts, events, and other cultural phenomena. As a field, it is largely oriented by the notion that popular media and everyday events offer rich sites for making sense of what we believe and why we believe it. Within cultural studies, then, usages of the word *power* then to be more toward "capacity to act."

Critical theory refers to an older movement that is actually rooted in studies of textual interpretation in the 1800s.[18] In contrast to cultural studies, within critical theory, references to power tend more toward the dominance-seeking, force-based senses of the word. Once again, however, this distinction is hardly a clear or fully consistent one. In fact, in some educational research contexts, cultural studies and critical theory are treated as synonyms.

With regard to their specific relevance to educational research, a prominent focus of post-structuralist-informed studies has been constructions of *normal* and *abnormal*, deployed in such familiar contexts as ability (e.g., normal intelligence, age-appropriatism), growth (e.g., normal development), and social background (e.g., normal family). For the most part, *normal* in these instances is linked to the statistical notion of arithmetic mean, and is thus a reference to "most common." The major problem with such usage, highlighted by cultural and critical theorists, is that "most common" is often interpreted as "natural," thereby drastically misrepresenting a number of likely complex phenomena.

Complexity thinking supports such critiques, and adds that there is a logical flaw with the practice of imposing a series of calculated norms on the agents that comprise a complex system. In a system made up of differentiated beings and where those differences are necessary to the system's viability—such as a culture— a truly *normal* agent would be truly abnormal. Indeed, it would be impossible to be normal on more than a handful of measured criteria. This particular issue is one of the core reasons that statistical methods are problematic in the study of complex unities. Such methods might provide a snapshot portrait of a dynamic unity. However, not only would such a representation be inaccurate by the time it could be presented (since the system is always transforming itself), it could well ignore or collapse diversities that afford a collective its distinct character.

Such is precisely the criticism made by critical theory and cultural studies discourses, and it is here that they break radically from most of the social constructionist discourses mentioned in the previous section. Post-structuralism-influenced theories tend toward much more pronounced concerns with moral and ethical action. Prominent themes in education have included the social construction of gender, race, class, sexuality, (dis)ability, identity, knowledge, and reality. For the most part, researchers who take on these concerns have pressed toward what Paulo Freire[19] called *conscientização*, a rendering explicit of the social habits that delimit possible worlds and acceptable identities. The main pedagogical strategy here is to turn language onto itself—to invite learners into critical examinations of the conventions that frame their experiences and into similarly critical examinations of their own complicity in those conventions. In effect, that is, both education and educational research are understood in this frame to be matters of deconstruction.

There is, of course, an irony here. Post-structuralist discourses can never be the dominant voices in academia, and critical education attitudes can never prevail among educationists. The foci of interrupting the status quo and deconstructing the structures of dominance means that these theories not only have their sights set on moving targets, but targets whose motions are influenced by such efforts to study them. In other words, critical theorists and others oriented by post-structuralism can never fall into the naïve belief that they have succeeded in their goals.

Discussion Box 6.4 • "Practice Makes Practice" An Example of Complex Educational Research at the Level of Cultural Dynamics

Given recent shifts in prevailing theories of learning, perceptions of "necessary knowledge," conceptions of the role of formal education, and so on, it should not be surprising that these sorts of issues should collect together as a sort of grand anxiety in teacher education programs. What does it mean to become a teacher? How does one prepare? What sorts of understandings will enable effective and appropriate pedagogy in this evolving world?

Deborah P. Britzman takes on such issues in *Practice Makes Practice: A Critical Study of Learning to Teach*.[20] The book is developed around the dramas of different individuals as they meet and negotiate the tensions, the constraints, and the possibilities that frame the context of their own constructs of who they might be as teachers.

Britzman writes as a critical ethnographer. She does not presume to present all of the relevant details or to have some sort of moral advantage over her protagonists or readers. Rather than adopting an authoritative voice, she invites her readers into a series of interwoven discussions of, as Maxine Greene describes is, "how *we* choose to be together and, in our emergent communicates, resist passivity and injustice as we learn what it is to teach."[21]

In other words, while raising important issues and presenting profound insights into the processes of constructing identities, the book does not permit closure. There are no comfortable answers, no unambiguous questions, no simple resolutions.

DISCUSSIONS OF PHENOMENOLOGY AND ECOLOGY WITHIN EDUCATIONAL RESEARCH

One of the interesting aspects of contemporary educational research is that relatively little of it pays much attention to the fact that humans are biological creatures. Obvious exceptions are studies of brain function and development, but reports of such investigations are at best a minor presence in the educational research literature. Rather, discussions tend to be delimited by interests in the learner's understandings at one extreme and society's needs at the other—bookends that, for the most part, exclude the biological.

In many ways, this constraint on discussions of learning and teaching is ironic. Even as structuralist and post-structuralist discourses have embraced biology-based evolutionary metaphors, the realm of the biological has not only been ignored, in some cases it has been deliberately excluded from discussions. This point is most obvious, and clearly justified in many ways, around issues of racism, sexism, ageism and related bases of discrimination and exclusion. More subtly, the displacing of the biological was a foundational part of Piaget's work, as he was clear that his theories were strictly about the emergence of personal interpretations, not about biological processes. He did not, however, deny the relevance of the biological; it simply was not what interested him.

In contrast, the biological is explicitly excluded in some post-structuralist discourses, and the principal reason for this rejection has to do with the lingering tendency to interpret references to genetic constitution and biological being as indicators of essentialist or determinist beliefs. As might be expected, then, the tendency to deny the role of the biological in matters of human subjectivity is most pronounced in those discussions that seek to interrupt cultural prejudices that are based on physical difference and inherited traits. This point is powerfully illustrated by the current taboos against, for example, suggesting that the females might have a neurological edge over males in matters of social competence or that one race might have a natural advantage in athletics. Discussions become even more volatile when the topic turns to general intelligence.

Of course, when such arguments are presented as statements of "raw fact," they are already deeply flawed, simply because one's complex neurophysiological structure is never a straightforward matter of either biology or experience, nor a dissociable combination of the two. Nevertheless, concerns around essentialist claims have rendered some topics touchy, if not forbidden. Indeed, so powerful is the tacit restriction that we find ourselves unwilling to cite researchers who have strayed into the territory of gender-, race-, and other body-based differences over the past few decades.

Specific issues of discriminations rooted in biological constitution aside, some important contributions to discussions of the biological bases of knowing and knowledge have been made over the past century. Notably, in the mid-1950s phenomenologist Maurice Merleau-Ponty[22] described humans as doubly-embodied. On the one hand, as physical-biological entities, humans embody the history of the species, and on this count it is interesting to note that there is stunningly little variation among members of the species on the level of genetics. On the other hand, as a social-cultural being, a human embodies experiences that have unfolded over a long cultural history and through countless social interactions. Both the biological history of the species and the social history of the culture are carried in the physical structure of the individual, melded through that individual's own idiosyncratic experience.

In effect, then, phenomenological inquiry prompts attentions in both microscopic and macroscopic directions, simultaneously embracing the insights of discourses focused on bodily subsystems (e.g., neurophysiology and immunology) and discourses concerned with the intertwining systems that constitute the biosphere. This expansion of the topics of conversation beyond the human (i.e., outside the bookends of self and society) has yet to have a broad impact on educational theory, research, and practice. However, some notable contributions have been made. Madeleine Grumet's *Bitter Milk*,[23] for example, draws on phenomenology and psychoanalysis to elaborate contributions of feminist discourses to education—in the process, providing a powerful example of how discourses focused on the biological and discourses focused on the cultural need not operate in tension, but can be made to inform and amplify one another.

Along compatible lines, a growing number of educational researchers have embraced ecological discourses in their studies of phenomena around schooling. The term *ecological* in these discussions is understood to have a specific meaning, referring to the study of relationships—which includes, but does not necessarily focus on the natural world. This refinement of definition is usually explained in terms of a recovery of the word's original meaning, which is typically traced back to the Greek *oikos*, "household." And, although the definition is more specific, it has allowed researchers to focus on a broad array of educational phenomena, occasioning the emergence of discussions of personal ecologies, classroom ecologies, and school ecologies alongside more familiar usages in reference to the physical contexts of learning, environmental issues, and the global ecosystem. In other words, in terms of the phenomena to which it has been applied, the term *ecology* has a very similar range of meaning as the term *complexity*. Moreover, emergent discussions of educational issues that are framed by ecological sensibilities, in general, are readily fitted to complexivist sensibilities. This point can be illustrated in the ecologist's suggestion that humanity might be metaphorically described as one of the organs (or, perhaps, cells) that constitute the body of the biosphere—a notion that invokes images of nested, scale independent forms.

> ## Discussion Box 6.5 •
> ## "Education, Cultural Myths, and the Ecological Crisis"
> ## An Example of Complex Educational Research at the Level of Ecology
>
> Many believe that humanity is in real danger of triggering changes to ecosystems that would be catastrophic to the species. What is worse, to date, the principal tool to respond to emergent problems seems to be the very mindset that prompted them in the first place: analytic science.
>
> In *Education, Cultural Myths, and the Ecological Crisis*, Chet Bowers[24] takes on the most cherished assumptions of liberal humanism, modernism, and progressivism, with his critique of such taken-for-granted core beliefs as individualism, abstract rational thought, emancipation, progress, and the elaboration and extension of technology. He draws on complex ideas from the sociology of knowledge, cultural anthropology, linguistics, and ecological theory in an examination of the multi-layered connections between culture, language, behavior, and thought—and, in particular, how the school functions as a reality-constructing process that projects and maintains a radical separation of human from natural.
>
> In particular, Bowers challenges conventional thinking about the use of information technology in the classroom and connections between addressing the ecological crisis and the challenges of cultural diversity. He explores reasons why the knowledge of traditional, ecologically oriented cultures has been marginalized, and presents a thoughtful and realistic appraisal of ways in which urban teachers might incorporate the wisdom of premodern cultures into the classroom.

COMPLEXITY THINKING AND *DESCRIPTIVE* EDUCATIONAL RESEARCH

We return now to a point made in the first pages of this book: Complexity thinking is not a metadiscourse that seeks to offer totalized explanations, but an umbrella notion that enables researchers to note profound similarities across a diversity of phenomena. As such, its immediate contribution to educational research is in the provision of a means to address and foreground the deep similarities of some heretofore disparate—and, at times, seemingly oppositional—theories and research foci. As it turns out, complexivist sensibilities were thoroughly represented in the educational literature long before the movement cohered.

That being said, however, it is significant that insights gleaned from neurological, constructivist, constructionist, critical theoretic, phenomenological, and ecological perspectives have been mainly *descriptive* in nature. They have, for the most part, offered accounts of learning and development that have departed radically from entrenched sensibilities. However, they have offered relatively little by way of *pragmatic* advice to educators and educational researchers, and it is here that we believe complexity thinking offers its most significant contribution to educational research. Such is the concern of the final two chapters.

CHAPTER SEVEN

Pragmatic Complexity Research:
CONDITIONS OF EMERGENCE

WHEN YOU COME TO A FORK IN THE ROAD,
TAKE IT.

—Yogi Berra[1]

There has been a longstanding problem with many of the theoretical frames imported by educational researchers from other domains. Very often, the discourses adopted and adapted from psychology, sociology, literary criticism, and elsewhere are not well fitted to the particular, pragmatic concerns of educationists. For the most part, those theories tend to be strictly descriptive, focused much more on the characterization of a specific phenomenon than on how one might go about affecting that phenomenon.

We have already mentioned the current, very problematic example of the incorporation of constructivist theories into discussions of teaching and schooling, but the same criticism could be extended to many emergent discourses, including those arising from cultural studies and critical theory. As authors and prominent explicators of such frameworks have repeatedly asserted, these theories cannot be construed as theories of education—at least insofar as teaching is understood in terms of the project of prompting learners toward particular, prespecified sets of competencies. Obviously it is useful to know about the dynamics of the process(es) involved, but just as obviously, complexity thinking compels an acknowledgment that an individual learner, a classroom, a disciplinary domain, and a culture are four among many qualitatively different systems. To derive guidelines for teaching based on an isolated knowledge of just one is simply to commit a category error. Even so, in spite of the frequent and unequivocal cautions against over-interpreting the practical utility of non-education-based theories, some educational writers have stretched and distorted descriptions of learning and knowledge into prescriptions for teaching—evidenced in now commonplace references to "constructivist teaching" and "critical pedagogy."[1]

A secondary problem, also already noted, is that unlike neurology, psychology, sociology, and anthropology—which are all developed in and focused on relatively well-delimited areas of interest—the field of education is greatly dispersed. It must be simultaneously attentive to issues and phenomena across many levels of organization. Simply put, an educator or an educational researcher cannot focus solely on brain function or individual sense-making or group process or cultural contexts. Quite the contrary, all of these concerns—along with many other aspects of existence—must be incorporated into effective educational theories and practices.

In other words, the field of education might be characterized as a domain that sits at the intersections of many other areas of inquiry, including, in addition to the ones just noted, various subject matter disciplines (e.g., mathematics, English literature, etc.), philosophy, sociology, and history. This point is, of course, reflected in the ranges of subdisciplines that are represented at major conferences, where the qualifiers *education* or *educational* are attached to psychology, history, sociology, leadership, physics, art, and many other conventionally recognized fields.

For these two main reasons—that is, the pragmatic (vs. descriptive) character of the educational project and the transdisciplinary nature of education—we believe that the umbrella offered by complexity thinking presents a powerful means to pull together a diversity of disciplines and discourses while enabling researchers and practitioners to deal with the practical aspects of the formal educational project. Having addressed the former aspect in previous chapters, in this one we turn our attentions to the sorts of practical advice that have emerged over the past several decades out of complexity-oriented research. To be clear about our project here, we are asserting that complexity thinking has evolved into a pragmatics of transformation—that is, a framework that offers explicit advice on how to work with, occasion, and affect complexity unities.

On this point, we do not mean to suggest that complexity thinking is the *only* discourse that offers advice on such issues. Others that have been taken up by educational researchers in recent decades include psychoanalysis[2] and, to a much lesser extent, Eastern mindfulness traditions.[3] Complexity thinking shares with these frames the conviction that transformations of learning systems cannot be understood in linear or mechanical terms and that any attempt at such transformations is necessarily a deeply ethical matter than must be undertaken with caution, humility, and care.

Of course, as has been foregrounded by critical theorists over the past several decades, the project of effecting change is neither innocent nor benign. Questions that must be addressed include, "Whose conception of change?", "Where does the authority rest?", and "Who benefits?" (We could go on.) Discussions of these issues are deferred to chapter 8, but we would note here that some of the discourses mentioned in chapters 5 and 6 ignore or appear oblivious to such topics of critical reflection, particularly those that focus exclusively on individual sense-making. Educational research that has been oriented by subject-centered constructivist theories, for example, tends to be aimed toward "doing things better"—ensuring better comprehension of topics, developing more effective assessment strategies, and so on— thereby side-stepping questions of the social impact or the cultural relevance of the topics to be taught and evaluated. In prompting attentions to the nested and co-implicated aspects of the educational project, questions of *how* to teach are often considered independently of questions of *why, who, where,* and *what.* As such, although this chapter is focused on issues of *how,* the discussion is not at all meant to be self-contained. Perhaps more than any other section in this book, if this chapter were to be read on its own, the possibilities for misunderstanding or underappreciating the lessons of complexity are most profound.

PROMPTING COMPLEX EMERGENCE

One of the preliminary issues that must be addressed before speaking to the potential contributions of complexity thinking to current efforts to effect change in social settings is the role of *specialization.*

As 18th-century economist Adam Smith developed in his immensely influential *The Wealth of Nations,* specialization can enable dramatic improvements in productivity. Concerned specifically with the organization of modern factories, Smith observed how different manufacturing plants were organized and noted how labor that is appropriately divided into specialized subtasks can be hundreds or even thousands of times more productive than work that is done holistically by skilled artisans. The example Smith used was the making of a pin, but the principles of division of labor are just as easily applied to almost any manufacturing task.

The reasons for increased productivity are simple and obvious. To begin, the specialist need only learn a small repertoire of skills, thus requiring less time to master the job and providing increased opportunity for high level (read: efficient) skills. Further, the specialized laborer requires very little transition-time between tasks. Rather than moving from one task to the next—which requires both physical and mental adjustment—the modern factory was organized around the realization that repetitive tasks can be moved to the worker. As well, sufficiently productive runs can justify the expenses associated with highly specialized equipment, thereby providing a means to even further accelerate production.

Much has been written about the way that formal education has been structured around the model of the modern factory, especially the idea of the division of labor as developed by Smith. With the teacher as worker, the learner as the incomplete product, and the topics to be learned parsed into the sequential tasks to be completed, the promise of efficient production of an educated populace has been used for centuries to rationalize the separation of students by age, subject matter, and social class, among other criteria. Correspondingly, teachers have become middle school science experts or early literacy specialists who are focused principally on how to present a narrow portion of a preset curriculum. And, as might be expected, the entire project has been subjected to various sorts of quality-control testing.

Clearly, it is easy to critique the application of an economist's model of specialized labor to the project of schooling. However, as it turns out, there is also a powerful critique of this model as it has been applied to manufacturing. Moreover, there is also a powerful alternative to thinking about the organization of labor, one that has been intensely studied over the past few decades. This research has had no shortage of sites for inquiry, as the monolithic, top-down, fragmented structures that dominated the manufacturing sectors of Western civilization until the 1970s have rapidly given way to a new manner of organization. Ford, General Motors, and IBM are among the many major companies that have been compelled to retool themselves on the fly, taking on more bottom-up, distributed, collective-oriented structures of Toyota, Honda, and Hewlett Packard. A principal reason for these rapid and pervasive transformations has been the emergence of a more volatile context in which such elements as fuel prices and technological possibilities can shift dramatically from one day to the next. Decades and centuries ago, in more socially unified and culturally static settings, the top-heavy factory was able to keep pace with unfolding circumstances. However, the current pace of cultural evolution demands that companies be capable of rapid change, able to transform ideas into products in once unthinkably brief spans of time.[4]

Such competencies require a more integrated response across all sectors of a manufacturing industry. In an era of slow-paced development, a corporate elite could issue a decree that would trickle down vertically through layers of management, squads of designers and engineers, and teams of machinists before reaching an army of assembly-line workers. A more rapid response requires a more horizontal structure in which representatives from all sectors are able to combine their respective areas of expertise. In other words, there is a need for a more flexibly adaptive—that is, a more intelligent—system. As discussed in previous chapters, decentralized structures are much better suited to such situations than centralized organizations.

These sorts of structural shifts have been directly and explicitly informed by complexity thinking—and on this count it is interesting to note how business and manufacturing were quick to realize the importance of complexity research. Education, by stunning contrast, lags well behind.

So why the discrepancy?

A number of reasons can be (and have been) given, ranging from the conscious and deliberate (e.g., privileged groups can retain their advantages in an educational system that is out of sync with cultural evolutions) to the unconscious and accidental (e.g., conventional practice has become so habitual and ritualized that is it simply locked in place). What is clear, and unfortunate, is that the circumstances have not yet emerged to compel a transformation similar to the one witnessed in the manufacturing sector over the past 30 years.

One pivotal issue in critical discussions of the issues appears to be common-sense beliefs around the purposes of schooling, which tend to be framed in terms of preparations of the young for an adult world. The obvious problem with this construct and its assumption of a linear developmental sequence is that the nature of the "adult world" is hardly stable—in marked contrast to the contents of most mandated curricula. As such schools find themselves perpetuating mathematics curricula that were mainly designed to prepare a workforce to work on assembly lines and in service industries, language arts curricula that are developed around rationalist assumptions about processes of meaning-making and representation, and science curricula that are organized around decontextualized factoids, outdated models, and analytic methods that are of limited use in a complex world. It could, of course, be argued that the conventional school's principal purpose has to do with maintaining the status quo by limiting prospects and by training learners to accept authority without question, but even these sorts of insidious goals seem geared to the work world of a century ago. Certainly the number of sites of employment for mindless labor gets smaller every day.

How, then, how might a complexivist respond to questions around the purposes of education? On this question, we turn first to Edgar Morin:

> Education for the future must make a concerted effort to regroup [humanity's] scattered knowledge—from the natural sciences, to situate the human condition in the world; from the social sciences, to shed light on human multi-

dimensionality and complexity—and integrate into this scientific knowledge the priceless contribution of the humanities, not only philosophy and history, but also literature, poetry, the arts.[5]

Morin's assertion is rooted in the complexivist attitude that a questioning of the human condition begins with a questioning of humanity's situation in the world. So framed, humans cannot be considered in terms of disjointed disciplines through which being is understood in terms of bioanatomical processes, cultural enframements, and so on. Nor can being be reduced to an amalgamation of such systems of interpretation. Rather, Morin argues, an education for a complex world entails a certain transdiscipinarity that avoids trivialized distinctions between self and other, individual and collective, art and science, biological and cultural, human and natural, and so on. Humanity, that is, must be radically contextualized.

This assertion is not intended as a reduction of humanity to biological processes or categories. On the contrary, although a remembrance of the biological is certainly entailed, it is just as much a call to recognize the dissimiliarities among humans and other species. Humanity, for example, is a teaching species—which, in complexivist terms, means that humanity has developed effective means not just to maintain its knowledge across generations, but to continuously elaborate its capacities. Among the varied means developed to enable such maintenance and elaboration are associative language and the written word, both of which appear to be unique to the species.[6]

Significantly, for the complexivist, these ongoing elaborations of knowledge are *not* understood in terms of closing in on a complete and totalized understanding of the universe. Quite the opposite, the point is that knowledge can be endlessly elaborated. The process of knowledge "production" might be described as an ever-expanding space of possibility that is opened and enlarged simply by exploring the space of what is currently possible. In this sense, humanity is presented with an ever-evolving horizon of possibility. The problem is that that horizon is often mistaken as stable and as marking the limit of the knowable.

Such perceived limits are perhaps better understood in terms of the boundaries of the currently imaginable—a point that is well illustrated by science fiction writings over the past decades and centuries. Consider the communications technologies used in *Star Trek* episodes from the late 1960s. Crew members' hand-held communicators now seem bulky and limited compared to current cell phones with text, imaging, and recording capacities. Many similar examples could be readily cited to demonstrate how once-cutting-edge imaginings have become dated, even hokey, in a matter of just years. Conversely, many examples of current technologies would simply have been unthinkable to the most creative imaginations of previous generations.

educate
the subject

The point? For a teaching species in a complex world, it is ridiculous to conceive of education in terms of top-down, ends-driven structures. This is not to say that formal education can do without formal organizations or explicit curricula. The point is, rather, that "an education for the future" (following Morin) is better understood as being oriented toward the as-yet unimagined—indeed, the currently unimaginable. Such a "goal" can only be understood in terms of exploration of the current spaces of possibility.

THE CONDITIONS NECESSARY FOR COMPLEX EMERGENCE

Education—and, by implication, educational research—conceived in terms of expanding the space of the possible rather than perpetuating entrenched habits of interpretation, then, must be principally concerned with ensuring the conditions for the emergence of the as-yet unimagined.

In recent years, there has actually been a rapid growth in understandings of the sorts of conditions that must be in place to allow the emergence of such expansive possibilities. Knowledge of these conditions has been applied, for example, in efforts to re-establish devastated ecologies[7] and, as already mentioned, within the corporate sector to improve the viability and productivity of various industries.[8] This knowledge has also been adapted and elaborated by a handful of educational researchers to structure classroom and research collectives.

On this count, developments in complexity science that are oriented toward occasioning the emergence and affecting the actions of complex collectives seem to be fitted to those research methodologies that are explicit and deliberate in their desires to effect and document transformations in group and collaborative settings—including, perhaps most prominently, action research and related participatory approaches to inquiry. With this assertion in mind, we illustrate the following discussions of some of the conditions for complex emergence with a research projects in which we and colleague Elaine Simmt have worked with a cross-grade cohort of practicing teachers to better understand the disciplinary knowledge that is necessary to effective teaching. Details of this study as they apply to the discussion are presented in the dialogue boxes throughout the chapter. Specifically, this account is used to underscore the relevancies of and the researchers' roles in affecting the following conditions:

- internal diversity,
- internal redundancy,
- neighbor interactions,
- distributed control,
- randomness, and

- coherence.

In the discussion that follows, we consider these conditions as sets of complementary pairs, under the following headings:

- specialization—living the tension of diversity and redundancy,
- trans-level learning—enabling neighbor interactions through decentralized control, and
- enabling constraints—balancing randomness and coherence.

Our reason for organizing the discussion around dyads is to foreground that complex emergence happens far-from-equilibrium. Indeed, as Waldrop describes it, complex emergence happens "on the edge,"

> where new ideas and innovative genotypes are forever nibbling away at the edges of the status quo, and where even the most entrenched old guard will eventually be overthrown … [in] the constantly shifting … zone between stagnation and anarchy … where a complex system can be spontaneous, adaptive, and alive.[9]

And so the discussion that follows is centrally concerned with what is involved in the transformation of a group of affiliated but independently acting agents into a unity in which personal aspirations contribute to grander collective possibilities. The discussion is oriented by the assumption that a successful collectivity is not just more intelligent than the smartest of its members, but that it presents occasions for all participants to be smarter—that is, to be capable of actions, interpretations, and conclusions that none would achieve on her or his own. In other words, each of the interdependent conditions discussed below is simultaneously a reference to global properties of a system and to the local activities of the agents. Such conditions are not easily pried apart. Indeed, as we have attempted to do so in our considerations of different moments in the collective activity, we have found ourselves caught up in tangled cross-references, repetitions, and qualifications.

One further orienting note: Our focus here is on the *conditions* of the collective work, as opposed to the *qualities* (i.e., structures and dynamics) of complex co-activity. Such concerns, of course, are vital for anyone considering this sort of research, and we recommend consulting texts that provide overviews of the past century of research into small groups.[10]

Discussion Box 7.1 • Developing Knowledge

The example that we use to illustrate the discussion in this chapter is based on an extended and ongoing study of practicing teachers' knowledge of mathematics, conducted by Davis, Simmt, and Sumara. At the time of the writing, the project is entering the fourth year of its six-year duration.

To date, most empirical studies concerned with teachers' knowledge of mathematics have been oriented by a "deficit" model of personal understanding, whereby teachers are examined according to a predetermined set of competencies. A different approach is taken in the research reported here, which is anchored in the assumption that experienced mathematics teachers enact a certain sort of mathematical knowledge that may never have been an explicit part of their own learning—or, for that matter, of their own teaching. Indeed, much of this knowledge may not be popularly recognized as part of the formal disciplinary body of knowledge. As such, the project, which involves a group of 24 teachers, is aimed explicitly at representing teachers' mathematics-for-teaching—that is, the sorts of mathematics that arise in the actual contexts of teaching.

The cohort is a diverse one, with grades from kindergarten through high school represented. In terms of professional experience, a few of the participants are at the beginning of their careers, several have taught for decades, and the rest fall somewhere in between. Most of the teachers are generalists, but two are mathematics specialists. Some teach in small urban centers, some teach in rural locations. The cohort meets for daylong seminars, scheduled every few months. The thread of the discussion that is presented through this chapter is developed around one of these sessions, in which the topic of discussion was "What is multiplication?"

SPECIALIZATION—
LIVING THE TENSION OF DIVERSITY AND REDUNDANCY

The condition of *internal diversity* has been used to discuss the importance of, for example, the tremendous amount of unexpressed "junk" DNA in the human genome, the range of vocational competencies in any large city, the biodiversity of the planet, and the specialized functions of different brain regions. In each case, the diversity represented among units/parts/agents is seen as a source of possible responses to emergent circumstances. For instance, if a pandemic were to strike humanity, currently unexpressed DNA sequences might bestow an immunity upon a few people, and hence ensure the survival of the species—an intelligent response to an unforeseeable shift in circumstances. A differently intelligent response to the same circumstances (and a 'more' intelligent response, from the perspective of most members of the species) might arise among the interactions of a network of researchers with expertise in such diverse domains as virology, immunology, sociology, entomology, and meteorology. A critical point here is that one cannot specify in advance what sorts of variation will be necessary for appropriately intelligent action, hence the need to ensure and maintain diversity in the current system.

Our linking of systemic intelligence with internal diversity in the preceding paragraph is deliberate. Internal diversity defines the range and contours of possible responses. On the level of collective human action, there are important and usually broad diversities in any social grouping, no matter how homogeneously conceived. However, as demonstrated by certain religious groups, classrooms, and other structures that are in one way or another rigidly governed and/or insulated from grander systems, the possibility for expression of relevant diversities can be readily suppressed, thereby minimizing the opportunities for innovative collective action.

With specific regard to classroom settings, we are once again prompted here to offer a critique of those "cooperative learning" and collaborate group-based strategies that are organized around formal roles and instrumental, close-ended tasks. One cannot impose diversity from the top down by naming one person a facilitator, another a recorder, and so on. Diversity cannot be assigned or legislated; it must be assumed to be present. Similarly, it is unlikely that diversity, even if expressed, will be recognized and valued if the task set for a collective is trivial. (We return to this point in the discussion of "enabling constraints.")

The complement of internal diversity of a system is *internal redundancy*, a term that is used to refer to duplications and excesses of those aspects that are necessary for complex co-activity. For example, in order for a group of historians to reconstruct some portion of Egypt's past, it is not necessary that everyone be able to interpret hieroglyphics. However, this sort of redundancy would likely be highly useful.

Unfortunately, in popular parlance, the word *redundancy* tends to be associated with aspects that are unnecessary or superfluous and that contribute to inefficiencies—a usage that is appropriate to descriptions of complicated (mechanical) systems, but that is not suitable for descriptions of complex unities. Indeed, redundancy among agents is one of the key qualities that distinguishes complex systems from complicated systems. The important difference is that, whereas it makes sense to think about mechanical operations in terms of *optimum* efficiency, complex systems obey a logic of *adequacy*. Indeed, it makes little sense to think in terms of "best" for systems that are constantly changing (and for systems whose contexts are constantly changing).

In a social grouping, redundancies include common language, similar social status of members, shared responsibilities, constancy of setting, and so on. Such redundancies tend to fade into the backdrop of social action and are only pulled into focus when there is some sort of rupture in one or more of them. In fact, at least among humans, there is vastly more redundancy than diversity. This sort of deep sameness is vital. A complex system's capacity to maintain coherence is tied to the deep commonalities of its agents. As demonstrated by the ways that some people's brains recover from strokes, some companies cope with employee disloyalty, and some ecosystems adapt to the loss or introduction of new species, redundancy among agents is what enables a system to cope with stress, sudden injury, and other impairments.

Redundancy thus plays two key roles. First it enables interactions among agents. Second, when necessary, it makes it possible for agents to compensate for others' failings. It is in these senses that redundancy is the complement to diversity. Whereas internal diversity is outward-oriented, in that it enables novel actions and possibilities in response to contextual dynamics, internal redundancy is more inward-oriented, enabling the habituated, moment-to-moment interactivity of the agents that constitute a system.

An upshot, perhaps obvious, is that educators and educational researchers who are interested in interactivity in a complex collective must attend to the common ground of participants. Again, much of the necessary redundancy can usually be assumed to be present. However, some aspects may need to be negotiated. As well, some aspects can be manipulated by, for example, introducing a common text or other artifact to focus attentions—a point that experienced teachers know well.

None of this is to say, however, that all members of a complex unity must "be on the same page" in terms of purpose, intentions, expectation, and so on. In fact, the vibrancy of complex unities arises in the mix of its redundant and its diverse elements—or, in systemic terms, the sources of its stability and its creativity. These elements and their balance, are not strictly dictated by the system itself, but are better understood in terms of a function of the system-in-context. Minimal redundancy among (i.e., high specialization of) agents is most valuable in relatively stable settings, but it can be associated with a loss of robustness and, hence, presents a risk of poor adaptability if the context were to become volatile. For instance, wide-scale extinctions are often linked to overspecialization (more precisely, over-speciation) and consequent inability to adapt to new conditions. Similarly, factories that are organized around highly specialized micro-tasks can be very efficient, but very difficult to update or upgrade in the face of changing consumer demands. On the flip side, maximum redundancy (i.e., highly interchangeable agents, and therefore low specialization) is more appropriate in more volatile situations. Increased redundancy can also engender decreased adaptability, however. Taken to an extreme, a reduction in internal diversity can diminish a system's capacity to respond quickly and intelligently, simply because it lacks a sufficient range of diverse responses. In such cases, even minor perturbations can trigger the collapse of a system.

Hence, to appreciate the importance of specialization—that is, the dynamic combination of diversity and redundancy—it is important to consider *simultaneously* the individual agents and the collective system. Somewhat ironically, this part-in-whole sensibility is one that has proven elusive within discussions of education, where debates are often framed in terms of such irresolvable tensions as self-interest versus societal-interest or learner-centeredness versus teacher-centeredness. Complexity thinking responds that there are inherent problems with dualities that are based on artificial separations of agents and the systems that they comprise. It simply does not make sense to assume that they are necessarily in tension with one another, given that they rely on one another. (This is not to say that there are no tensions. Rather, the point is that a this-or-that mentality is often inappropriate and counterproductive when thinking about such matters.)

Noticing and supporting *specialization*, then, can help educators avoid the tendency to dichotomize parts and wholes. Specialization entails a balancing of individual obsession and collective necessity—that is, a balancing of internal diversity and internal redundancy. This manner of argument is also useful for thinking through concerns around equity in complex social unities. In complexity terms, equity is not about sameness of opportunity, influence, or expression; it is about freedom to pursue particular interests in the service of group possibility. In our own experiences, this point is most evident in work with practicing teachers. In such contexts, whereas we usually frame our own involvements in terms of better understanding some aspect of formal education (along with the concomitant professional need to publish, secure grants, and so on), teacher-participants in shared projects usually frame their own participations quite differently. Rationales have included opportunities for professional development, curiosity, breaks from the classroom, improved chances of promotion, and so on. In other words, there should be ample room for self-interest in a complex collective—but the global project should never be reducible to those self-interests.

Discussion Box 7.2 • Developing Specialized Knowledge

In the study of teachers' mathematics knowledge, the research sessions with the teachers are regarded in different ways by the various participants. For most part, the teachers see the meetings as "in-service sessions"; their principal reasons for taking part revolve around their professional desires to be more effective mathematics teachers. In contrast, for Davis, Simmt, & Sumara, these events are "research sessions"—that is, sites to gather data on teacher knowledge. The researchers are explicit in the fact that they are there to try to make sense of teachers' understandings of mathematics and how that knowledge might play out in their teaching. The common ground, as developed through the course of these discussion boxes, arises in the joint production of new insights into mathematics and teaching. Topics have ranged from general issues (e.g., problem-solving) to specific curriculum topics (as in the case of multiplication, developed here).

In regard to the explicit research agenda of assessing teachers' mathematics, the investigation team often finds that teachers' first responses to a question like "What is multiplication?", while usually appropriate, represent just one of many possibilities, and usually a possibility that is redundant to every member of the system—that is, one that is automatized and requires little thought. In response to the "What is multiplication?" prompt, for instance, almost everyone answered "repeated addition" or "groups of," and was surprised when asked the follow-up question, , "And what else?" However, when this same group of teachers is asked to share their responses or explain for others, in general a much greater diversity of responses comes to be represented.

With regard to the redundant elements of the collective, the session that serves as the focus of this discussion unfolded early in the second year of the collaboration, and so there had been ample opportunity to establish routines and expectations. The topic of multiplication had been selected by the teachers themselves in a previous session, and so it represented a matter of shared interest and concern. The researchers' decision to begin with question, "What is multiplication?" was intended as means to have participants represent their common knowledge on the topic—to explicitly announce the common or redundant elements around the issue-at-hand, as it were.

Participants certainly understood it in this way. What they were not expecting was that follow-up question, "And what else?"—which, as elaborated in subsequent discussion boxes, turned out to be an occasion to represent a diversity of images, applications, and other associations used to give shape to the topic of multiplication at various grade levels. It was in the this diversity of responses that new, emergent possibilities for conceptual interpretation began to arise.

TRANS-LEVEL LEARNING—INCORPORATING
DECENTRALIZED CONTROL AND NEIGHBOR INTERACTIONS

Learning, in complexity terms, is always a trans-level phenomenon. For example, for a social collective to expand its repertoire of possibilities, the individuals that comprise it must themselves learn and adapt.

This point is not a new one, but what complexity thinking offers is some insight into how certain conditions might be manipulated to ensure that individual interests and collective interests need not be placed in competition with one another. It is possible to foster individual agency and possibility at the same time as addressing collective potential. A key is the structure of the system, and a first consideration is the manner in which neighbors are able to interact.

It goes without saying that agents within a complex system must be able to affect one another's activities. Clearly, neighbors that come together in a grander unity must communicate. However, what is not so obvious is what might constitute a *neighbor* in the context of a knowledge-producing community such as a research collective, a classroom grouping, or even an individual's psyche. In our own ongoing efforts to interpret and prompt complex activity around educational topics, we have come to realize that the neighbors in knowledge-oriented communities are not physical bodies or social groupings. That is, although undeniably important, personal and group interactions for their own sake may not be as vital or as useful as is commonly assumed. Rather, *the neighbors that must interact* with one another are ideas, hunches, queries, and other manners of representation.

We recognize that there are dangers with the phrasing of the previous sentence. The claim that notions can "interact" might be interpreted as invoking a knowledge-as-object metaphor or as ascribing intentions to ideas. As already developed, we understand knowledge in terms of potentials to action—necessarily dynamic, even volatile, subject to continuous revisions as the knowing agent integrates/embodies new experiences. The principle that we are developing here is more about the importance of activating these potentials in the hope that they might trigger others and, in the process, be blended into more sophisticated possibilities. One need only look to the academic world for many examples of these sorts of mechanisms, including conferences, seminars, journals, hallway interactions, and visiting professorships, to mention only a few. A prominent metaphor that is used to point to such interactive structures is that of the conversation, foregrounding the contingent and engaged nature of the phenomenon.[11] Unfortunately, a more descriptive English vocabulary for this manner of ideational interaction has not yet emerged, hence our reliance on the somewhat troublesome, but nonetheless productive, notions of bumping, colliding, and juxtaposition of ideas.

All that said, there is often a physical component to the interaction of ideas. For notions to bump against one another, they must be represented in some way—for example, as oral expressions at conferences or as written statements in published texts. The juxtaposition of varied representations might then trigger other interpretations, which when represented might trigger still others. In other words, by underscoring the conceptual character of the agents in a knowledge-producing system, we do not mean to ignore or minimize the role of social interaction. The ideational network rides atop the social network. The point is that they should not be collapsed, in the same way that a personal web of meaning cannot be reduced to a neurological network or a body of knowledge cannot be reduced to practitioners. Brian Rotman's description of the relationship among mathematics (an ideational network), mathematicians (a social network), and mediating representations is cogent:

> Mathematics is an activity, a practice. If one observes its participants, then it would be perverse not to infer that for large stretches of time they are engaged in a process of communicating with themselves and one another; an inference prompted by the constant presence of standardly presented formal written texts (notes, textbooks, blackboard lectures, articles, digests, reviews, and the like) being read, written, and exchanged, and all informal signifying activities that occur when they talk, gesticulate, expound, make guesses, disagree, draw pictures, and so on.[12]

Not only must there be neighbor interactions, there must be a sufficient density of neighbors to interact. By way of familiar examples, in a traditional instruction-driven or an administration-heavy work setting, it would seem that conceptual possibilities are rarely crowded enough to occasion the emergence of rich interpretive moments. (Note that our point is not that such conceptual diversity is not present. It likely is. The issue is that the means to represent and blend extant insight may not be available.)

A perhaps surprising implication here is that the critical point is that mechanisms be in place to ensure that ideas will stumble across one another, *not* that there must be a particular sort of organizational structure in a social collective. Small group meetings, round-table discussions, face-to-face interactions, and so on may be no more effective than large conventions, straight rows, and text-mediated exchanges. Indeed, in some instances, the latter can be considerably more effective. To restate this vital point, then, complexity thinking explicates the importance of neighbor interactions, but offers little generalizable advice on means to accomplish the meeting and blending of ideas. Teachers and educational researchers must make provision for the representation and interaction of ideas, but the means of doing so must be considered on a case-by-case basis, contingent on the particular issues, contexts, and participants involved.

Our experience is that one of the first lessons of enabling neighboring interactions is that one must relinquish any desire to control the structure and outcomes of the collective. Consistent with such unities as brains, anthills, cities, and ecosystems, control in a knowledge-producing collective must be understood as decentralized, arising in localized activities.

Note that in this discussion of knowledge-producing systems, just as "neighbors" is used to refer to ideas, "control" has to do with emergent conceptual possibilities. We are in no way suggesting that teachers or educational researchers should abandon their responsibilities for organizing physical structures and spaces. Rather, we are talking about the development of interpretive reach, and that may entail rather rigid constraints on the physical system (as we discuss in the next section). The point is simply that *interpretive* possibilities (as opposed to physical conditions) cannot be managed. To impose a singular or centralized authority would be to extinguish the potential of the collective as a knowledge-producer.

An example of this issue is provided by current artificial intelligence research, where efforts to manage outcomes through speedy central processors and massive data bases have given way to projects developed around the parallel linking of small, specialized subsystems that are capable of learning and affecting one another (i.e., co-adapting and self-organizing)—in effect, to create systems that figure out what to do on their own by coordinating their specializations. Although researchers are still far from achieving the sorts of super intelligence projected by scientists and science fiction writers in the 1950s, considerably more progress has been made in the past decade with this decentralized, self-organized approach than was made in the preceding half-century with the massive computer approach.[13] Many other examples could be cited of the importance of decentralized control to the viability of a complex unity. In fact, Kelly[14] develops his account of the history of complexity science around the slow emergence of the realization that one must give up control if complexity is going to happen.

In the context of this discussion of education, it might seem that an immediate implication of this condition of complex emergence is that the teacher-centered classroom and the researcher-led study group are inherently problematic. Such may well be the case, at least insofar as the desire to achieve preset objectives, but the conclusion is not fully justified. In fact, the condition of decentralized control also serves to problematize the constructs of student-centered classrooms and participant-driven research. This condition of complex emergence compels us to question an assumption that underlies both teacher/researcher-centered and student/participant-centered arguments—namely, that the locus of learning is the individual. Learning occurs on other levels as well, and to appreciate this point one must be clear on the nature of the complex unities that might be desired in educational collectives. For us, these complex unities are shared ideas, insights, projects, concepts, and understandings that collectively constitute the group's *body* of knowledge. To underscore this point, the goal is not interpersonal collectivity, but collective knowing, noting once again that a knowledge-producing systems is not the same as the knowledge produced by the system.

Shared is a key notion here, and we use it deliberately as a synonym of *decentralized*. Commonly, expressions such as "shared knowledge" or "shared understandings" are taken to suggest samenesses in interpretation. However, the meaning intended here is consistent with usages in relation to responsibilities, meals, opportunities, and other objects or identifications. Just as such phenomena might be shared/distributed, so might collective projects and knowledge. But this suggestion only makes sense if the observer allows knowing and knowledge to be spread across agents in collective contexts.

This conception of shared/decentralized control prompts our attentions away from matters of a leader's actions and toward consensual domains of authority. Within a structure-determined complex system, external authorities cannot impose, but merely condition or occasion possibilities. The system itself "decides" what is and is not acceptable. Pragmatically speaking, with regard to shared/distributed work or understandings, the upshot is that a person should never strive to position herself or himself (or a text or other figurehead) as the final authority on matters of appropriate or correct action. Structures can and should be in place to allow students to participate in these decisions. For us, then, an important element in effective educational and research practices is the capacity to disperse control around matters of intention, interpretation, and appropriateness.

This issue is not a new one to education or to educational research. Indeed, as was developed in chapter 6, it has been thoroughly developed by a number of theorists and researchers who have adopted critical and liberatory stances—including, prominently, Paulo Freire, William Pinar, Madeleine Grumet, Michael Apple, and Elizabeth Ellsworth. Rejecting such dichotomies as child-versus-society, teacher-versus-learner, and knowledge-versus-knower, these theorists have offered alternative interpretations of authority. For example, instead of seeing it as an external and monological imposition, authority might be described in terms of capacities to invoke prevailing discourses—or, in complexity terms, to act within a consensual domain. Once again, the explicit purpose of these theorists' rhetorical gestures is to render problematic the assumption that the locus of learning is the individual. Within complexity thinking, just as learning is distributed among agents and across levels of organization, so is authority.

Or, perhaps more provocatively, just as learning is distributed, so is *authorship*. In a complex social system, the "object" at the center is never an individual, but an idea, a shared commitment, a common purpose, a collective orientation, an emergent possibility. That means that almost every social grouping, assuming adequate redundancy to enable some level of meaningful interaction, is always and already a complex unity. As any teacher will attest, for example, from the first days of the term, the members of each new classroom grouping are engaged in the complex activity of negotiating social positionings, establishing group norms, and inscribing a collective identity. These sorts of social activities unfold whether encouraged or not (indeed, in a conventional classroom, they tend to be discouraged; hence the obsessions with classroom management—that is, control of the knowledge-producing system—rather than decentralized control of the knowledge produced). The issue, then, is not whether the condition of decentralized control is present in a social collective—it is *always* there. Rather, the question is whether or not that condition can be meaningfully brought to bear on the development of concepts and interpretive possibilities.

Discussion Box 7.3 • Developing Trans-Level Knowledge

As noted in the previous discussion box, the teachers' responses to the "What is multiplication?" prompt were at first limited and seemed to offer little promise for discussion, let alone elaboration. However, when participants were asked to interact and to explore other interpretations, in rather short order they generated several other possibilities.

To enable the interactions of ideas, the researchers asked small discussion groups to prepare lists of their interpretations on posters. After an appropriate time to prepare these posters, the products were put on display at the front of the room. Through a combination of explanation, discussion, and questioning, key points were collected into a single summary poster, the contents of which follow:

Multiplication has to do with ...

- repeated addition: e.g., $2 \times 3 = 3 + 3$ or $2 + 2 + 2$;
- equal grouping: e.g., 2×3 can mean "2 groups of 3";
- number-line hopping: e.g., 2×3 can mean "make 2 hops of length 3";
- sequential folding: e.g., 2×3 can refer to folding a page in two parts and then into 3;
- many-layered: e.g., 2×3 means "2 layers, each of which contains 3 layers";
- the basis of proportional reasoning: e.g., 3 L at \$2/L costs \$6;
- the inverse of division—which makes division about repeated subtraction, equal separations, number-line fragmentation, etc.;

- a sort of intermediary of addition and exponentiation—i.e., multiplication is repeated addition, and exponentiation is repeated multiplication;
- array-generating: e.g., 2 × 3 gives you 2 rows of 3 or 2 columns of 3;
- area-producing: e.g., a 2 unit by 3 unit rectangle has an area of 6 units^2;
- dimension-changing;
- number-line stretching or compressing: e.g., 2 × 3 = 6 can mean that "3 corresponds to 6 when a number-line is stretched by a factor of 2".

By the end of the lengthy discussion, there was consensus that the concept of multiplication was anything but transparent. In particular, it was underscored in the interaction that multiplication was not the sum of these interpretations. It was some sort of complex conceptual blend. Teachers at all levels of schooling participate in the development and elaboration of the idea.

More significantly, perhaps, through the course of the research activity, it became more and more apparent that the mathematics of individual participants could not be distinguished from the emergent mathematical understanding of the collective itself. It became impossible to attribute authorship of particular understandings to one person or another. Moreover, the final product surpassed the knowledge of any single individual present. Its authorship was decentralized.

And even though the product was clearly a collective one, *every participant* attested to having learned a great deal about the topic. Several commented that they had learned more about multiplication through the session than they had learned at any other time. The learning, that is, occurred across at least two different levels of organization.

ENABLING CONSTRAINTS—
BALANCING RANDOMNESS AND COHERENCE

At first hearing, *enabling constraints* might sound like an oxymoron. It is, however, a notion that is critical to the potential for complex emergence. It refers to the structural conditions that help to determine the balance between sources of coherence that allow a collective to maintain a focus of purpose/identity and sources of disruption and randomness that compel the collective to constantly adjust and adapt.

Complex systems are rule-bound. Whether at the sub-cellular or super-species level, these unities are subject to imposed constraints. Some constraints are dictated by context, others by the structures of the unities, still others through co-implicated action of agents and setting. Regardless of source, however, the common feature of these constraints is that they are not prescriptive, but proscriptive. They are not imposed rules that one must obey in order to survive, but conditions that one must avoid in order to remain viable. To maintain coherence, for instance, a human must not leap off tall buildings, assault other humans, or ingest poisons. As Johnson phrases it, complex emergence occurs in

> rule-governed systems: their capacity for learning and growth and experimentation derives from their adherence to low level rules…. Emergent behaviors, like games, are all about living within boundaries defined by the rules, but also using that space to create something greater than the sum of its parts.[15]

There are many examples of proscriptive rule structures in social systems. Perhaps the most prominent instance for those raised within Judeo-Christian traditions are the Ten Commandments, a list of what one must not do (proscription), not what one must do (prescription). By proscribing unacceptable action rather than prescribing acceptable action, not only are the conditions for group identification (i.e., *coherence*) set, but an unexplored space of possibility (i.e., *randomness*) is opened.

To put a finer point on this matter, consider the following statements of research objectives:

1) Through this study, we will use Sleeman's protocol to determine the relative importance of key factors that contribute to success in young learners capacities to read—where reading is understood in terms of capacities to accurately decode age-appropriate texts.
2) In this study, we will investigate early literacy.

In complexity terms, both statements are flawed. The first, while clearly coherent, is too constrained and limiting. Its conclusions are assured, and in many ways presumed, in the manners in which the objective is articulated and the interpretive frame is specified. In order to pursue such a study, researchers would likely have to begin with already-formulated (prescriptive) lists of "factors" that would be observed and measured—and would therefore likely do little more than confirm the status quo or to verify common sense. The latter, by contrast, is likely much too undefined and ambiguous, opening the study to neurophysiological, psychological, sociological, and critical discussions that are simply too diverse to provide a meaningful shape to the research activity.

The structures that define complex social systems, in contrast, maintain a delicate balance between sufficient coherence to orient agents' actions and sufficient randomness to allow for flexible and varied response. Such situations are matters of neither "everyone does the same thing," nor "everyone does their own thing," but of "everyone participates in a joint project." In our experience, minor modifications in statements of purpose are sometimes all that is needed to transform tasks that are either too narrow or too open into enabling constraints. By way of example, a statement such as

> In this study, we will examine and contrast conceptions of "literacy" and the means to assess reading competence that are explicit and implicit in two prominent contemporary theories of learning: cognitivism and social constructivism.

Actually, we could have come up with literally dozens of possibilities. The critical features are (1) sufficient coherence based on a sufficiently constrained domain (i.e., in this case, discourses around "literacy") and (2) an openness to randomness in order to allow for the emergence of unanticipated possibilities (e.g., the juxtaposition of distinct discourses on learning).

The sort of randomness that we are discussing here is more a condition of the system's context that of the system itself. To reiterate an earlier point, the behavior of a complex unity is neither fixed nor chaotic. Rather, such systems are influenced by and take advantage of random contextual noise. Such noise can trigger a diversity of possibilities that might not otherwise arise. (In fact, the pervasive desire to minimize random noise is one of the reasons that some classrooms do not operate as intelligent collectives.) It is due to the inevitable presence of random noise that research problematics can rarely be rigidly set in advance, but must be subject to continuous revision through the course of the research as new insights emerge and new questions arise.

On this point, it is relevant to contrast approaches to defining questions between researchers in the physical sciences and researchers in the humanities and social sciences. The subjects of the latter tend to be considerably more dynamic—moving targets as it were—and thus generally call for a more flexible attitude toward both the posing of the question and the articulation of a methodology. This flexibility is neither a weakness nor a limitation. It is a necessary characteristic of being part of a complex emergent unity. That said, however, we would also highlight the tensions that can arise when a proscriptive attitude toward research is embraced in the contemporary, largely prescriptive educational context. The fit is not always a good one, especially when there are expectations for measurable results and demonstrations of methodological rigor. Yet the fact of the matter is that an educational research culture overshadowed by such insistences for more than a century seems to have generated little by way of stable and generalizable conclusions backed by irrefutable evidence. Complexity thinking would suggest that that will never happen.

Discussion Box 7.4 •
Enabling Constraints for Developing Knowledge

During research sessions, teachers are invited to work on shared interpretive and problem-solving tasks. These tasks are developed around mathematical topics that are selected by the teachers themselves and they are designed in ways that allow the researchers to map out some of the contours of their mathematical knowledge.

At first glance, it might seem that some of these tasks are rather narrow. Many of them—like the "What is multiplication?" example that has served as the focus of this linked series of discussions—appear to have immediate and well-established responses. Indeed, in most mathematics assessment contexts, they would likely be seen as questions as close-ended, with singular correct answers.

That quality is actually important. The participants need to perceive of the tasks as both relevant and do-able—that is, as coherent. At the same time, there must be sufficient play in the questions to open spaces for broader discussion. In the multiplication example, this quickly proved to be the case as teachers realized that their immediate responses did not reflect the actual conceptual complexity represented by the notion of multiplication. In other words, the follow-up "And what else?" served to flag a certain openness or ambiguity—a sort of inherent randomness.

Further to this point, as new interpretations were suggested and others blended, it grew increasingly apparent that not only is there no definitive response to the question, "What is multiplication?", but that the answer was always a moving target that is subject to endless recursive elaboration as new applications, images, and metaphors are tossed into the mix.

So framed, the principal role of the researchers is understood in terms of structuring tasks that are meaningful and appropriate to participants and to organize the settings in ways that allow participants and their ideas to interact. In the context of these discussions, the researchers listen in particular for teachers' commentaries on how they teach, might teach, and should teach. Embedded in such articulations are profound understandings of not just mathematical concepts, but the manner in which mathematical concepts are developed and learned. In other words, teachers' knowledge of established mathematics and their knowledge of how mathematics is established are inextricably intertwined. In different terms, for us, the phrase mathematics-for-teaching refers not just to a mastery of content, but also to teachers' understandings of the development of that knowledge on both individual and collective levels—a truly complex phenomenon.

OTHER CONDITIONS

The six conditions that we have presented in this chapter—that is, diversity, re-dundancy, neighbor interactions, decentralized control, coherence, and random-ness—are just part of a much longer list. Complexity researchers have identified many others, including

- negative feedback loops (mechanisms to keep systems in check, so that as-pects do not spiral out of control);
- positive feedback loops (means to amplify specific qualities or dynamics that may be of use to the system);
- the possibility of dying (given the interdependency of agents, a significant rupture in their interactivity—such as a shift in the relational web arising from the failure or departure of an agent—presents the possibility of cas-cading failure and catastrophic collapse of the system);
- means to preserve information (complex unities embody their histories and identities, so an inability to preserve relevant information will precipitate a collapse of the system);
- stability under perturbations (although existing far from equilibrium, the pat-terns of activity and interactivity that constitute a system must have some measure of stability);
- reproductive instability (there must be room for "error"—that is, for the emergence of variations on relatively stable patterns—if a system is going to be adaptable).

We could go on,[16] but will suffice it to say that our basis for selection of the conditions discussed in this chapter is the extent to which the educator or educa-tional researcher can affect or tinker. For instance, as the extended example illus-trates, we might readily occasion the expression of diverse understandings in a research collective or a classroom. However, by contrast, it is not (yet) clear to us how we might tinker with negative and positive feedback loops. For those, and the others listed above, we rely on conditions that are already present and well-developed in human social systems, but that tend to operate on biological or tacit levels.

A FEW CLOSING REMARKS: ON THE CONSTANT NEED TO RESTRUCTURE STRUCTURES

Accounts of complexity-informed research, such as the narrative we have used to illustrate this chapter, can never be offered as events to be replicated or even held up as models. At best, they can serve as illustrations, not exemplars. Indeed, we ourselves have failed in efforts to "replicate" studies in different settings, in large part because of inabilities to accommodate to the particularities of varied contexts. Encouraged by the fecundity of specific projects, we have on occasion misinterpreted or failed to perceive the ambiguities that arise between settings and, in the process, assumed a coherence that simply was not there.

In retrospect, in these instances, we failed to attend to the six conditions and the three dynamic balances discussed in this chapter. Yet even if we had, there was no guarantee that a similar richness would have been achieved. Complexity cannot be scripted or managed into existence.

Yet it can sometimes be occasioned. The critical issue developed in this chapter is that such occasioning is contingent not only on the appropriate conditions being in place, but for attentions to be oriented toward the appropriate level(s) of complex activity. In the example developed here, we focused on group collectivity and the consequences of such a focus for individual understanding and broader social contexts. Several other levels of complex co-activity remain to be addressed, and such is the topic of our closing chapter.

CHAPTER EIGHT

Pragmatic Complexity Research: VITAL SIMULTANEITIES

HISTORY AND MEMORY SHARE EVENTS;
THAT IS, THEY SHARE TIME AND SPACE.
EVERY MOMENT IS TWO MOMENTS

—Anne Michaels[1]

In this final chapter, we further develop the assertion made at the start of chapter 7—namely that complexity thinking might properly be construed as an educational discourse.

We organize this chapter around several vital simultaneities offered by complexity thinking, which we believe render it very well suited to the projects and concerns of educators and educational researchers. The word *simultaneity* refers to events or phenomena that exist or operate at the same time. It is used here as a contrast to the modern and Western habit of thinking in terms of *discontinuities* around such matters as theory and practice, knowers and knowledge, self and other, mind and body, art and science, and child and curriculum. In the context of popular debate, the terms of these sorts of dyads tend to be understood as necessarily distinct, opposed, and unconnected, even though they always seem to occur at the same time. In other words, such simultaneities tend to be seen as coincidental, not co-implicated. Complexity thinking troubles such an interpretation and, in the process, offers important advice on the projects of education and educational research.

A first simultaneity, the capacity of complexity thinking *both* to orient observational-descriptive work *and* to inform pragmatic concerns, was developed in the preceding chapters. This quality distinguishes complexity from most of the discourses that have been imported into education from other domains. In this chapter, which serves as both summary and elaboration of the rest of the book, we develop several other simultaneities, all of which have been introduced in some manner in preceding discussions:

- Knower & Knowledge,
- Transphenomenality,
- Transdisiplinarity,
- Interdiscursivity,
- Representation & Presentation,
- Affect & Effect, and
- Education and Research.

SIMULTANEITY 1 • KNOWER AND KNOWLEDGE

Through most of the history of Western thought, it has been assumed that knowers and knowledge are discontinuous. They have most often been cast in terms of two separate domains that must somehow be bridged. (We attempted to represent the figurative underpinnings of this conception in fig. 2.1.) The assumption of such a gap is particularly troublesome for educators who, within such a frame, are assumed to straddle the two realms. The role of educators is thus typically described in terms of the dual responsibility of representing objective knowledge and fostering subjective knowing, but these roles are usually understood as existing in tension. This knowledge/knower dichotomy has been institutionalized in the commonplace distinction between *curriculum* (generally used in reference to the educator's responsibilities toward established knowledge) and *pedagogy* (used in reference to the teacher's task of affecting knowers).

Not surprisingly, in efforts to cope, researchers and teachers have often downplayed or ignored the particularities of either knowledge or knowers. Alternatively, knowledge and knowers have sometimes been conflated, collapsed, or prioritized. In contrast, complexity thinking provides an alternative frame to this simultaneity, and it does so by noting that they belong to two different categories of phenomena—namely, as we described them in chapter 5, *knowledge-producing systems* and *systems of knowledge produced.*

Knowledge-producing systems—that is, knowers—are among the phenomena that are studied by those interested in *systems theory*, one of the major tributaries to complexity thinking. Systems theorists focus mainly on living systems, seeking to understand the manners in which *physical* systems self-organize and evolve. These systems include brains, individuals, social collectives, and cultures (among many others, such as beehives and slime molds). As noted in chapters 5 and 6, this area of inquiry also has a certain prominence among educational researchers, particularly those who have investigated the relational dynamics of students in classroom groupings.

Unfortunately, in broader discussions of the sociology of knowledge, there has been some confusion around the relationships between knowledge-producing systems and the systems of knowledge they produce. For example, studies of the tools, symbols, and interactive strategies of scientists have not often been undertaken alongside critical interrogations of the nature of science—or, if they have been simultaneously addressed, the knowledge-producing system (scientists) has often been conflated with the system of knowledge produced (science). This latter sort of system is among the core interests within cybernetics, which like systems theory is a major tributary to complexity thinking. In contrast to systems theory, cybernetics is more concerned with *ideational* systems than physical systems. Particular attentions are paid to the networked structures of ideas/concepts/information that, in a sense, "pass through" knowledge-producing systems. For example, personal knowledge tends to remain highly stable even though the physical system supporting it completely regenerates itself many times through a typical lifespan. Similarly, disciplinary knowledge can maintain its coherence through many generations of the thinkers and researchers.

We have attempted to portray some aspects of the dynamic and reflexive relationships between knowing systems and knowledge systems in figure 8.1. To reiterate the simultaneity, a knower is a physical system that might be described as a stable pattern in a stream of matter; a body of knowledge is an ideational system and might be understood in terms of stabilized but mutable patterns of acting that are manifest by a knower. In offering these descriptions, we in no way mean to gesture toward the body/mind or material/ideal dichotomies of ancient Western (esp. Greek) metaphysics. Quite the contrary, our point is that the ideational is inseparable from the material, but that their inseparability does not mean they are the same thing. In effect, we are offering a complexivist reading of an ancient intuition. A system of ideas is indeed transcendent of a material system; hence, knowers and knowledges can be considered separately, even if they cannot be considered separate. One cannot exist without the other; they are enfolded in and unfold from one another.

Throughout this text, we have been using the word *learning* to refer to ongoing transformations of both *knowledge-producing systems* and *systems of knowledge produced*. We might refine that usage by noting that learning can be understood more explicitly in terms of the continuous process through knower and knowledge are simultaneously redefined in relation to one another. Education, with its funda-

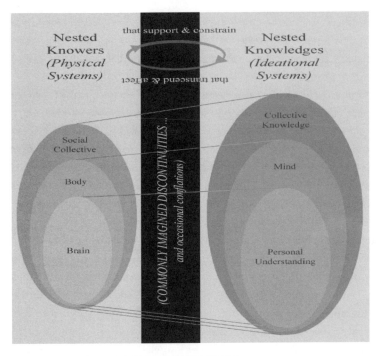

FIGURE 8.1 SOME KNOWERS AND THE KNOWLEDGES
Knowlede-producing systems (knowers) and the systems of knowledge they produce (knowledges) can both be understood as complex phenomena.

mental interest in matters of learning, is always already dealing with the knower-knowledge simultaneity—an insight that, as Dewey developed, is hardly new:

> Abandon the notion of subject-matter as something fixed and ready-made in itself, outside the child's experience; ... see [the child's experience] as something fluent, embryonic, vital; and we realize that the child and the curriculum are simply two limits which define a single process.[2]

SIMULTANEITIES 2, 3, AND 4 • TRANSPHENOMENALITY, TRANSDISCIPLINARITY, AND INTERDISCURSIVITY

One of our favorite "research" activities is to listen in on how practicing teachers use the word "they" during our visits to school staffrooms. The term might be in reference to individual students, or to clusters of neurons, or to classrooms, or to the world of adolescents, or to society, or any of a number of coherent collectives that are of relevance to the educational project. To cope with the task of educating, one must be able to jump fluidly among and across these levels of coherence.

Some roots of a personal understanding of multiplication:	Specific contributions
Innate capacities:	· distinction-making ability · pattern-noticing ability · rudimentary quantity sense
Pre-school (recursive) elaborations:	· experiences of collecting, ordering, sharing, etc. · refinement of object/quantity permanence · learning of a counting systems · preliminary development of number sense · preliminary development of binary operations (esp. addition)
Early grades (recursive) elaborations:	· physical action-based metaphors for binary operations · mastery of a symbol system for numbers and operations · grouping, repeated addition, and skip counting
Middle grades (recursive) elaborations:	· Introduction to range of images and applications · In particular, shift from discrete to continuous contexts · Conceptual blending of old and new metaphors, including ... grouping processes ... sequential folds ... many-layered ... ratios and rates ... grid-generating ... dimension-changing ... number-line-stretching or -compressing ... rotating ...
Senior grades (recursive) elaborations:	· broader range of applications · algebraic and graphical representations · distinguishing arithmetic, geometric, and exponential growth · severing of ties to concrete realm

TABLE 8.1 A SUMMARY OF THE ORIGINS OF PERSONAL UNDERSTANDINGS OF MULTI-PLICATION, AS UNDERSTOOD BY A COLLECTIVE OF MATHEMATICS TEACHERS

In a more formal attempt to study such *transphenomenal* hopping, we recently posed the question, "Where does a learner's understanding of multiplication come from?" during a meeting of the mathematics teachers' research collective that we introduced in chapter 7's discussion boxes. Their collective response, generated over the course of an hour of discussion, is presented in Table 8.1. As the entries in the table illustrate, these teachers are well aware that an individual's understanding of multiplication (or any other concept) only makes sense when considered in transphenomenal terms, as

- rooted in biological structure (genetic predisposition),
- framed by bodily activity (personal experience),
- elaborated within social interactions (symbolic tools),

- enabled by cultural tools (societal usages), and
- part of an ever-unfolding conversation of humans and the biosphere.

Unfortunately, in the main, the education literature simply does not treat such topics in this manner. Rather, investigations of issues such as personal understanding of multiplication tend to be oriented by an assumption that one level of analysis (e.g., the neurological level, or the symbolic-linguistic level) is sufficient for making sense of the matter.

An interesting aspect of the piece of research that we use to illustrate this point is that the teacher-participants did not seem to be aware that they were jumping among different levels of phenomena in their discussion of the origins of one's understanding of multiplication. We surmise that a reason for this unconscious but fluid level-hopping is that the relevant phenomena evolve at radically different paces (see fig. 2.3)—a realization that demands many categories of expertise and diverse methodologies if the overarching phenomena is to be studied in detail. In other words, a phenomenon as "simple" as personal understanding of multiplication demands a *transdisciplinary* approach.

Just as transphenomenality entails a sort of level-jumping, transdisciplinarity compels a sort of border-crossing—a need to step outside the limiting frames and methods of phenomenon-specific disciplines. We attempt to illustrate this point in the second column of Table 8.2, in which we list a few of the disciplines that are of immediate relevance to the issue of personal understanding of multiplication. Such a listing presents a powerful refutation of the early 19th-century assertion that education is an "applied psychology," or the more recent contention that teaching should be construed as an "applied science of the brain."[3] Clearly, such formulations engender profound ignorances of the complexity of the phenomenon at hand.

The third column of Table 8.2 is likely the one that would be troubling to most researchers. The discourses that support and are supported by the various disciplines are commonly seen as incompatible, if not flatly contradictory. Complexity thinking provides a means around this apparent impasse, and it does so by emphasizing the need to study phenomena at the levels of their emergence, oriented by the realizations that new stable patterns of activity arise and that those patterns embody emergent rules and laws that are native to the system.

This piece of advice requires that researchers pay particular attention to the paces of evolution at hand. For example, biological structure transforms over millennia and eons, and is thus sufficiently stable to lend itself to the assumptions of analytic science. By contrast, other phenomena, such as a culture's symbolic tools, not only evolve more quickly, but are subject to very different sets of influ-

Transphenomenality	Transdisciplinarity	Interdiscursivity
Personal understandings of multiplication are:	*Relevant disciplines include:*	*Relevant discourses include:*
· rooted in GENETIC structure (biological predisposition),	Neurology	Analytic Science
· framed by BODILY activity (personal experience),	Psychology	Phenomenology
· elaborated in SOCIAL interactions,	Sociology	Post-structuralism
· enabled by CULTURAL tools, and	Anthropology	Cultural Studies
· part of an ECOLOGICAL, ever-unfolding conversation of humans and the biosphere.	Ecology	Ecosophy (Ecological Philosophy)

TABLE 8.2 ONE ILLUSTRATION OF THE LEVELS OF PHENOMENA, INTERSECTIONS OF DISCIPLINES, AND INTERLACINGS OF DISCOURSES THAT ARISE IN THE STUDY OF EDUCATIONAL ISSUES

ences. Analytic methods are simply inappropriate to make sense of such disperse, rapidly changing, intricately entangled sets of phenomena.

It is thus that we would describe complexity thinking as a sort of *interdiscourse*. To remind, a *discourse* is a structurally coherent domain of language use—along with the activities associated with the use of that language—that organizes and constrains what can be said, done, and thought. Every discourse has its own distinctive set of rules, usually operating implicitly, that govern the production of what is to count as meaningful and/or true. Discourses always function in relation to or in opposition to other discourses. No discourse stands alone, although some (such as fundamentalist religion, scientism, or modernism) lay claim to a certain totalized and exclusive understanding of the universe.

Post-structuralist theory has contributed to understandings of interdiscursivity—that is, how discourses intersect, overlap, and interlace. But post-structuralism has been less effective at providing insight into how discourses intersect, overlap, and intersect with phenomena, in part because of a habit within post-structuralist thought of limiting discussions to the realm of human interest and interpretation. Phrased in terms of the contents of Table 8.2, post-structuralism is very useful for interpreting the mutual affects of disciplines discourses (columns 2 and 3). However, it has been less useful or effective in untangling the influences of disciplines and discourses (columns 2 and 3) on phenomena (column 1). Complexity thinking helps here by pressing beyond the boundaries of intersubjective constructions, as it refuses to collapse *phenomena* with *knowledge of phenomena*. These are inextricably entangled, but not coterminous.

As such, complexity thinking enables a simultaneous appreciation of the insights of such disparate discourses as post-structuralism and analytic science. Notably, as a collective, educational researchers have acknowledged this point. The discourses mentioned in the third column of Table 8.2 (among many, many others) are prominently represented in the current research literature. What is not so well represented—within single publications, at least—is the necessity of interdiscursivity. Indeed, most often in the contemporary literature, discourses are presented as oppositional rather than complementary. This sort of conclusion is inevitable if the transphenomenal character of educational "objects" is not taken into consideration.

SIMULTANEITY 5 • REPRESENTATION AND PRESENTATION

Of course, if one takes seriously the transphenonenal concerns, the transdisciplinary nature, and the interdiscursive character of education, one would quickly find oneself faced with unwieldy reports that would almost certainly undermine the practicality of important insights.

Complexity thinking, then, requires that the teacher or researcher seek out a balance between attention to and ignorance of detail. Indeed, the preceding three chapters were all organized around an implicit assumption that acts of perception and interpretation are always more about bracketing out possibilities than about being comprehensive. But, clearly, such bracketing can be troublesome.

The underlying issue here, however, is not really about bracketing; it's about the role of the published work. In our ongoing efforts to make sense of our particular responsibilities in this regard, we have found Albert Borgmann's commentary useful. He notes:

> What remains unexamined … is the power of products, of the material results of production, to shape our conduct profoundly. Any moral theory that thinks of the material setting of society as an essentially neutral stage is profoundly flawed and unhelpful; so, in fact, is most of modern and contemporary ethics.[4]

The written product, then, is not an endpoint, but a particular sort of participation—one that, by virtue of its lingering presence, may well have a more profound influence on life than that actual act of producing.

It is our assertion that this understanding must be brought to bear on understandings of academic discussions. That is, rather than thinking of scholarly engagement in terms of depictions of the way things are, research reports and theoretical accounts must be considered as forms that contribute to the shape of possibility. They are partial rather than comprehensive, active rather than inert, implicated rather than benign. In complexity terms, one cannot represent things as they are, simply because the representation contributes to the transformation of an always evolving reality. How, then, might one structure one's representations in ways that are mindful of such moral layerings?

We confess to have few answers here. As this text demonstrates, we are clearly comfortable with many of the *standard* and *normal* (cf. chap. 3) tools of the academic trade.[5] However, we have explored a few other (re)presentational strategies, and present some thoughts on them here, insofar as the forms of these strategies have enabled us to be attentive to our own complicity in the projects of education and educational research.

We proceed by acknowledging and further borrowing from post-structuralist thought, in particular the notion of deconstruction. Developed (mainly) by Jacques Derrida,[6] deconstruction refers to an interpretive approach to textual representations through which one attempts to flag the multitude of diverse and often conflicting "voices" that are speaking in a text—that is, its interdiscursivity. An example of this sort of work is our chapter 3, in which we foregrounded the hegemony of Euclidean-based imagery in academic writing.

Derrida and others have steadfastly avoided formal definitions or fixed strategies for deconstruction. As such, definitive statements on deconstruction as an attitude or method are impossible (and undesirable). It can be said that they engender a certain suspicion of metaphysical assumptions and internal contradictions of texts. In particular, Derrida saw dichotomies (binary oppositions) and hierarchies as hallmarks of Western thought. He sought to expose them in this writing while, at the same time, avoiding the creation of new ones (hence the need for fluidity of the notion of deconstruction—to fix it would be to suggest it complete or sufficient, thus superior to other approaches and attitudes). The refusal to create hierarchies or binaries and the attentiveness to flexible possibilities are obvious sites of compatibility between deconstruction and complexity thinking. (A difference is that complexity compels attentiveness to the biological as well as the social, whereas deconstruction is overwhelmingly focused on human-made texts.)

A further post-structuralist contribution is the notion of rhizomes, developed by Gilles Deleuze and Felix Guattari[7]—who actually borrow extensively from the language and imagery of complexity theory in their work. In brief, they point to the need to be aware of multiple interacting flows that, like the concealed root structures of some plants, give rise to similar structures in diverse domains, even though the interconnections and shared reliances of those structures remain hidden from view. Mindsets, Deleuze and Guattari argue, are fractal-like, concealing intricate patterns of supposition and conjecture beneath a veneer of coherence.

A lesson of deconstruction, rhizomatics, and associate notions is that the expository text (such as this one) is just one of many possible forms—one that tends to fall into traps of reductive explanation and conclusive certainty. Other modes are thus encouraged, provided that they too are subject to the same sort of deconstructive scrutiny. One would not want to critique one form only to be seduced by another.

One means to avoid such a seduction/reduction is articulated by Hans-Georg Gadamer[8] in his description of the work of art. For him, art has a two-fold function. It both *represents* (in the sense of calling something to mind, not in the sense of precise or fixed depiction) at the same time that it *presents* (that is, it opens up new interpretive possibilities). It is our conviction that the two-fold function of representation and presentation—this vital simultaneity—can (and should) also be a possibility for texts written in standard academic prose.

Such has, in fact, been our intention and hope with this text, throughout which we have operated mainly in an expository mode. In other writings we have attempted to present deconstructive readings, rhizomatics, and level-jumping more poetically, in manners that more actively and explicitly implicate readers or audiences. One example is a readers' theatre performance in which we made use of the literary/dramatic technique of "multiple threading."[9] Multiple threading involves the presentation of several narrative strands by, for example, moving from one setting to another between scenes or chapters. In a standard academic paper, the reader is typically expected to attend to a single thread of thought (see fig. 8.2) or possibly a few strands that might include discussions of related literature, methodological considerations, and data reporting (see fig. 8.3). In a multiple threaded paper, many strands are involved, some may be only brief phrases or single images that punctuate the text, and strands may overlap or interlink at times. An illustration of this sort of strategy is provided in figure 8.4, in which we present a mapping of the aforementioned readers' theatre.

The intention with this sort of presentational strategy is to "marry complex narrative structure with complex subject matter," as Johnson puts it.[10] More familiar examples of multiple threaded texts include such popular television series as *Seinfeld*, *Six Feet Under*, and *The Sopranos*. Within such a text, there is no dominant theme or plot, no clear distinctions among coincident threads. However, a single "scene" might serve to connect two or more strands at the same time, layering them atop one another. Notably, it is expected that each of these strands will have its own coherence. The driving idea is essentially complexivist: New

FIGURE 8.2 A REPRESENTATION OF A STANDARD ACADEMIC ARGUMENT
The horizontal axis is time (as experienced by the reader); the vertical axis points to the threads of discussion (as presented by the author). Each horizontal row represents a discrete thread of the discussion.

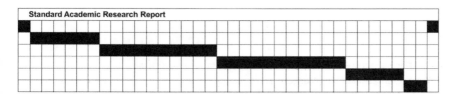

FIGURE 8.3 A REPRESENTATION OF A STANDARD ACADEMIC RESEARCH REPORT
The standard research report generally consists of several threads (e.g., statement of the problem, literature review, methodology, etc.) that are each engaged separately.

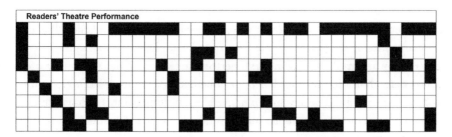

FIGURE 8.4 A REPRESENTATION OF OUR READERS' THEATRE PERFORMANCE
As with figures 8.2 and 8.3, each row represents a coherent thread of the discussion. Unlike the sorts of texts represented in those figures, the strands of the multiple threaded text might overlap and intersect. One purpose of this sort of simultaneous narrative threading is to render more apparent the complicity of the researchers/presenters and the interpretive engagement of the listeners/readers.

interpretive possibilities can arise in the interplay of already-coherent threads of thought.

Every complex phenomena can in some way be characterized as multiply threaded. Walter Gershon provocatively illustrates this point with a moment-by-moment transcription of simultaneous and overlapping interactions during a classroom episode, the first 12 seconds of which are presented in figure 8.5.[11] Gershon's example provides a cogent reminder that, as complex beings, we are always already caught up in and contributing to multiply threaded existences.

Seconds :01	:02	:03	:04	:05	:06
Participants:					
Conversation A					
Teacher		T: If Ihaveeleveninches and I takeawayeightinches/whaddo I have			
					thei
S1:/S9:					S1: Ahhh
S2:/S10:					
S3:/S11:					
S4:/S12:					
S5:/S13:					
S6:/S14:					
S7:					
S8:					
Juan					
Elsa					
Conversation B					
Marc	Do you think I'd be				Drawing
	able to beat you?				
Researcher (W)			At what?		

FIGURE 8.5 A MULTIPLY-THREADED TEXT FROM A CLASSROOM
This representation of simultaneous and overlapping interactions was developed by Walter Gershon. With it, he provocatively illustrates how, as complex beings who inhabit complex social and cultural spaces, our existences are multiply threaded.

This manner of presentation does not assume or pretend to offer a complete, unambiguous argument or depiction of some aspect of reality that is somehow intended to stand on its own, independent of author or audience. Rather, the partialities of the presenters are foregrounded at the same time as the listeners/readers are implicated in the text/performance. This is not to say that presenters are abdicating responsibility for coherence or interpretation. Quite the contrary, there should be a point (or, more likely, multiple points). However, the mode of presentation (vs. representation) does not allow for simplistic reductions of complex issues.

We offer this structure as merely one of many possibilities—and we re-emphasize that we do not mean to suggest that the standard format of an academic paper is inappropriate for addressing complex phenomena. It is more a case of it being *inadequate* for *all* reporting, especially when a vital aspect of that reporting is level-jumping. We see multiple threaded texts as a complement to, not a substitute or replacement for more conventional academic reporting strategies.

With current and emergent technologies, it is not difficult to imagine other modes of representation—involving, for example, hypertext or interactive web pages. As well, a number of powerful techniques have been developed in the dramatic and visual arts, many of which might be appropriate for use in academic and educational contexts. Other structures that we have explored have been drawn explicitly from fractal geometry.[12]

In brief, we do not perceive of our or anyone else's work in strictly *representational* terms, regardless of the intentions of the author. Even those research products oriented by a desire to depict or replicate the existing possible inevitably

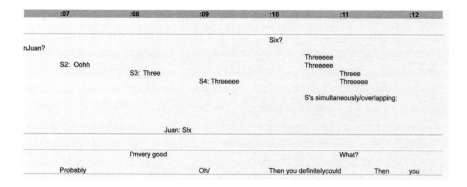

contribute to the expansion of the space of the possible—that is, as presentational as well as representational. For us, then, complexity thinking is eminently well-suited to education. Education is, after all, simultaneously representational and presentational.

SIMULTANEITY 7 • AFFECT AND EFFECT

In terms of conceptual influence, education is a net importer of theory and research. Indeed, the domain has a rather startling trade deficit. One rarely encounters the insights of educators or educational researchers in academic literatures outside the field.

The situation is unlikely to change any time soon, in part because description-oriented and phenomenon-specific disciplines may not have the means to embrace the transphenomenal and pragmatic character of educational inquiry. Nevertheless, complexity thinking offers a challenge to the mindset that seems to underlie educationists' willingness to take on methods and discourses developed elsewhere, without seeking to influence those methods and discourses.

We see this as an ethical issue. Educators and educational researchers are uniquely positioned to contribute to complexity thinking, in several ways. The most obvious arises in the transphenomenal nature of the educational project, the transdisciplinary character of educational research, and the necessarily interdiscursive nature of educational thought. Educational research thus provides an opportunity to complexify the methods and discourses that it draws on, and we would argue it has a concomitant responsibility to in some manner "reply" to the domains to which it listens.

Just as important, education sits at the intersection of virtually all domains of inquiry, including the disciplines that serve as source domains for curricula. It is becoming increasingly clear that the knowledge needed to teach these disciplines might be understood as a legitimate branch of inquiry within those disciplines, as evidenced by journals devoted to engineering education, medical education, and so on. This point has perhaps been best developed within mathematics education, where teachers' mathematics knowledge is coming to be recognized as a legitimate branch of mathematical inquiry[13] in which attentions are paid to the largely tacit bits of knowledge—the metaphors, analogies, images, applications, and gestures—that bubble to the surface in moments of teaching. The fact that educational insights are being, in effect, exported to domains such as mathematics is instructive. The relationship between education and other domains need not be understood strictly in terms of unidirectional affect. Educators and educational researchers can and should have some effect on other realms.

Complexity thinking provides the elaboration that, not only *should* this be the case, it inevitably *is* the case. This assertion is informed by emergent realizations that initiates exert profound influences on knowledge domains. For example, children, not adults, represent the most potent force in the ongoing evolution of language as they even out inconsistencies in grammar, invent new associations, and impose other modifications to render verbal communication more user-friendly.[14] Similarly, with regard to specific disciplinary domains, such pedagogical acts of selecting topics, structuring classroom experiences, and defining acceptable standards of academic performance contribute profoundly to the shape of a realm of knowledge—especially those realms that are included in grade school curricula. Formal education does much more than draw from disciplinary knowledge; it helps to shape them. The dimension we are highlighting here is that the effects of educational inquiry on other domains should be more conscious and deliberate. Educationists, that is, must be more attuned to their complicity in the academic world.

The implications of this assertion extend to the realm of complexity thinking itself. Educationists must take care to go beyond importation of insights (and the associated responsibility for accurate representations), to think in terms of elaboration of those insights (that is, presentation). We can point to a few emerging possibilities that are organized around a recognition of relationships among biological and social processes. By way of illustration, interpretations of classroom dynamics in terms of life cycles or the body's circadian rhythms could not only help to make sense of the temporally synchronized social behaviors of individuals within groups, but to inform other domains in which social-coactivity is central. To this end, Darren Stanley has offered the notion of "comparative dynamics," a sort of inter-systemic examination of similarities and differences on the level of the dynamical patterns—by which, for example, the profile of a healthy heart's activity might be compared with the profile of activity in a school.[15]

Similar could be said about both other qualities of complex unities (developed in chap. 5) and conditions of complex emergence (introduced in chap. 7). We suspect that one of the major contributions of educators and educational researchers to complexity thinking will be in this regard. After all, few others are so centrally concerned and intimately familiar with the working of human collectivities. The fact that some educators can be so effective at prompting the co-activity of humans under such artificial, mechanically-conceived conditions suggests a depth of (enacted) knowledge that is waiting to be rendered available for others.

We anticipate that another aspect of this contribution will be around the temporal qualities of complex unities. What is the pace of life at the level of social collectivity? Of knowledge? Once again, educationists would seem to be uniquely positioned to address these sorts of questions.

SIMULTANEITY 8 • EDUCATION AND RESEARCH

Over the past decade, we have experienced a deep compatibility between complexity thinking and hermeneutic inquiry. Hermeneutics is oriented by the entangled questions, "What is it that we believe?", "How is it that we came to think this way?", and "What is being taken for granted about the nature of reality, truth, and existence?"[16] Complexity thinking addresses each of these questions—and, importantly, does not settle on conclusive answers. The point, then, is not that everyone should agree, but that there must be an attitude of openness toward new possibilities.

Over recent years, an increasing number of educators and educational researchers have demonstrated just such an openness.[17] For our own part, the need to attend to theory has meant endeavoring to keep pace with the latest literature in the field. As well, we feel there to be an obligation to tinker with vocabulary. In this regard, we follow Richard Rorty's description of *ironists*:

> The ironist ... takes the unit of persuasion to be a vocabulary rather than a proposition. Her method is redescription rather than inference. Ironists specialize in redescribing ranges of objects or events in partially neologistic jargon, in the hopes that by the time she is finished using old words in new senses, not to mention introducing brand new words, people will no longer ask question phrased in the old words.[18]

A brief illustration of how one might take up Rorty's exhortation: Consider, for a moment, human consciousness, a phenomenon that depends on social collectivity at the same time as it is always personal and individual. As Donald[19] explains, human cognitive systems (or minds) are hybrid; they depend on both an individual brain and various levels of collectivity. To understand consciousness, one must be willing and able to think in transphenomenal terms and engage in transdiscipinary ways. Yet it is only recently that consciousness studies have developed into a domain in which, for example, neurologists routinely work with psychologists and anthropologists to better understand how electronic technologies are transforming the very nature of human awareness.[20]

Endeavoring to put an ironical twist on the notion, we would assert that education falls into the same class of phenomena as consciousness and thus demands a similar attitude of its practitioners and its researchers. In fact, it is tempting to suggest a metaphor of "formal education as cultural consciousness." Just as one's consciousness serves to bring certain aspects of personal experience to awareness, formal education is a means by which certain aspects of collective experience are foregrounded within the body politic. Developing the analogy a bit further, it is interesting to note that one's consciousness does not control one's experience,[21] although it does play an important orienting role. Phrased differently, perception, interpretation, and identity are not *determined by* consciousness, but they are *dependent on* consciousness. In a similar sense, formal education does not play a deterministic role in the unfolding of society, but does play an important orienting role that profoundly affects culture.

An obvious problem with this analogy is, of course, the deliberate nature of formal education: It can be understood, in effect, in recursive terms of conscious efforts to organize individual consciousnesses. In comparison, human self-awareness seems much more contingent, even accidental. Yet even here the contrast is probably less pronounced than might be expected. For example, the extent to which curricula reflect emergent worldviews, knowledge, technologies, and social issues illustrates that formal education is highly dependent on evolving circumstances. Just as individual consciousness seems to lag behind the personal experience,[22] in a very strong sense, formal education lags behind the events of the world. Like consciousness, education offers commentary, it orients, it helps to render events sensible, it contributes to the ongoing reorganization of the system's resources, and it assists in the coordination of other aspects of the grander unity—all while dealing with only a tiny portion of the vast corpus of knowledge of the grander body.

Our purpose in presenting this example of irony, in Rorty's sense of the word, is to develop the suggestion that educational research and educational practice might be considered aspects of the same project—namely, expanding the space of human possibility by exploring the space of the existing possible.

A CLOSING NOTE ON COMPLICITY:
THE NEED FOR CRITICAL REFLECTION

One of the grand errors of classical inquiry has been the mistaking of the theo-retical, the descriptive, and/or the experimental result with stable and secure knowl-edge. Complexity thinking does not permit this error—and not only because phenomena that learn cannot be pinned down with certainty. The major issue here is the tendency for the theorist/observer/experimenter to write himself or herself out of the research result. The complexity researcher has an obligation—an ethical imperative, we would argue—to be attentive to how she or he is impli-cated in the phenomenon studied.[23]

This is especially the case for educational research, which must become more aware of its consequences. As developed in previous chapters, interpretive frames that are powerful at the level of research have been distorted in textbooks and other resources for teachers, giving rise to claims and practices that are simply indefensible. Yet one hears very little from the theorists and researchers who continue to publish at pace, either oblivious to the troublesome consequences of their efforts or unwilling to accept any responsibility.

In foregrounding the overlapping and interlaced characters of social sys-tems—such as research communities and teacher collectives—complexity think-ing does not allow for such ignorances and abdications. To the extent possible, complexity researchers are obligated to be attentive to the consequences and im-plications of their efforts. As such, among the intertwining questions that we ask ourselves within any research project are the following:

- How am I complicit (i.e., affecting or hoping to affect) the phenomenon that I study?
- How is this research *educational*—that is, how does it educate?
- How might his research be taken up?
- How might I represent/present these interpretations?

In brief, this issue is a moral one, and we use the word *moral* in the complexified sense of implying an "ethics of care, responsiveness, and responsibility."[24] As David Michael Levin explains, there are two different ways of thinking about moral problems:

> (1) a competitive model, which gives primacy to the individual and relies on the supervenience of formal and abstract rules to achieve co-operation and consensus and (2) a cooperative model, which given primacy to relation-ships and relies on contextual narratives and dialogue—communication....[25]

The notion of complicity invokes the latter conception of morality. And that is where we will leave this discussion—not with a sense of conclusion or finality, but with an acknowledgment that in the profoundly moral-ethical domain of education, we must give primacy to relationship and rely on communication.

ENDNOTES

PREFACE

1. J. Derrida, *Limited, Inc.* (Evanston, IL: Northwestern University Press, 1988): 119.
2. The Complexity and Education site is organized and maintained by a collective of faculty members, graduate students, and postdoctoral fellows at the University of Alberta. **<http://www.complexityandeducation.ca>**
3. As developed in chapter 2, the phrase "complexity thinking" was proposed by K.A. Richardson & P. Cilliers in their editorial, "What is complexity science? A view from different directions," in a special issue of *Emergence*, vol. 3, no. 1 (2001): 5–22. Available at <http://www.kurtrichardson.com/Editorial_3_1.pdf>.

CHAPTER ONE — WHAT IS "COMPLEXITY"?

1. Albert Einstein, quoted in *Reader's Digest*, October, 1977.
2. Cited in B. Chui, "'Unified theory' is getting closer, Hawking predicts," *San Jose Mercury News*, Sunday Morning Final Editions, January 23, 2000, p. 29A.
3. For additional information, see the Complexity and Education website <http://www.complexityandeducation.ca> or the Complexity Digest page <http://www.comdig.org/>. Both offer links to sites of a number of institutes and centers devoted to the study of complexity.
4. This particular phrase is adapted from the controversial *No Child Left Behind* educational initiative of the George W. Bush administration. In the documents accompanying the initiative, the term is used to frame an argument that educational research should measure up to the same standards as medical research—an assertion that is absurd within a complexity science frame. See chapter 3.
5. M.M. Waldrop, *Complexity: the emerging science on the edge of order and chaos.* (New York: Simon & Schuster, 1992).
6. See, e.g., R. Lewin, *Complexity: life at the edge of chaos* (New York: Macmillan, 1992); Waldrop, 1992; K. Kelly, *Out of control: the new biology of machines, social systems, and the economic world* (Cambridge, MA: Perseus, 1994); S. Johnson, *Emergence: the connected lives of ants, brains, cities, and software* (New York: Scribner, 2001).
7. W. Weaver, "Science and complexity," in *American Scientist*, vol. 36, 536–544. Available online at <http://www.conceptualinstitute.com/genre/weaver/weaver-1947b.htm>.

8. Weaver actually used the terms *simple, disorganized complexity*, and *organized complexity*. The terms *simple, complicated*, and *complex* reflect more current usages. See, e.g., Waldrop, 1992 or Johnson, 2001.

9. P.S. de Laplace, *A philosophical essay on probabilities*, translated by F.W. Truscott & F.L. Emory (New York, Dover, 1951; published in the original French in 1814).

10. H. Poincaré, *Science and hypothesis* (London: Walter Scott Publishing, 1905).

11. Significantly, Poincaré did not problematize the assumption of a determinate universe—that is, a universe like the one described by Laplace. Rather, Poincaré seriously questioned the belief that humans would ever be able to determine anything but the simplest of phenomena.

12. S. Kauffman, quoted in R. Ruthen, "Trends in nonlinear dynamics: adapting to complexity," in *Scientific American*, vol. 269 (January, 1993): 130–140.

13. Ibid.

14. C. Dyke, *The evolutionary dynamics of complex systems* (Oxford: Oxford University Press, 1988).

15. Of course, it is possible to take the discussion further in both the micro and macro directions, eventually meeting up with the phenomena that are difficult to classify as either complicated (mechanical) or complex (learning). As our purpose in this text is to focus on those phenomena that are of interest and relevance to educational researchers, we deliberately avoid this phenomena and the theoretical and philosophical debates that emerge when the discussion is pressed further.

16. J. Cohen & I. Stewart, *The collapse of chaos: discovering simplicity in a complex world* (New York: Penguin, 1994): p. 414.

17. Ibid., p. 412.

18. Ibid., p. 414.

CHAPTER TWO—WHAT IS "SCIENCE"?

1. D. Dennett, *Darwin's dangerous idea: evolution and the meanings of life* (New York: Touchstone, 1995): p. 21.

2. Richardson & Cilliers, 2001.

3. Waldrop, 1992; Johnson, 2001.

4. J. Jacobs, *The death and life of great American cities* (New York: Vintage, 1961).

5. D. Gordon, *Ants at work: how an insect society is organized* (New York: Free Press, 1999).

6. F. Engels, *The condition of the working class in England* (New York: (Penguin, 1987).

7. R. Carson, *Silent spring* (New York: Houghton Mifflin Company, 1962).

8. H. Maturana, "Autopoiesis: reproduction, heredity and evolution," in *Autopoiesis, dissipative structures, and spontaneous social orders*, edited by M. Zeleny (Boulder, CO: Westview, 1980).

9. See, e.g., the "Sims" website, <http"//thesims.ea.com/>, or the "interactive and

visual representations link at the website of the New England Complex Systems Institute, <http://necsi.org/>.

10. E.g., Lewin, 1992; Waldrop, 1992.

11. See Kelly, 1994, for a survey of these sorts of research projects.

12. Ibid. See also R. Lewin & B. Regine, *Weaving complexity and business: engaging the soul at work* (New York: Texere, 2000).

13. In fact, it seems that this conception of the project of modern science may be 'true' only in the popular imagination. A number of prominent scientists view the project quite differently. See, e.g., E.F. Keller, *Making sense of life: explaining biological developments with models, metaphors, and machines* (Cambridge, MA: Harvard University Press, 2002).

14. See B. Davis, *Inventions of teaching: a genealogy* (Mahwah, NJ: Lawrence Erlbaum Associates, 2004) for a fuller account of this worldview discussed alongside associated and contrasting sensibilities.

15. See, e.g., J.H. Holland, *Emergence: from chaos to order* (Reading, MA: Helix, 1998); S. Kauffman, *At home in the universe: the search for the laws of self-organization and complexity* (New York: Oxford University Press, 1995).

16. D. Osberg, *Curriculum, complexity and representation: rethinking the epistemology of schooling through complexity theory* (unpublished doctoral dissertation, Open University, Milton Keynes, UK, 2005).

17. Cohen & Stewart, 1994. See chapter 1 for a discussion of these notions.

18. S.Y. Auyang, *Foundations of complex-system theories in economics, evolutionary biology, and statistical physics* (Cambridge: Cambridge University Press, 1998).

19. R. Rucker, in *Mind tools: the mathematics of information* (New York: Penguin, 1987), discusses and illustrates the "memories as fractally structured" metaphor.

20. See D. Watts, *Six degrees: the science of the connected age* (New York: W.W. Norton, 2003).

21. E.g., S.A. Barab & M. Cherkes-Julkowski, "Principles of self-organisation: learning as participation in autocatakinetic systems," in *The Journal of the Learning Sciences*, vol. 8, nos. 3 & 4 (1999): 349–390; C.D. Ennis, "Reconceptualizing learning as a dynamical system," in *Journal of Curriculum and Supervision*, vol. 7, (1993): 115–130; M. Resnick, *Turtles, termites, and traffic jams: explorations in massively powerful microworlds* (Cambridge, MA: The MIT Press, 1995); M. Resnick, "Beyond the centralized mindset," in *Journal of Learning Sciences*, vol. 5, no. 1 (1996): 1–22; D. Sawada & M.T. Caley, "Dissipative structures: new metaphors for becoming in education," in *Educational Researcher*, vol. 14, no. 3 (1985): 13–19; U. Wilensky & M. Resnick, "Thinking in levels: a dynamic systems approach to making sense of the world," in *Journal of Science Education and Technology*, vol. 8, no. 1 (1999): 3–19.

22. E.g., M. Cherkes-Julkowski, "The child as a self-organizing system: the case against instruction as we know it," in *Learning Disabilities*, vol. 7, no. 1 (1996): 19–27; M. Cherkes-Julkowski & N. Mitlina, "Self-organization of mother-child instructional

dyads and later attention disorder," in *Journal of Learning Disabilities*, vol. 32, no. 1 (1999): 6–21; B. Davis & E. Simmt, "Understanding learning systems: mathematics teaching and complexity science," in *Journal for Research in Mathematics Education*, vol. 34, no. 2 (2003): 137–167; W.E. Doll, Jr., "Complexity in the classroom," in *Educational Leadership*, vol. 47, no. 1 (1989): 65–70; E.B. Mandinach & H.F. Cline, *Classroom dynamics: implementing a technology-based learning environment* (Hillsdale, NJ: Lawrence Erlbaum Associates, 1994); J. Rasmussen, "The importance of communication in teaching: a system-theory approach to the scaffolding metaphor," in *Journal of Curriculum Studies*, vol. 33, no. 5 (2001): 569–582; M. Resnick & U. Wilensky, "Diving into complexity: developing probabilistic decentralized thinking through role-playing activities," in *Journal of Learning Sciences*, vol. 7, no. 2 (1998): 153–172.

23. E.g., J.D. Dale, "The new American school: a learning organization," in *International Journal of Educational Reform*, vol. 6, no. 1 (1997): 34–39.; B. Davis & D. Sumara, "Cognition, complexity, and teacher education," in *Harvard Educational Review*, vol. 67, no. 1 (1997): 105–125; B. Davis, D.J. Sumara, & T.E. Kieren, "Cognition, co-emergence, curriculum," *Journal of Curriculum Studies*, vol. 28, no. 2 (1996): 151–169; M.J. Jacobson, K. Brecher, M. Clemens, W. Farrell, J. Kaput, K. Reisman, & U. Wilensky, *Education in complex systems* (Nashua, NH: New England Complex Systems Institute, 1998).

24. E.g., G.A. Cziko, "Unpredictability and indeterminism in human behavior: arguments and implications for educational research," in *Educational Researcher* (1989 April): 17–25; J.A. Middleton, D. Sawada, E. Judson, I. Bloom, & J. Turley, "Relationships build reform: Treating cleassroom research as emergent systems," in L.D. English (ed.), *Handbook of International Research in Mathematics Education* (Mahwah, NJ: Lawrence Erlbaum Associates, 2002): 409–431.

25. Sawada & Caley, 1985.

26. W. Doll, Jr., *A post-modern perspective on curriculum* (New York: Teachers' College Press, 1993).

27. See, e.g., R. Rorty, *Contingency, irony, solidarity* (New York: Cambridge University Press, 1989).

28. By some accounts, these limitations are extreme. It appears that fewer than one out of every million sensorial possibilities—that is, events that are sufficiently intense to activate some part of a human being's sensory system—actually bubbles to the surface of consciousness. See T. Norretranders, *The user illusion: cutting consciousness down to size* (New York: Viking, 1998), for an overview of the research into consciousness.

29. Adapted from B. Davis, D. Sumara, & R. Luce-Kapler, 2000, p. 73.

30. See C. Seife, *Zero: the biography of a dangerous number* (New York: Viking Penguin, 2000).

31. The significance of the varied temporal dimensions of these nested and mutually embedded phenomena is not merely a matter of speculation. In his research into

subpersonal, personal, and interpersonal processes, neurophenomenologist Francisco Varela has examined the "sizes" of the three different scales of lived time. According to Varela, the time scale for one's personal feeling of "nowness"—that is, the time scale a conscious moment, during which one's awareness begins to play a role in one's actions—is in the range of one (10^0) second. The time scale of separable perceptual events, which can affect one's actions but which may not register in consciousness, is in the order of 0.1 (i.e., 10^{-1}) seconds. And, according to Varela, *narrative time*—that is, the temporal scale at which personal experience is knitted into the fabric of social collectivity—is in the range of 10 (i.e., 10^1) seconds.[1] In somewhat different terms, as one moves from automatic regulation of perceptual events to/through conscious regulation of awarenesses to/though social regulation of interpretations, the time required increases approximately by factors of 10. (As is developed in chap. 3, there are corresponding decreases in the numbers of events as one moves upward through these levels. They obey what is known as a *power distribution*.) See D. Rudhauf, A. Lutz, D. Cosmelli, J.-P. Lachaux, & M. le van Quyen, "From autopoiesis to neurophenomenology: Francisco Varela's exploration of the biophysics of being," in *Biological Research*, vol. 36 (2003): pp. 27–65.

32. See Davis, 2004, for a fuller discussion and an extended illustration of bifurcations.

33. F. de Saussure, *Course in general linguistics*, trans. W. Baskin (New York: Philosophy Library, 1959).

34. T. Kuhn, *The structure of scientific revolutions* (Chicago: University of Chicago Press, 1962).

35. K. Popper, *Conjectures and refutations* (London: Routledge & Kegan Paul, 1963).

36. See, e.g., A. Sokal & J. Bricmont, *Intellectual impostures: postmodern philosopher's abuse of science* (London: Profile Books, 1998).

37. See, e.g., H.R. Maturana, "Science and daily life: the ontology of scientific explanations," in W. Krohn & G. Kuppers (eds.), *Self-organization: portrait of a scientific revolution* (Dordrecht: Kluwer Academic Publishers, 1990).

38. P. Cilliers, *Complexity and postmodernism* (London: Routledge , 1998), p. 11.

39. Ibid., p. 72.

40. J.-F. Lyotard, *The postmodern condition: a report on knowledge*, Trans. G. Bennington & B. Massumi. (Minneapolis: University of Minnesota Press, 1984), p. *xxiv*.

CHAPTER THREE—THE SHAPE OF COMPLEXITY

1. B.B. Mandelbrot, *The fractal geometry of nature* (San Francisco: W.H. Freeman and Co., 1982), p. 4.

2. The act and associated discussion papers can be found online at <http://www.ed.gov/policy/elsec/leg/esea02/index.html>.

3. V. Reyna, *What is scientifically based evidence? What is logic?* Full text available at <http://www.ed.gov/nclb/methods/whatworks/research/page_pg3.html>.
4. E.g., Lyotard, 1984; A. Borgmann, *Crossing the postmodern divide* (Chicago: University of Chicago Press, 1989).
5. E.g., Rorty, 1989.
6. E.g., G. Lakoff & M. Johnson, *Philosophy in the flesh: the embodied mind and its challenge to Western thought* (New York: Basic Books, 1999).
7. Rorty, 1989.
8. R.L. Chapman (editor), *Roget's international thesaurus, fourth edition* (Toronto: Fitzheny & Whiteside, 1977).
9. E.g., Davis, Sumara, Luce-Kapler, 2000; M. Foucault, *Abnormal: lectures at the Collège de France, 1974–1975,* trans. G. Burchell (New York: Picador, 2003).
10. See M. Gardner, "In which 'monster' curves force redefinition of the word 'curve'," in *Scientific American,* vol. 235 (December 1976), 124–129.
11. Mandelbrot, 1982.
12. See J. Gleick, *Chaos: making a new science* (New York: Penguin, 1987).
13. Mandelbrot, 1982.
14. I. Stewart, *Life's other secret: the new mathematics of the living world* (Cambridge, UK: Cambridge University Press, 1998).
15. See I. Stewart, *Does God play dice?* (Cambridge, MA: Blackwell, 1989).
16. Ibid., p. 83.
17. Ibid.
18. I. Stewart & J. Cohen, *Figments of reality: the evolution of the curious mind* (New York: John Wiley & Sons, 1997), p. 187.
19. See, e.g., P.R. Ehrlich, *Human natures: genes, cultures, and the human prospect* (New York: Penguin, 2000).
20. See., e.g., D.D. Hoffman, *Visual intelligence: how we create what we see* (New York: W.W. Norton, 1998).
21. Cohen & Stewart, 1994, p. 369.
22. M. Buchanan, *Ubiquity: The science of history … or why the world is simpler than we think* (London: Phoenix, 2000), p. 184. See also P. Bak, *How nature works: the science of self-organized criticality* (New York: Springer-Verlag, 1996).
23. Watts, 2003, p. 25.
24. E.g., A.-L. Barabàsi, *Linking: how everything is connected to everything else and what it means for business, science, and everyday life* (New York, Penguin, 2002); M. Buchanan, *Nexus: small worlds and the groundbreaking theory of networks* (New York: W.W. Norton, 2002); Watts, 2003.
25. See S. Milgram, "The small world problem," in *Psychology Today,* vol. 2 (1967): 60–67; J. Guare, *Six degrees of separation: a play* (New York: Vintage, 1990).
26. Barabàsi, 2002. For a gallery of images of the evolving internet, visit <http://research.lumeta.com/ches/map/gallery/>.

27. W. Calvin, *How brains think: evolving intelligence, then and now* (New York: Basic Books, 1996), p. 120.

28. Based on P. Baran, *Introduction to distributed communications networks*, available at <http://www.rand.org/publications/RM/baran.list.html>.

29. R. Upitis, "School architecture and complexity," in *Complicity: An International Journal of Complexity and Education*, vol. 1, no. 1 (2004): 19–38.

30. Barabàsi, 2002, p. 237.

31. For an example of this sort of work, see M. de Landa, *A thousand years of nonlinear history* (New York: Zone Books, 2000).

32. See Buchanan, 2000, for a fuller account.

33. J. Surowiecki, *The wisdom of crowds: why the many are stronger than the few and how collective wisdom shapes business, economies, societies, and nations* (New York: Doubleday, 2004), p. 161.

34. D.J. de Solla Price & D.B. Beaver, "Collaboration in an invisible college," in *American Psychologist*, vol. 21 (1966): 1107–1117. See also, H. Zuckerman, "Nobel laureates in science: patterns of productivity, collaboration and authorship," in *American Sociological Review*, vol. 32 (1967): 391–403.

35. See, e.g., B.V. Carolan & G. Natriello, "Data-mining journals and books: using the science of networks to uncover the structure of the educational research community," in *Educational Researcher*, vol. 34, no. 3 (2005 April), 25–33, C. Chen & R.J. Paul, "Visualizing a knowledge domain's intellectual structure," in *IEEE* (2001 March), 65–71.

CHAPTER FOUR—THE NETWORK OF COMPLEXITY

1. J. Muir, *My first summer in the Sierras* (New York: Houghton Mifflin, 1911/1998).

2. See Surowiecki, 2004 for several case studies of this point, both inside and outside of science.

3. J. Dewey, "The influence of Darwin on philosophy," in *The influence of Darwin on philosophy and other essays* (New York, Henry Holt, 1910): 1–19.

4. P. Freire, *Pedagogy of the oppressed* (New York: Seaview, 1971).

5. See, e.g., Lyotard, 1984; Sokal & Bricmont, 1997.

6. Nicolas Bourbaki is not a single person, but a collective. The name was adopted by a group of mathematicians in the early 1900s who were intent on redefining all of mathematics in terms of a formal propositional system.

7. For a more thorough discussion of this issue, see B. Davis & D. Sumara, "Constructivist discourses and the field of education: problems and possibilities," in *Educational Theory*, vol. 52, no. 4 (2002): 409–428.

8. Any text from Foucault's considerable opus would illustrate this point, e.g., *Discipline and punish: the birth place of the modern prison* (New York: Pantheon, 1977), *The history of sexuality, an introduction* (New York, Vintage, 1990).

9. E.g., D. Britzman, *Practice makes practice: a critical study of learning to teach* (Albany, NY: State University of New York Press, 1991).

10. E.g., C. Cherryholmes, *Power and criticism: poststructural investigations in education* (New York: Teachers College Press, 1988); P. Lather, *Getting smart: feminist research and pedagogy with/in the postmodern* (New York: Routledge, 1991).

11. H. Maturana, "Everything is said by an observer," in W.I. Thompson (ed.), *Gaia: a way of knowing* (Hudson, NY: Lindisfarne Press, 1987): 65–82.

12. B. Latour, "On objectivity," in *Mind, Culture, and Activity*, vol. 3, no. 4 (1996): 228–245.

13. B. Davis & D. Sumara, "Why aren't they getting this? Working through the regressive myths of constructivist pedagogy," in *Teaching Education*, vol. 14, no. 2 (2003): 123–140; B. Davis & D. Sumara, "Listening to how you're heard: on translations, mistranslations, and really bad mistranslations (A response to Stuart McNaughton and Nicholas Burbules)," in *Teaching Education*, vol. 14, no. 2 (2003): 149–152.

14. M. Merleau-Ponty, *Phenomenology of perception* (London: Routledge & Kegan Paul, 1962; published in the original French in 1948).

15. E.g., see M. Grumet, *Bitter milk: women and teaching* (Amherst, MA: University of Massachusetts Press, 1988).

16. Johnson, 2001.

17. Morphogenesis refers to the ability of life-forms to develop more and more complex bodies out of vastly simpler beginnings.

18. Jacobs, 1961.

19. Literally, self-creating.

CHAPTER 5—DESCRIPTIVE COMPLEXITY RESEARCH: QUALITIES OF LEARNING SYSTEMS

1. D.W. Thomson, *On growth and form* (London: Cambridge University Press, 1917).

2. Several articles have been published out of this work, including: Davis & Sumara, "Cognition, complexity, and teacher education,"; D. Sumara & B. Davis, "Enactivist theory and community learning: toward a complexified understanding of action research," in *International Journal of Educational Action Research*, vol. 5, no. 3 (1997): 403–422; D. Sumara, B. Davis, & D. van der Wey, "The pleasure of thinking," in *Language Arts*, vol. 76, no. 2 (1998): 135–143.

3. P. Senge, N. Cambron-McCabe, T. Lucas, B. Smith, J. Dutton, & A. Kleiner, *Schools that learn: a fifth discipline fieldbook for educators, parents, and everyone who cares about education* (New York: Doubleday, 2000).

4. Davis & Simmt, 2003.

5. See, e.g., Lewin & Regine, 2000.

6. See., e.g., Watts, 2003; R.J. Eidelson, "Complex adaptive systems in the behavioral and social sciences," in *Review of General Psychology*, vol. 1, no. 1 (1997): 42–71.

7. For a provocative examination of processes and dynamics of group identification, see J.R. Harris, *The nurture assumption: Why children turn out the way they do* (New York: Free Press, 1998).

8. L. Lowry, *The giver* (New York: Bantam Doubleday, 1993).

9. Surowiecki, 2004.

10. Ibid., pp. 189–190.

11. Ibid., p. 203.

12. Ibid., p. 205.

13. Ibid., p. 212–213.

14. Ibid., p. 212.

15. Ibid., p. 231.

16. Ibid., p. xx.

17. Barabàsi, 2002.

18. J. Fuite, "Network education: understanding the functional organization of a class," paper presentation given at the Complexity, Science & Society Conference, The University of Liverpool, UK, September 12, 2005.

19. From B. Davis & E. Simmt. "Mathematics-for-teaching: an ongoing investigation of the mathematics that teachers (need to) know," in press in *Educational Studies in Mathematics*.

20. For a more fulsome account of this co-teaching event, see Sumara, Davis, & van der Wey, "The pleasure of thinking."

21. See, e.g., R. Barthes, *S/Z* (New York: Hill & Wang, 1974); R. Luce-Kapler, *Writing with, through, and beyond the text: an ecology of language* (Mahwah, NJ: Lawrence Erlbaum Associates, 2004); W. Iser, *The act of reading* (Baltimore, MD: The Johns Hopkins University Press, 1978); L. Rosenblatt, *The reader, the text, the poem* (Carbondale, IL: Southern Illinois University Press, 1978); D. Sumara, *Why reading literature in school still matters: imagination, interpretation, insight* (Mahwah, NJ: Lawrence Erlbaum Associates, 2002).

22. In such cases, the result invariably comes out to about a 50-50 split—that is, apparently equal contributions of nature on nurture—on quantified conceptions of intelligence, personality, and so on. The consistency of result might be taken by a cynic to be more a reflection of a consistency of expectation than anything else.

23. For a review of some of this literature, see D. Sumara, *Private readings in public: schooling the literary imagination* (New York: Peter Lang, 1996).

24. For a review of some of this research, see B. Davis, *Teaching mathematics: toward a sound alternative* (New York: Garland, 1996).

25. We develop this point in much greater detail in an article exploring the compatibility of complexity thinking and action research. See B. Davis & D. Sumara, "Complexity science and educational actions research," in *Educational Action Research*, vol. 13, no. 3 (2005): 453–464.

26. M. Donald, A mind so rare: the evolution of human consciousness (New York: W.W. Norton, 2002).

27. J. Mason, *Practitioner research using the discipline of noticing* (London: Routledge-Falmer, 2001); I. Namukasa, *Attending in mathematics: a dynamic view about students' thinking* (Edmonton, AB: University of Alberta, unpublished doctoral dissertation, 2004).

28. See Davis & Sumara, 2002 for a discussion of the issue of the responsibility of educational researchers. Their discussion is developed around the specific example of the imposition of constructivist discourses on educational phenomena.

CHAPTER 6 — DESCRIPTIVE COMPLEXITY RESEARCH: LEVEL-JUMPING

1. I. Prigogine, *The end of certainty: time, chaos, and the new laws of nature* (New York: The Free Press, 1997), p. 7.

2. See F. Varela, E. Thompson, & E. Rosch, *The embodied mind: cognitive science and human experience* (Cambridge, MA: The MIT Press, 1991).

3. The resilience of this centuries-old belief is frequently acted out in fantasy and science fiction tales in which, for example, identities are exchanged (e.g., mother–daughter, male–female, adult–child, human–dog, human–alien, human–machine, etc.). Such plotlines make no sense when brains are understood in terms of complex, nested systems that embody their histories.

4. These numbers are expressed in North American terms. In UK terms, they are 100 thousand million neurons and billions of connections.

5. For an elaborated description of the "Increasing Human Potential Project," see E. Goldberg and members of the Santa Fe Institute Consortium, "Increasing human potential," in B. Davis (ed.), *Proceedings of the First Conference on Complexity Science and Educational Research* (Edmonton: AB: University of Alberta: 2003): 11–19; available at <http://www.complexityandeducation.ca>.

6. J. Piaget, *The construction of reality in the child* (New York: Basic Books, 1954).

7. See Davis & Sumara, 2003 for an overview of this work.

8. Although Piaget did not explicitly develop the point, assimilations and accommodations might be discussed in terms of power law distributions (cf. fig. 3.4). The vast majority of learning events are minor, analogous to barely measurable earth tremors. These Piaget referred to as assimilations—event that were too slight to register in conscious awareness. Some, however, were major—Piaget's accommodations. These were vastly fewer in number, but weighty enough to compel conscious reformulation of one's understandings of the world.

9. E. von Glasersfeld, *Radical constructivism: a way of knowing and learning* (London: The Falmer Press, 1995), p. 59.

10. See. L.P. Steffe, "The constructivist teaching experiment: illustrations and implications," in E. von Glasersfeld (ed.), *Radical constructivism in mathematics education* (Dordrecht, the Netherlands: Kluwer, 1991): 177–194.

11. There are literally hundreds of research reports that could be cited. A volume that provides a reasonably balanced treatment of pragmatic research issues and inter-

preted accounts of observational studies is L.P. Steffe & P. Cobb (eds.), *Construction of arithmetical meanings and strategies* (New York: Springer, 1988).

12. Lakoff & Johnson, 1999, p. 3.

13. "Social construc*tion*ist" theories are also commonly called "social construc*tivist*" theories. A majority of researchers oriented by these discourses have opted for the former phrase in order to distinguish their interests from those whose work is based in subject-centered (Piagetian) constructivist theories.

14. See J. Lave & E. Wenger, *Situated learning: legitimate peripheral participation* (Cambridge, UK: Cambridge University Press, 1991), p. 40.

15. Davis & Simmt, 2003.

16. J.A. O'Day, "Complexity, accountability, and school improvement," in *Harvard Educational Review*, vol. 72 (Fall 2002): 293–329.

17. See, e.g., Jacobson et al., 1998.

18. See Davis, 2004 for a fuller account of this historical note.

19. Freire, 1971, p. 54.

20. Britzman, 1991.

21. M. Greene, "Foreword," in Britzman, 1991, p. ix.

22. See esp. Merleau-Ponty, 1962.

23. Grumet, 1988.

24. C.A. Bowers, *Education, cultural myths, and the ecological crisis: toward deep changes* (Albany, NY: State University of New York Press, 1993).

CHAPTER 7—PRAGMATIC COMPLEXITY RESEARCH: CONDITIONS OF EMERGENCE

1. For a critique of common prescriptions of "critical pedagogy," see E. Ellsworth, "Why doesn't this feel empowering? Working through the repressive myths of critical pedagogy," in *Harvard Educational Review*, vol. 59, no. 3 (1986): 297–324. One of our own critiques of "constructivist teaching" (i.e., Davis & Sumara, "Why aren't they getting this? Working through the regressive myths of constructivist pedagogy") is structured after Ellsworth's work.

2. See, e.g., D. Britzman, *Lost subjects, contested objects: toward a psychoanalytic inquiry of learning* (Albany, NY: State University of New York Press, 1998); Grumet, 1988.

3. See, e.g., T.T. Aoki, *Curriculum in a new key: the collected works of Ted T. Aoki*. Edited by W.F. Pinar & R.L. Irwin (Mahwah, NJ: Lawrence Erlbaum, 2004).

4. See, e.g., Lewin & Regine, 2000; Watts, 2003.

5. E. Morin, *Seven complex lessons in education for the future* (Paris: UNESCO, 1999), p. 21.

6. Cf. D.R. Olson, *The world on paper: the conceptual and cognitive implications of writing and reading* (Cambridge, MA: Cambridge University Press, 1996).

7. See Kelly, 1994.

8. See Lewin & Regine, 2000.

9. Waldrop, 1992, p. 12.

10. E.g., H. Arrow, J.E. McGrath, & J.L. Berdhahl, *Small groups as complex systems: formation, coordination, development, and adaptation* (Thousand Oaks, CA: Sage, 2000). Significantly, they address such pragmatic issues as group size, articulation of roles, definitions of projects, and evolutions of social collectives.

11. The metaphor of conversation as the means and context of joint knowledge production is particularly well developed in the hermeneutics literature. See, e.g., R.E. Palmer, *Hermeneutics: interpretation theory in Schleiermacher, Dilthey, Heidegger, and Gadamer* (Evanston, IL: Northwestern University Press, 1969).

12. B. Rotman, *Mathematics as sign: writing, imagining, counting* (Stanford, CA: Stanford University Press, 2000), pp. 7–8.

13. See R. Brooks, *Flesh and machines: how robots will change us* (New York: Pantheon Books, 2002); A. Clark, *Being there: putting brain, body, and world together again* (Cambridge, MA: The MIT Press, 1997).

14. Kelly, 1994.

15. Johnson, 2001, p. 181.

16. See Kelly, 1994 and Johnson, 2001 for extended lists and discussions.

CHAPTER 8—COMPLEXITY AND EDUCATION: VITAL SIMULTANEITIES

1. A. Michaels, *Fugitive pieces* (Toronto: McClelland & Stewart, 1996), p. 138.

2. J. Dewey, "The child and the curriculum," in J. Dewey, *The child and the curriculum and The school and society* (Chicago: University of Chicago Press, 1956; originally copyrighted in 1902), p. 11.

3. See J.E. Zull, *The art of changing the brain: enriching the practice of teaching by exploring the biology of learning* (Sterling, VA: Stylus: 2002).

4. Borgmann, 1989, p. 110.

5. Although principally expository, we would note that we hardly limited ourselves to logical/rational/deductive modes of argumentation in this text. Notably, we also appealed to the following modes in various portions of the writing:

   • empirical/experimental/demonstrative,
   • analogical/figurative/metaphorical,
   • episodic/experiential/narrative,
   • allegorical/lyrical/mythological,
   • phenomenological/redescriptive, and
   • post-structuralist/deconstructive.

6. See, e.g., J. Derrida, *Writing and difference* (trans. Alan Bass) (Chicago: The University of Chicago Press, 1980).

7. See G. Deleuze & F. Guattari, *anti-Oedipus: capitalism and schizophrenia* (Minneapolis:

University of Minnesota Press, 1983).

8. Gadamer, 1990.

9. For a text-based version of this readers' theatre, see The Counternormativity Discourse Group, in press.

10. Johnson, 2005, p. 68.

11. W. Gershon, "Collective improvisation: a theoretical lens for classroom observation," in press in *Journal of Curriculum and Pedagogy*. The images are used with the permission of W. Gershon.

12. See, e.g., Davis, 2004, which is organized around a recursive bifurcation (branching) motif.

13. See Davis & Simmt, in press.

14. See T. Deacon, *The symbolic species: the co-evolution of language and the human brain* (New York: W.W. Norton, 1997).

15. D. Stanley, "The body of a 'healthy' education system," in *JCT: Journal of Curriculum Theorizing*, vol. 20, no. 4 (2004): 63–74.

16. Cf., Palmer, 1969; H.-G. Gadamer, *Truth and method* (New York: Continuum, 1990).

17. E.g., M.J. Fleener, *Curriculum dynamics: recreating heart.* (New York: Peter Lang, 2002); W.E. Doll, Jr. & N. Gough, *Curriculum visions* (New York: Peter Lang, 2003); W.E. Doll, Jr., M.J. Fleener, D. Trueit, & J. St. Julien (eds.), *Chaos, complexity, curriculum, and culture: a conversation* (New York: Peter Lang, 2005).

18. Rorty, 1989, p. 78.

19. Donald, 2002.

20. See Johnson, 2005.

21. Cf. Norretranders, 1998.

22. Consciousness studies have demonstrated that awareness lags about a half-second behind worldly happenings. That lag is needed for nonconscious processes to sort through, interpret, and select what will become conscious. See Norretranders, 1998.

23. We develop this issue at much greater length elsewhere. See B. Davis & D. Sumara, "From complexity to complicity: reading complexity theory as a moral and ethical imperative," in *JCT: Journal of Curriculum Theorizing*, vol. 15, no. 2 (1999), 19–38.

24. M. Johnson, *Moral imagination: implications of cognitive science for ethics* (Chicago, The University of Chicago Press, 1993), p. 207.

25. D.M. Levin, *The listening self: personal growth, social change and the closure of metaphysics* (London: Routledge, 1989), p. 110.

REFERENCES

Aoki, T.T. *Curriculum in a new key: the collected works of Ted T. Aoki.* (eds. W.F. Pinar & R.L. Irwin). Mahwah, NJ: Lawrence Erlbaum Associates, 2004.

Arrow, H., J.E. McGrath, & J.L. Berdhahl. *Small groups as complex systems: formation, coordination, development, and adaptation.* Thousand Oaks, CA: Sage, 2000.

Auyang, S.Y. *Foundations of complex-system theories in economics, evolutionary biology, and statistical physics.* Cambridge: Cambridge University Press, 1998.

Bak, P. *How nature works: the science of self-organized criticality.* New York: Springer-Verlag, 1996.

Barab, S.A. & M. Cherkes-Julkowski. "Principles of self-organisation: learning as participation in autocatakinetic systems," in *The Journal of the Learning Sciences,* vol. 8, nos. 3 & 4 (1999): 349–390

Barabàsi, A.-L. *Linking: How everything is connected to everything else and what it means for business, science, and everyday life.* New York, Penguin, 2002.

Barthes, R. *S/Z.* New York: Hill & Wang, 1974.

Borgmann, A. *Crossing the postmodern divide.* Chicago: University of Chicago Press, 1989.

Bowers, C.A. *Education, cultural myths, and the ecological crisis: toward deep changes.* Albany, NY: State University of New York Press, 1993.

Britzman, D. *Practice makes practice: a critical study of learning to teach.* Albany, NY: State University of New York Press, 1991.

Britzman, D.P. *Lost subjects, contested objects: toward a psychoanalytic inquiry of learning.* Albany, NY: State University of New York Press, 1998.

Brooks, R. *Flesh and machines: how robots will change us.* New York: Pantheon Books, 2002.

Buchanan, M. *Ubiquity: the science of history ... or why the world is simpler than we think.* London: Phoenix, 2000.

Buchanan, M. *Nexus: small worlds and the groundbreaking theory of networks.* New York: W.W. Norton, 2002.

Burton, L. (ed.). *Learning mathematics: from hierarchies to networks.* London: Falmer, 1999.

Calvin, W. *How brains think: evolving intelligence, then and now.* New York: Basic Books, 1996.

Carolan, B.V. & G. Natriello, "Data-mining journals and books: using the science of networks to uncover the structure of the educational research community," in *Educational Researcher,* vol. 34, no. 3 (2005 April), 25–33.

Carson, R. *Silent spring.* New York: Houghton Mifflin Company, 1962.

Chapman R.L. (ed.). *Roget's international thesaurus, fourth edition.* Toronto: Fitzhenry & Whiteside, 1977.

Chen, C. & R.J. Paul, "Visualizing a knowledge domain's intellectual structure," in *IEEE* (2001 March), 65–71.

Cherkes-Julkowski, M. "The child as a self-organizing system: the case against instruction as we know it," in *Learning Disabilities,* vol. 7, no. 1 (1996): 19–27.

Cherkes-Julkowski, M. & N. Mitlina. "Self-organization of mother-child instructional dyads and later attention disorder," in *Journal of Learning Disabilities,* vol. 32, no. 1 (1999): 6–21.

Cherryholmes, C. *Power and criticism: poststructural investigations in education.* New York: Teachers College Press, 1988.

Chui, B. "'Unified theory' is getting closer, Hawking predicts." *San Jose Mercury News,* Sunday Morning Final Editions, January 23, 2000, p. 29A.

Cilliers, P. *Complexity and postmodernism.* London: Routledge , 1998.

Clark, A. *Being there: putting brain, body, and world together again.* Cambridge, MA: The MIT Press, 1997.

Cohen, J. & I. Stewart. *The collapse of chaos: discovering simplicity in a complex world.* New York: Penguin, 1994.

Counternormativity Discourse Group (The). "Performing an archive of feeling: experiences of normalizing structures in teaching and teacher education. In press in *Journal of Curriculum and Pedagogy.*

Cziko, G.A. "Unpredictability and indeterminism in human behavior: arguments and implications for educational research," in *Educational Researcher* (1989 April): 17–25.

Dale, J.D. "The new American school: a learning organization," in *International Journal of Educational Reform,* vol. 6, no. 1 (1997): 34–39.

Davis, B. *Teaching mathematics: toward a sound alternative.* New York: Garland, 1996.

Davis, B. *Inventions of teaching: a genealogy.* Mahwah, NJ: Lawrence Erlbaum Associates.

Davis, B. & E. Simmt. "Understanding learning systems: mathematics teaching and complexity science," in *Journal for Research in Mathematics Education,* vol. 34, no. 2 (2003): 137–167.

Davis, B. & E. Simmt. "Mathematics-for-teaching: an ongoing investigation of the mathematics that teachers (need to) know," in press in *Educational Studies in Mathematics.*

Davis, B. & D. Sumara. "Cognition, complexity, and teacher education," in *Harvard Educational Review,* vol. 67, no. 1 (1997): 105–125.

Davis, B. & D. Sumara. "From complexity to complicity: reading complexity theory as a moral and ethical imperative," in *JCT: Journal of Curriculum Theorizing,* vol. 15, no. 2 (1999), 19–38.

Davis, B. & D. Sumara, "Constructivist discourses and the field of education: problems and possibilities," in *Educational Theory,* vol. 52, no. 4 (2002): 409–428.

Davis, B. & D. Sumara, "Why aren't they getting this? Working through the regressive myths of constructivist pedagogy," in *Teaching Education*, vol. 14, no. 2 (2003): 123–140.

Davis, B. & D. Sumara, "Listening to how you're heard: on translations, mistranslations, and really bad mistranslations (a response to Stuart McNaughton and Nicholas Burbules)," in *Teaching Education*, vol. 14, no. 2 (2003): 149–152.

Davis, B. & D. Sumara, "Complexity science and educational action research," in *Educational Action Research*, vol. 13, no. 3 (2005): 453–464.

Davis, B. & D. Sumara., "Challenging images of knowing: complexity science and educational research," in *Qualitative Studies in Education*, vol. 18, no. 3 (2005): 305–321.

Davis, B., D.J. Sumara, & T.E. Kieren. "Cognition, co-emergence, curriculum," *Journal of Curriculum Studies*, vol. 28, no. 2 (1996): 151–169.

Davis, B., D. Sumara, & R. Luce-Kapler. *Engaging minds: learning and teaching in a complex world*. Mahwah, NJ: Lawrence Erlbaum Associates: 2000.

Deacon, T. *The symbolic species: the co-evolution of language and the human brain*. New York: W.W. Norton, 1997.

Deleuze, G. & F. Guattari, *Anti-Oedipus: capitalism and schizophrenia*. Minneapolis: University of Minnesota Press, 1983.

Dennett, D. *Darwin's dangerous idea: evolution and the meanings of life*. New York: Touchstone, 1995.

Derrida, J. *Writing and difference* (trans. Alan Bass). Chicago: The University of Chicago Press, 1980.

Derrida, J. *Limited, Inc*. Evanston, IL: Northwestern University Press, 1988.

Dewey, J. "The influence of Darwin on philosophy," in *The influence of Darwin on philosophy and other essays*. New York, Henry Holt, 1910: 1–19.

Dewey, J. *The child and the curriculum and The school and society*. Chicago: University of Chicago Press, 1956.

Doll, Jr., W.E. "Complexity in the classroom," in *Educational Leadership*, vol. 47, no. 1 (1989): 65–70.

Doll, Jr., W. *A post-modern perspective on curriculum*. New York: Teachers' College Press, 1993.

Doll, Jr., W.E., M.J. Fleener, D. Trueit, & J. St. Julien (eds.), *Chaos, complexity, curriculum, and culture: a conversation*. New York: Peter Lang, 2005.

Doll, Jr., W.E. & N. Gough, *Curriculum visions*. New York: Peter Lang, 2003.

Donald, M. *A mind so rare: the evolution of human consciousness*. New York: W.W. Norton, 2002.

Dyke, C. *The evolutionary dynamics of complex systems*. Oxford,: Oxford University Press, 1988.

Eidelson, R.J. "Complex adaptive systems in the behavioral and social sciences," in *Review of General Psychology*, vol. 1, no. 1 (1997): 42–71.

Ehrlich, P.R. *Human natures: genes, cultures, and the human prospect.* New York: Penguin, 2000.

Ellsworth, E. "Why doesn't this feel empowering? Working through the repressive myths of critical pedagogy," in *Harvard Educational Review,* vol. 59, no. 3 (1986): 297–324.

Engels, F. *The condition of the working class in England.* New York: Penguin, 1987.

Ennis, C.D. "Reconceptualizing learning as a dynamical system," in *Journal of Curriculum and Supervision,* vol. 7 (1993): 115–130.

Fleener, M.J. *Curriculum dynamics: recreating heart.* New York: Peter Lang, 2002.

Foucault, M. *Discipline and punish: the birth place of the modern prison.* New York: Pantheon, 1977.

Foucault, M. *The history of sexuality, an introduction.* New York, Vintage, 1990.

Foucault, M. *Abnormal: lectures at the Collège de France, 1974–1975* (trans. G. Burchell). New York: Picador, 2003.

Freire, P. *Pedagogy of the oppressed.* New York: Seaview, 1971.

Fuite, J. "Network education: understanding the functional organization of a class." Paper presented at the Complexity, Science & Society Conference, The University of Liverpool, UK, September 12, 2005.

Gadamer, H.-G. *Truth and method.* New York: Continuum, 1990.

Gardner, M. "In which 'monster' curves force redefinition of the word 'curve'," in *Scientific American,* vol. 235 (December 1976), 124–129.

Gershon, W. "Collective improvisation: a theoretical lens for classroom observation," in press in *Journal of Curriculum and Pedagogy.*

Gleick, J. *Chaos: making a new science.* New York: Penguin, 1987.

Goldberg, E. & Members of the Santa Fe Institute Consortium. "Increasing human potential," in *Proceedings of the First Conference on Complexity Science and Educational Research* (ed. B. Davis) (Edmonton, AN: University of Alberta, 2003): 11–19. Available at http://www.complexityandeducation.ca.

Gordon, D. *Ants at work: how an insect society is organized.* New York: Free Press, 1999.

Grumet, M. *Bitter milk: women and teaching.* Amherst, MA: University of Massachusetts Press, 1988.

Guare, J. *Six degrees of separation: A play.* New York: Vintage, 1990.

Harris, J.R. *The nurture assumption: Why children turn out the way they do.* New York: Free Press, 1998.

Hoffman, D.D. *Visual intelligence: how we create what we see.* New York: W.W. Norton, 1998.

Holland, J.H. *Emergence: from chaos to order.* Reading, MA: Helix, 1998.

Iser, W. *The act of reading.* Baltimore, MD: The Johns Hopkins University Press, 1978).

Jacobs, J. *The death and life of great American cities.* New York: Vintage, 1961.

Jacobson, M.J., K. Brecher, M. Clemens, W. Farrell, J. Kaput, K. Reisman, & U. Wilensky. *Education in complex systems.* Nashua, NH: New England Complex Systems Institute, 1998.

Johnson, M. *Moral imagination: implications of cognitive science for ethics*. Chicago, The University of Chicago Press, 1993.

Johnson, S. *Emergence: the connected lives of ants, brains, cities, and software*. New York: Scribner, 2001.

Johnson, S. *Everything bad is good for you: how today's popular culture is actually making us smarter*. New York: Riverhead Books, 2005.

Kauffman, S. *At home in the universe: the search for the laws of self-organization and complexity*. New York: Oxford University Press, 1995.

Keller, E.F. *Making sense of life: explaining biological developments with models, metaphors, and machines*. Cambridge, MA: Harvard University Press, 2002.

Kelly, K. *Out of control: the new biology of machines, social systems, and the economic world*. Cambridge, MA: Perseus, 1994.

Kuhn, T. *The structure of scientific revolutions*. Chicago: University of Chicago Press, 1962.

Laidlaw, L. *Reinventing curriculum: a complex perspective on literacy and writing*. Mahwah, NJ: Lawrence Erlbaum Associates, 2005.

Lakoff, G. & M. Johnson. *Philosophy in the flesh: the embodied mind and its challenge to Western thought*. New York: Basic Books, 1999.

Landa, M. de. *A thousand years of nonlinear history*. New York: Zone Books, 2000.

Laplace, P.S. de. *A philosophical essay on probabilities* (trans. F.W. Truscott & F.L. Emory). New York, Dover, 1951. Published in the original French in 1814.

Lather, P. *Getting smart: feminist research and pedagogy with/in the postmodern*. New York: Routledge, 1991.

Latour, B. "On objectivity," in *Mind, Culture, and Activity*, vol. 3, no. 4 (1996): 228–245.

Lave, J. & E. Wenger. *Situated learning: legitimate peripheral participation*. Cambridge, UK: Cambridge University Press, 1991.

Levin, D.M. *The listening self: personal growth, social change and the closure of metaphysics*. London: Routledge, 1989.

Lewin, R. *Complexity: life at the edge of chaos*. New York: Macmillan, 1992.

Lewin, R. & B. Regine, *Weaving complexity and business: engaging the soul at work*. New York: Texere, 2000.

Lowry, L. *The giver*. New York: Bantam Doubleday, 1993.

Luce-Kapler, R. *Writing with, through, and beyond the text: an ecology of language*. Mahwah, NJ: Lawrence Erlbaum Associates, 2004.

Lyotard, J.-F. *The postmodern condition: a report on knowledge* (trans. G. Bennington & B. Massumi). Minneapolis: University of Minnesota Press, 1984.

Mandelbrot, B.B. *The fractal geometry of nature*. San Francisco: W.H. Freeman and Co., 1982.

Mandinach, E.B. & H.F. Cline. *Classroom dynamics: implementing a technology-based learning environment*. Hillsdale, NJ: Lawrence Erlbaum Associates, 1994.

Mason, J. *Practitioner research using the discipline of noticing*. London: Routledge-Falmer, 2001.

Maturana, H.R. "Autopoiesis: reproduction, heredity and evolution," in *Autopoiesis, dissipative structures, and spontaneous social orders* (ed. M. Zeleny). Boulder, CO: Westview, 1980.

Maturana, H.R. "Everything is said by an observer," *Gaia: a way of knowing* (ed. W.I. Thompson). Hudson, NY: Lindisfarne Press, 1987: 65–82.

Maturana, H.R. "Science and daily life: the ontology of scientific explanations," in *Self-organization: portrait of a scientific revolution* (eds. W. Krohn & G. Kuppers). Dordrecht: Kluwer Academic Publishers, 1990.

Merleau-Ponty, M. *Phenomenology of perception*. London: Routledge & Kegan Paul, 1962 (published in the original French in 1948).

Michaels, A. *Fugitive pieces*. Toronto: McClelland & Stewart, 1996.

Middleton, J.A., D. Sawada, E. Judson, I. Bloom, & J. Turley. "Relationships build reform: Treating classroom research as emergent systems," in *Handbook of International Research in Mathematics Education* (ed. L.D. English). Mahwah, NJ: Lawrence Erlbaum Associates, 2002: 409–431.

Milgram, S. "The small world problem," in *Psychology Today*, vol. 2 (1967): 60–67.

Morin, E. *Seven complex lessons in education for the future*. Paris: UNESCO, 1999.

Muir, J. *My first summer in the Sierras*. New York: Houghton Mifflin, 1911/1998.

Namukasa, I. *Attending in mathematics: a dynamic view about students' thinking* (unpublished doctoral dissertation). Edmonton, AB: University of Alberta, 2004.

Norretranders, T. *The user illusion: cutting consciousness down to size*. New York: Viking, 1998.

O'Day, J.A. "Complexity, accountability, and school improvement," in *Harvard Educational Review*, vol. 72 (Fall 2002): 293–329.

Olson, D.R. *The world on paper: the conceptual and cognitive implications of writing and reading*. Cambridge, MA: Cambridge University Press, 1996.

Osberg, D. *Curriculum, complexity and representation: rethinking the epistemology of schooling through complexity theory* (unpublished doctoral dissertation) Open University, Milton Keynes, UK, 2005.

Palmer, R.E. *Hermeneutics: interpretation theory in Schleiermacher, Dilthey, Heidegger, and Gadamer*. Evanston, IL: Northwestern University Press, 1969.

Piaget, J. *The construction of reality in the child*. New York: Basic Books, 1954.

Phelps, R. & S. Hase, "Complexity and action research: exploring the theoretical and methodological connections," in *Educational Action Research*, vol. 10, no. 3 (2003): 507–523.

Poincaré, H. *Science and hypothesis*. London: Walter Scott Publishing, 1905.

Popper, K. *Conjectures and refutations*. London: Routledge & Kegan Paul, 1963.

Prigogine, I. *The end of certainty: time, chaos, and the new laws of nature*. New York: The Free Press, 1997.

Rasmussen, J. "The importance of communication in teaching: a system-theory approach to the scaffolding metaphor," in *Journal of Curriculum Studies*, vol. 33, no. 5 (2001): 569–582.

Resnick, M. *Turtles, termites, and traffic jams: explorations in massively powerful microworlds.* Cambridge, MA: The MIT Press, 1995.

Resnick, M. "Beyond the centralized mindset," in *Journal of Learning Sciences*, vol. 5, no. 1 (1996): 1–22.

Resnick, M. & U. Wilensky, "Diving into complexity: developing probabilistic decentralized thinking through role-playing activities," in *Journal of Learning Sciences*, vol. 7, no. 2 (1998): 153–172.

Reyna, V. *What is scientifically based evidence? What is logic?* Full text available at <http://www.ed.gov/nclb/methods/whatworks/research/page_pg3.html>.

Richardson, K.A. & P. Cilliers. "What is complexity science? A view from different directions," in *Emergence*, vol. 3, no. 1 (2001): 5–22.

Rorty, R. *Contingency, irony, solidarity.* New York: Cambridge University Press, 1989.

Rosenblatt, L. *The reader, the text, the poem.* Carbondale, IL: Southern Illinois University Press, 1978.

Rotman, B. *Mathematics as sign: writing, imagining, counting.* Stanford, CA: Stanford University Press, 2000.

Rucker, R. *Mind tools: the mathematics of information.* New York: Penguin, 1987.

Rudhauf, D., A. Lutz, D. Cosmelli, J.-P. Lachaux, & M. le van Quyen, "From autopoiesis to neurophenomenology: Francisco Varela's exploration of the biophysics of being," in *Biological Research*, vol. 36 (2003): pp. 27–65.

Ruthen, R. "Trends in nonlinear dynamics: adapting to complexity," in *Scientific American*, vol. 269 (January, 1993): 130–140.

Saussure, F. de. *Course in general linguistics* (trans. W. Baskin). New York: Philosophy Library, 1959.

Sawada, D. & M.T. Caley. "Dissipative structures: new metaphors for becoming in education," in *Educational Researcher*, vol. 14, no. 3 (1985): 13–19.

Seife, C. *Zero: the biography of a dangerous number.* New York: Viking Penguin, 2000.

Senge, P., N. Cambron-McCabe, T. Lucas, B. Smith, J. Dutton, & A. Kleiner, *Schools that learn: a fifth discipline fieldbook for educators, parents, and everyone who cares about education.* New York: Doubleday, 2000.

Sokal, A. & J. Bricmont. *Intellectual impostures: postmodern philosopher's abuse of science.* London: Profile Books, 1998.

Solla Price, D.J. de & D.B. Beaver. "Collaboration in an invisible college," in *American Psychologist*, vol. 21 (1966): 1107–1117.

Stanley, D. "The body of a 'healthy' education system," in *JCT: Journal of Curriculum Theorizing*, vol. 20, no. 4 (2004): 63–74.

Steffe, L.P. "The constructivist teaching experiment: illustrations and implications," in *Radical constructivism in mathematics education* (ed. E. von Glasersfeld). Dordrecht, the Netherlands: Kluwer, 1991: 177–194.

Steffe, L.P. & P. Cobb (eds.). *Construction of arithmetical meanings and strategies.* New York: Springer, 1988.

Stewart, I. *Does God play dice?* Cambridge, MA: Blackwell, 1989.

Stewart, I. *Life's other secret: the new mathematics of the living world.* Cambridge, UK: Cambridge University Press, 1998.

Stewart, I. & J. Cohen, *Figments of reality: the evolution of the curious mind.* New York: John Wiley & Sons, 1997.

Sumara, D. *Why reading literature in school still matters: imagination, interpretation, insigh.* Mahwah, NJ: Lawrence Erlbaum Associates, 2002.

Sumara, D. *Private readings in public: schooling the literary imagination.* New York: Peter Lang, 1996.

Sumara, D. & B. Davis. "Enactivist theory and community learning: toward a complexified understanding of action research," in *International Journal of Educational Action Research*, vol. 5, no. 3 (1997): 403–422.

Sumara, D., B. Davis, & D. van der Wey. "The pleasure of thinking," in *Language Arts*, vol. 76, no. 2 (1998): 135–143.

Surowiecki, J. *The wisdom of crowds: why the many are stronger than the few and how collective wisdom shapes business, economies, societies, and nations.* New York: Doubleday, 2004.

Thomson, D.W. *On growth and form.* London: Cambridge University Press, 1917.

Upitis, R. "School architecture and complexity," in *Complicity: An International Journal of Complexity and Education*, vol. 1, no. 1 (2004): 19–38.

Varela, F., E. Thompson, & E. Rosch. *The embodied mind: cognitive science and human experience.* Cambridge, MA: The MIT Press, 1991.

van Manen, M. *Researching lived experience: human science for an action sensitive pedagogy.* London, ON: The Althouse Press, 1990.

von Glasersfeld, E. *Radical constructivism: a way of knowing and learning.* London: The Falmer Press, 1995.

Waldrop, M.M. *Complexity: The emerging science on the edge of order and chaos.* New York: Simon and Schuster, 1992.

Watts, D. *Six degrees: the science of the connected age.* New York: W.W. Norton, 2003.

Weaver, W. "Science and complexity," in *American Scientist*, vol. 36, 536–544.

Wilensky U. & M. Resnick. "Thinking in levels: a dynamic systems approach to making sense of the world," in *Journal of Science Education and Technology*, vol. 8, no. 1 (1999): 3–19.

Zuckerman, H. "Nobel laureates in science: patterns of productivity, collaboration and authorship," in *American Sociological Review*, vol. 32 (1967): 391–403.

Zull, J.E. *The art of changing the brain: enriching the practice of teaching by exploring the biology of learning.* Sterling, VA: Stylus: 2002.

ACKNOWLEDGMENTS

The idea to write this book first arose after a series of seminars for the Education and Social Research Institute at Manchester Metropolitan University in September, 2004. Bridget Somekh had invited us some months earlier to speak to issues around complexity thinking and education as part of a broader exploration of developments for research methodology in the social sciences—and the warm, but not uncritical reception of our presentations provided both an opportunity to formulate some new thoughts and an occasion to interrogate much of what it seems we had been taking for granted. On those counts, we extend a special thanks to Bridget, Maggie MacLure, John Shostak, Ian Stronach, Harry Torrance, Michael Totterdell, and their colleagues at MMU. In particular, we wish to acknowledge Harry who was the one who challenged us to assemble this sort of book.

Much of the thinking developed herein has arisen and been elaborated in conversations and collaborations with colleagues and co-researchers. We would like, in particular, to recognize the contributions of Elaine Simmt, Rebecca Luce-Kapler, and Tom Kieren.

The Complexity Science and Educational Research annual conference has been an important location for our thinking over the past several years. In this regard, we would like once again to acknowledge the collaborative and conceptual contributions of Elaine and Rebecca, as well as Bill Doll, Tara Fenwick, Jayne Fleener, Linda Laidlaw, and Rena Upitis.

Others whose contributions to our thinking and to joint projects include those who have helped to assemble and maintain the Complexity and Education website (www.complexityandeducation.ca), among them Angus McMurtry, Deborah Osberg, and Kris Wells. Special thanks as well to Clay Kropp who designed both the site and the book's front cover.

Finally, we would like to acknowledge the rich and vibrant thinking space that has emerged in the Department of Secondary Education at the University of Alberta, prompted in large part by the contributions of an exceptional cohort of graduate students. In addition to those already mentioned, we would also like to thank current and past students, including Jim Fuite, Khadeeja Ibrihim-Didi, Tammy Iftody, Helena Miranda, Elizabeth Mowat, Immaculate Namukasa, and Jérôme Proulx.

Finally, we are grateful to the Social Sciences and Humanities Research Council of Canada for its support of several of the research projects discussed herein.

NAME INDEX

Aoki, T.T., 181
Apple, M., 145
Aristotle, 32
Arrow, H., 182
Auyang, S.Y. 173

Bacon, F., 9, 23, 63
Barab, S.A., 173
Barabàsi, A., 54, 88–89
Baran, P., 177
Barthes, R., 179
Beaver, D.B., 55
Berdhahl, J.L., 182
Berra, Y., 129
Bloom, I., 174
Borgmann, A., 160, 176
Bourbaki, N., 63, 64, 177
Bowers, C.A., 127
Brecher, K. 174
Bricmont, J., 175
Britzman, D., 124, 178, 181
Brooks, R., 182
Buchanan, M., 48–49
Bush, G.W., 27, 49–50

Caley, M., 25, 173
Calvin, W., 51
Cambron-McCabe, N., 178
Carolan, B.V., 177
Carson, R., 19
Chapman, R.L., 176
Chen, C., 177
Cherkes-Julkowski, M., 173

Cherryholmes, C., 178
Cilliers, P., 18–19, 21, 25, 34
Clark, A., 182
Clemens, M., 174
Cline, H.F., 174
Cobb, P., 180
Cohen, J., 16, 22, 46, 59
Cosmelli, D., 175
Cziko, G.A., 174

Dale, J.D., 174
Darwin, C., 12, 21–22, 32, 33, 58–60,
    63, 73
de Landa, M., 177
Deacon, T., 183
Deleuze, G., 161–162
Dennett, D., 17
Derrida, J., ix, 161, 182
Descartes, R., 9, 23, 45, 63, 71, 76
Dewey, J., 59, 73, 74, 156
Diderot, D., 58
Doll, Jr., Wm., 25, 174, 183, 193
Donald, M., 103, 168
Dutton, J., 178
Dyke, C., 14

Ehrlich, P.R., 176
Eidelson, R.J., 178
Einstein, A., 3
Ellsworth, E., 145, 181
Engels, F., 19, 74
Ennis, C.D., 173
Euclid, 38–39, 42–43

Farrell, W., 174
Fenwick, T., 193
Fleener, M.J., 183, 193
Foucault, M., 67–177
Freire, P., 61, 123, 145
Freud, S., 12, 72
Fuite, J., 89, 193

Gadamer, H.-G., 162
Galileo, 9
Gardner, M., 176
Gershon, W., 163–165
Gleick, J., 176
Goldberg, E., 180
Gordon, D., 19, 20, 74
Gough, N., 183
Greene, M., 124
Grumet, M., 126, 145, 178
Guare, J., 176
Guattari, F., 161–162

Harris, J.R., 179
Hawking, S., 3
Hoffman, D.D., 176
Holland, J.H., 173
Husserl, E., 72

Ibrahim-Didi, K, 193
Iftody, T., 193
Iser, W., 179

Jacobs, J., 19, 74
Jacobson, M.J., 174
James, W., 73
Johnson, M., 116–117
Johnson, S., 59, 148, 162
Judson, E., 174

Kant, I., 114
Kaput, J., 121, 174
Kauffman, S., 12

Keller, E.F., 74, 173
Kelly, K., 144
Kepler, J., 24
Kieren, T.E., 174, 193
Kleiner, A., 178
Kropp, C., 193
Kuhn, T., 33

Lachaux, J.-P., 175
Laidlaw, L., 193
Lakoff, G., 116–117
Lamarck, J.-B., 58
Laplace, P.S. de, 9
Latour, B., 69
Lave, J., 118–119, 181
le van Quyen, M., 175
Levin, D.M., 169
Lewin, R., 173
Linnaeus, 30
Locke, J., 61–62
Lowry, L., 83–84
Lucas, T., 178
Luce-Kapler, R., 174, 175, 176, 193
Lutz, A., 175
Lyell, C., 58
Lyotard, J.-F., 35, 68

MacLure, M., 193
Mandelbrot, B., 37, 43
Mandinach, E.B., 174
Marx, K., 119
Mason, J., 180
Maturana, H., 19, 69, 74
McGrath, J.E., 182
McMurtry, A., 193
Merleau-Ponty, M., 72, 125–126
Michaels, A., 153
Middleton, J.A., 174
Milgram, S., 51
Minsky, M., 74
Miranda, H., 193

Mitlina, N., 173
Morin, E., 133–134, 135
Mowat, E., 193
Muir, J., 57

Namukasa, I., 180, 193
Natriello, G., 177
Newton, I., 9, 10, 24, 45, 57, 59
Norretranders, T., 174

O'Day, J., 121
Olson, D.R., 181
Osberg, D., 22, 193

Paul, R.J., 177
Peano, G., 43
Peirce, C.S., 73
Piaget, J., 63, 64, 65, 74, 112–114, 117–
    118, 120, 125
Pinar, Wm., 145
Plato, 39, 42, 59, 71
Poincaré, H., 10–11, 172
Popper, K., 33
Prigogine, 25, 107
Proulx, J., 193

Rasmussen, J., 174
Regine, B., 173
Reisman, K., 174
Resnick, M., 173, 174
Reyna, V., 176
Richardson, K.A., 18–19, 21, 25
Rorty, R., 39, 167–168
Rosch, E., 180
Rosenblatt, L., 179
Rotman, B., 143
Rucker, R., 173
Rudhauf, D., 175

Saussure, F. de, 32–33, 63, 64, 67, 113
Sawada, D., 25, 173, 174

Seife, C., 174
Senge, P., 81–82
Shostak, J., 193
Simmt, E., 82, 90–91, 120–121, 135,
    137, 140–141, 174, 193
Smith, A., 131–132
Smith, B., 178
Sokal, A., 175
Solla Price, D.J. de, 55
Somekh, B., 193
Stanley, D., 166–167
Steffe, L.P., 180
Stewart, I., 16, 22, 45, 46, 49
Stronach, I., 193
Suroweicki, J., 54, 84–85

Thompson, E., 180
Thomson, D.W., 79
Torrance, H., 193
Totterdell, M., 193
Trueit, D., 183
Turing, A., 74
Turley, J., 174

Upitis, R., 53, 193

van der Wey, D., 93, 104
Varela, F., 174, 180
Vico, G., 63–64
von Glasersfeld, E., 114
Vygotsky, L.S., 63, 64, 65, 117–120

Waldrop, M.M., 5, 136
Watts, D., 49
Weaver, W., 9, 74
Wells, K., 193
Wenger, E., 118–119, 181
Wilensky, U., 121, 173, 174

Zuckerman, H., 177
Zull, J.E., 182

SUBJECT INDEX

accommodation, 114, 180

action research, 101

activity theory, 118

actor-network theory, 119

adequacy: optimality vs., 138

analytic method, 9

argumentation: modes, 182; structures of, 40, 163

artificial intelligence, 8, 110–111, 144

assimilation, 114, 180

authorship/authority, 95, 145–146

autopoiesis, 74, 175

behaviorism, *xi*, 12, 70, 103, 115, 120

bell curve: see *normal distribution*

bifurcation, 31–32

biology: educational research and, 108–112; metaphors from, 13–14, 125

border-crossing, 158–159

bottom-up, 84–88

boundaries: ambiguous, 5, 94–98; individual/collective, 96; specification of, 15

brain: function, 109–110; metaphors for, 108–109, 111; research, *ix*, 108; structure, 51, 97, 102, 108

butterfly effect, 10

centralized networks, 52–53, 88–89

chaos theory, 8

classroom: collectivity, 82; control, 103; organization, 53, 89, 92, 105

co-authorship, 95

co-emergence, 100

cognitive science, 116

cognitivism, 109

coherence: of complex unities, 148–149; theories, 32–34, 63, 113

collectivity, 58, 80–81, 85, 90, 95, 98, 101: classroom, 82, 135–152; individuality vs., 140; intelligence and, 136, 149, knowledge and, 117–121, 143

comparative dynamics, 166–167

complex phenomena: complicated vs., 172; qualities of, 5–6, 79–105

complexity: definition, *ix*, 3–7; history, 3, 8–12, 19–21, 73–74

Complexity and Education website, *xii*, 171

Complexity Digest website, 171

complexity science: hard, 18, 21–23; soft, 18, 23–25

complexity thinking, 18–19, 25–30, 33–35

complicated: complex vs., 10–11

complicity, 14–16, 22, 25, 32, 70, 73, 166, 169–170

computer simulation, 20, 22

conditions of emergence, 129–152

connected classroom, 121

conscientização, 123

consciousness, *ix*, 26, 42, 67, 103, 167–168

consensus: problems with, 84

constructionism, 28, 30, 63, 117–120,

181: metaphors of, 118; subdiscourses fo, 118–120
constructivism, 28, 30, 65, 70, 112–114, 118: metaphors of, 118; trivial, 62
corporatism: curriculum and, 132–133
correspondence theories, 32–33
critical: pedagogy, 131; reflection, 169; theory, 122–123
cultural: studies, 121–122; theory, 121–122
culture, 121–124
currere, 25
curriculum, 25, 53, 91, 97, 100, 154
cybernetics, 8, 81

Darwinism, 21–22, 31–32, 34, 58–62, 101
decentralized, 85: classrooms, 89; control, 88, 142, 144–146; networks, 52–54, 88–90
deconstruction, 38, 122, 161–162
determinism, 9, 13, 168, 172
dichotomies, 31–32, 153, 161
discourse, 66, 122, 159
disequilibrium, 6, 102–104
disorganized complexity, 172
distributed networks, 52–53, 88–89
distributions: normal, 47–48; power law, 48–49
diversity, 4, 6–7, 137–138: conceptual, 138, 143; social 138

ecology, 70, 124–127: etymology, 126
education: metaphors for, 168
educational research, 76, 92, 104, 166, 167–168, 169–170
embodiment, 65, 100, 116, 125–126
emergence, 5, 73–76, 81–84, 129–152, 158
enabling constraints, 138, 147–150
Enlightenment, 4, 9, 23–24, 63

environment, 14–15
ERIC, 113
essentialism, 125
ethics, 16, 70, 160, 165, 169–170: see also *complicity*
Euclidean geometry, 38–42, 92, 161
evolution: learning as, 44–45; see also *Darwinism*
existentialism, 64

far-from-equilibrium, 6, 102–104
feedback loops, 151: negative, 102–103; positive, 102–103
Ford Motor Company, 132
fractal geometry, 8, 24, 42–47

General Motors, 132
geometry: Euclidean, 38–42, 92, 161; fractal, 8, 24, 42–47
Giver, The, 86–88, 93–94, 98–99, 101, 104, 105–106
gold-standard of medical research, 37

hermeneutics, 167
Hewlett Packard, 132
Honda, 132
hypertext, 164

IBM, 132
identity, 58, 86, 98, 114, 180: collective, 146; fictive, 87; reading and, 93–94
incompressibility, 14, 26, 34, 45
intelligence, 42, 74, 85–86, 111, 123: collective, 26, 85–86, 133, 136, 141, 149; multiple, 110; systemic, 138; tests, *x*
intentionality, 72
interdisciplinarity, 3
interdiscursivity, 156–160
internet, 51–55

interobjectivity, 15, 34, 69–71
intersubjectivity, 15, 34, 69
irony, 167–168

knowledge, 29–30, 97: bodies and, 66; collective, 117–121, 143, 145, 154–155; evolution of, 4, 134; knower and, 154–156; metaphors of, 27, 51–52, 57, 62, 182; networks and, 97; power and, 66, 67; shared, 145; sociology of, 155

learners, 12–14, 79–106, 142–147
learning, 12–14, 74, 86, 92, 103, 144–145: biology and, 109; conceptions of, 61, 109; evolution and, 44–45; modalities, 110; systems, 79–106, 142–147; trans-level, 142–147
level-jumping, 26, 107–128, 156–158, 162
linearity, 24, 40–41, 45, 46
literary engagement, 87

mathematics, 143: school, 90–91; teachers' knowledge of, 120–121, 136–137, 140–141, 146, 150, 157, 166
memory: intelligence and, 111; types, 110
metadiscourses, 7
metanarratives, 35
metaphor, 116–117: of learning, 109; research and, 38; science and, 24
metaphysics, 58–59, 67, 155
mob mentality, 103
morphogenesis, 74
multidisciplinarity, 3
multiple threading, 162–165
multiplication, 141, 146, 157

naturalism, 68, 96
nature/nurture, 96–97

negative feedback loops, 102–103
neighbor interactions, 142–143
nestedness, 5–6, 15, 29, 90–94
network theory, 24, 42–50
networks, 49–53: centralized, 52–53; de-centralized, 52–54, 88–90; distributed, 52–53; scale-free, 88–90; types, 52–54
neurology, 108–112, 126
neurophenomenology, 173–174
New England Complex Systems Institute, 173
No Child Left Behind, 27, 28, 49–50, 171
nonlinear dynamics, 8
nonlinearity, 45–46
non-representationism, 114, 160–165
normal, 41–42, 48: abnormal vs., 123; distributions, 42, 47–48; synonyms for, 41
norms/normativity, 73, 104, 146, 161

objectivity, 15, 62–63, 117
optimality: adequacy vs., 138
organizational: closure, 94–98; management, 85

participatory epistemologies, 70
pedagogy, 100, 105, 154: see also *teaching*
perception, 46, 71, 174
phenomenology, 71–73, 124–127
positive feedback loops, 102–103
positivism, 69
postmodernism, 35
post-structuralism, 30, 38, 64–68, 122–125, 159
power, 66, 67, 122: metaphors of, 122
power law distributions, 48–49, 180
pragmatism, 26, 34, 38, 64, 72–73
proscription, 148
psychoanalysis, 38, 64, 71–73, 130

qualitative/quantitative, 37, 41–42, 46

radical constructivism: see *constructivism*
randomness, 148–149
rationalism, 39, 40–41
reader-response, 83–84, 87
reading, acts of, 93
recursion, 25, 43, 46
reductionism, 39–40
redundancy, 20, 138–140
religion, 67
replicability, 17–18, 101, 152
representations, 34, 68, 160–165
rhizomatics, 161–162
right: synonyms of, 40–41
rigor, 21, 149
robustness, 51–52, 138–140

Santa Fe Institute, 4, 112, 180
scale-free, 46–49: networks, 88–90
scale independence, 43–44, 48
schools: organization of, 53, 92
science, 17–35, 38, 119, 149: concep-
    tions of, 17–18, 30–35, 68–71; ety-
    mology of, 31; modern, 11, 22, 173
Scientific Revolution: see *Enlightenment*
Scientism, 25, 69
Seinfeld, 162
self-organization, 5, 81–84
self-similarity, 44–45, 92, 119
shared knowledge, 145
short-range relationships, 104–105
simple systems, 9
simplexity, 16, 22
Sims, 172
simultaneities, 153–170: definition, 153
situated learning, 118–119

"six degrees of separation", 51
Six Feet Under, 162
"small world" phenomenon, 51
social constructivism: see *constructionism*
social movements, 102
sociocultural theories, 119
Sopranos, The, 162
specialization, 131–132, 137–141
Star Trek, 134
statistical methods, 10, 24, 41–42, 46,
    97
straight: synonyms for, 40–41; see also
    linearity
structuralism, 32, 38, 63–66, 113, 118,
    122
structure, 64–65: definition, 13–14
structure determinism, 6, 99–101
subjectivity, 15, 62–63, 117: understand-
    ing and, 112–117
systems: complicated, 10–11; complex,
    11–12; ideational, 155; physical,
    155; simple, 9; types, 9–12
systems theory, 8, 81–82, 154–155

teaching, 100, 103, 115, 20–121, 124:
    see also *pedagogy*
teaching experiments, 116
time: narrative, 175; varied scales, 28–
    29, 91, 175
Toyota, 132
transdisciplinarity, 3–4, 7–8, 72, 130,
    156–160
transphenomenality, 30, 156–160
truth: theories of, 26, 32–34, 73, 167

weak links, 52
win-win logic, 105